MAKING FOREIGN POLICY

Thank you,
Mom and Dad

Making Foreign Policy
Presidential Management of the Decision-Making Process

DAVID MITCHELL
Bucknell University, USA

Routledge
Taylor & Francis Group

LONDON AND NEW YORK

First published 2005 by Ashgate Publishing

Reissued 2019 by Routledge
2 Park Square, Milton Park, Abingdon, Oxon, OX14 4RN
52 Vanderbilt Avenue, New York, NY 10017

Routledge is an imprint of the Taylor & Francis Group, an informa business

Publisher's Note
The publisher has gone to great lengths to ensure the quality of this reprint but points out that some imperfections in the original copies may be apparent.

Disclaimer
The publisher has made every effort to trace copyright holders and welcomes correspondence from those they have been unable to contact.

A Library of Congress record exists under LC control number:

ISBN 13: 978-0-8153-9034-3 (hbk)
ISBN 13: 978-1-138-35835-5 (pbk)
ISBN 13: 978-0-429-19940-0 (ebk)

Contents

List of Tables

Tables

List of Abbreviations

ABM	Anti-Ballistic Missile
ACDA	Arms Control and Disarmament Agency
ALCM	Air-Launched Cruise Missile
ARVN	Army of the Republic of Vietnam
CIA	Central Intelligence Agency
COVN	Central Offices for South Vietnam
CSG	Counterterrorism Strategy Group
DC	Deputies Committee
DCI	Director of Central Intelligence
DMZ	Demilitarized Zone
DRV	Democratic Republic of Vietnam
ICBM	Inter-Continental Ballistic Missile
IG	Interagency Group
JCS	Joint Chiefs of Staff
MIRV	Multiple Independent Targeted Re-entry Vehicle
NLF	National Liberation Front
NSC	National Security Council
NSDD	National Security Decision Directive
NSPD	National Security Presidential Directive
NSPG	National Security Planning Group
NVA	North Vietnam Army
OSD	Office of the Secretary of Defense
PC	Principals Committee
PCC	Policy Coordination Committee
PDD	Presidential Decision Directive
PRC	Policy Review Committee
PRD	Policy Review Directive
PRG	Policy Review Group
SACPG	Special Arms Control Policy Group
SALT I	Strategic Arms Limitation Treaty One
SALT II	Strategic Arms Limitation Treaty Two
SCC	Special Coordinating Committee
SDI	Space Defense Initiative
SLBM	Submarine Launched Ballistic Missiles
SLCM	Submarine Launched Cruise Missile
SRG	Senior Review Group
START	Strategic Arms Reduction Talks

UNPROFOR	United Nations Protection Force
VBB	Vance, Brzezinski, and Brown
VSSG	Vietnam Special Studies Group

Chapter 1

Presidents and Foreign Policy Processes

Disinterest in the day-to-day activities of leaders and advisors has characterized mainstream International Relations since the late 1950s when systemic explanations came to dominate much of intellectual thinking on international politics (Waltz 1959; Singer 1961); however this has not been true for the study of foreign policy, in which many scholars have closely examined the actions of individual decision-makers. The interest in individuals and small groups has been clearly demonstrated by those who have chosen to focus on the Kennedy administration's decision-making during the Cuban Missile Crisis (Kennedy 1969; Allison 1971; May and Zelikow 1997; Garthoff 1988; Blight 1989; Welch 1989; Chang 1998; White 1998). The Cuban Missile Crisis perfectly demonstrates how crucial it is to study the relationships between leadership and advisors, because it is these interactions that are essential factors in determining a government's behavior. However, the recognition that leaders and advisors matter is only the first step in explaining how states behave. At a public forum on presidential decision-making, Ted Sorenson—legal counsel and policy advisor during the Kennedy administration—makes a set of informative points regarding the decision-making process.

> **Questioner:** Is there a larger lesson to be learned from the structure of the decision-making process during the crisis? Should American foreign policy be conducted in the informal manner of the ExComm, or should it be organized more formally?
>
> **Ted Sorensen:** I don't think there is a single answer to that. I think that was the best organization and the best group for John F. Kennedy. That is the way he made decisions, that is the way he operated. President Eisenhower had a far more structured system. He was accustomed to that from the military and he was more comfortable with that. I don't second guess him, because I think every president ought to be able to make those decisions in the way which he is most comfortable, which will be most effective for him. (Lobel et al. 2000: 40)

Sorensen's comments, first, indicate that the relationship between leaders and advisors varies based on the president's needs. Kennedy, upon learning of the placement of Soviet missiles in Cuba, recognized that the gravity of the situation required that a range of views be assessed and that in a time of crisis he needed to surround himself with those individuals that could provide him with the best informed views. Thus, Kennedy brought together an informal group of individuals he thought could provide the best advice. This action was partially driven by the crisis, but it was also partially a result of learning from the poor decision making that occurred during the planning of the Bay of Pigs invasion. As Sorensen points out, Eisenhower had a different approach to decision making that used a more formalized procedure, where deliberations over options took place within a set of committees that had specialized responsibilities, and options generated in those committees were presented to Eisenhower for choice.

In a similar dialogue, Brent Scowcroft (2001), former deputy national security advisor in the Nixon administration and national security advisor in the Ford and Bush administrations, notes the ways successive presidents organized their advisors to facilitate the making of decisions. Scowcroft points out, Nixon instituted a system of committees that formulated options allowing him to 'take papers to his study, come back with them marked up.' Only after this private deliberation would Nixon decide on a course of action. Ford and Bush, Scowcroft continues, were 'just the opposite,' because both presidents preferred to make decisions 'in the course of hearing debate over the issues involved.' Thus, differences among presidents' leadership styles result in the formation of different advisory systems, with the important consequence that different advisory systems result in variations in presidential decision-making process.

This study is motivated by a simple yet vitally important question for an understanding of US foreign policy. Quite simply, how does a president's choice of management style influence the US foreign policy decision-making process and decision outcomes? Presidents play a critical role in the formulation of United States foreign policy, however presidential studies and foreign policy analysis literature arrive at very different conclusions regarding how presidents influence the policy process and both are often inaccurate. This study develops an Advisory Systems Decision Framework to address how presidents influence the decision-making process. Four types of decision-making processes can be exhibited by a president at any given point in time based on the president's choice of advisory structure and the degree of centralization that the president exercises over the decision-making process. Foreign policy analysts have addressed the relationship between presidential management style and the decision-making process, but have failed to seriously take into account centralization as a key variable in determining the nature of the decision-making process. Furthermore, previous studies have only dealt superficially with the connection between the decision process and decision outcomes. This study addresses this issue by arguing that the way in which president and advisors resolve disagreements has implications for the outcome of the process. Specifically, the choice of "unstructured solution" or method for resolving disagreements results in variations in decision outcomes.

A reasonable response to the proposed centrality of the president in organizing his advisors based on individual characteristics is that it is the president that ultimately matters and not the advisors. Why take an interest in advisors, if the variables that matter to the nature of foreign policy are found in the president and the president is the locus of decision making in any administration? The simple answer is that the president may organize their advisors, but once constituted the president's decisions will be influenced and shaped by the interactions with and among advisors (Walcott and Hult 1987).

Traditionally, scholars have spoken of different structures, which were meant to describe the relationships between advisors and leaders, however their description of different structures reveals that these scholars were conflating two different dimensions of the advisor–leader relationship. The first dimension, structure, focuses on the organization of the advisors in relation to the president, for example some structures are hierarchic. The second dimension, operation, focuses on the nature of the interaction between advisors and leaders during the decision-making process within a given structure (i.e., the leader does not reach down to gain information, the leader participates in deliberation or the leader and advisors collectively pursue feasible options). Collectively, the two dimensions—structure and operation—form the advisory system, which is a distinct and more comprehensive concept than advisory structure. The use of the term system is deliberately chosen because a system or a complex decision-unit composed of smaller parts better represents the unit of analysis in this study.

A word on the definition of advisors is important at this juncture. A wide range of individuals have access to the president and during any given interaction have the ability to present the president with advice that can have a significant influence on the president's thinking. Aside from members of the cabinet and the White House staff, the First Lady, personal friends, members of Congress, other heads of state are often in the position to advise the president. Nancy Reagan is known to have had a significant amount of influence on Ronald Reagan's thinking about policy issues, while Richard Nixon often discussed, over drinks, issues he was confronting with his personal friend Bebe Rebozzo. Although many of these individuals are not formally considered advisors, these interactions can have a critical influence on presidential thinking. Given this state of affairs, the definition of advisor remains purposefully broad and includes all those individuals that have access to the president; however, this study focuses on those individuals who have been given the authority and whose job it is to give advice to the president. More specifically, the term advisor is meant to refer to the National Security Council Staff, White House Staff, and sub-cabinet appointees and those civil servants who are participating in the decision-making process at the highest level. These are the individuals who attend committee meetings and have the closest interaction with the president regarding the formulation of policy. Again, this focus is not meant to exclude the consideration of other individuals in the sense that when a non-formal advisor participates in the process their contribution is duly noted.

On its own, the advisory system framework is a valuable tool because it better specifies the links between management structure and decision-making process than the frameworks presented by Johnson and George. By the inclusion of the centralization variable, the advisory system framework expands the identified range of management structures and decision-making processes, while presenting an explanation of the variations in decision-making processes. The implications of such a framework is that it explains the consequences of the choices made by leader's when they choose the means to formulate foreign policy, by constructing a set of ideal types that function as a baseline to understand both variations in management and processes. The Advisory Systems framework has a value beyond explaining how structure and centralization produce a particular kind of decision-making process; it has implications for how we think about other decision-making theories and models. If the framework's explanation of the decision-making process is accurate, then it is possible to address a range of questions regarding the decision-making process. For example, are some advisory systems more or less prone to engage in bureaucratic politics? Likewise, which advisory systems are more prone to lead to breakdowns or policy failures? In what ways do advisors go about influencing the decision-making process given a type of presidential management? An investigation of these types of questions presents the future possibility that once a set of management characteristics are identified, it is then possible to not only explain how decisions are made by a leader and advisors, but whether the policy process will deadlock, result in groupthink, or be captured by a faction within the advisory system.

The Advisory System Decision-making Framework is examined using cases of US presidential decision making over five different administrations, Nixon, Carter, Reagan, Clinton, and George W. Bush. In addition, the new framework includes an explanation of the type of "unstructured solution" or decision outcome associated with each decision-making process, an aspect of the decision-making process that previous typologies have not fully addressed. Before moving on to a discussion of the reformulation of the existing advisory system typology, a discussion of group decision-making research is necessary in order to highlight the gap in the literature that the new Advisory System Framework fills.

Foundations of Group Decision Making

The recognition of differences between decision-making groups found in Sorenson's comments, have not been lost on all foreign policy analysts, as previously noted. Scholars interested in decision making recognized that individual decision-making takes place within a context that must be taken into account in order to understand the decision-making process and its outcomes (Snyder, Bruck, and Sapin 1962; Golembiewski 1962; Verba 1962; Stodgill 1981). These early assessments of small group decision making were wide ranging in their scope and were not linked to an empirical assessment of their claims. 't Hart, Stern, and Sundelius (1997) have pointed out that these works and others written since by social psychologists and management theorists have been overshadowed by a focus on groupthink and bureaucratic politics. Thus, a serious effort to examine the decision-making processes within the context of different advisory settings, which is the object in this study, has not taken place. Groupthink (Janis 1971; 't Hart et al. 1997) and bureaucratic politics (Allison 1971; Allison and Halperin 1972; Halperin, Clapp, and Kanter 1974), and to a lesser extent organization theories (Cyert & March 1963; Steinbrunner 1974; Cyert and March 1976; March 1994) have in fact been given more attention by foreign policy analysts. Of these three different approaches, groupthink, a social psychological approach has been given the most attention.

Irving Janis (1972) presented the concept of groupthink as an explanation for policy fiascos where small cohesive groups seek to maintain unanimity and group cohesion in the face of external stress. The pursuit of concurrence on an issue comes at the expense of a thorough search and evaluation of all the options available to the group. This process, Janis explains, functions as an explanation for fiascos; specifically he cites the inability to foresee the possibility of an attack by the Japanese on Pearl Harbor and the failed Bay of Pigs invasion, to name two examples. Groupthink can be identified by a set of eight symptoms: illusion of invulnerability, a belief in the group's superior morality, a shared illusion of unanimity, collective efforts at rationalizing the group's actions, self-censorship of deviant views, pressure to conform, stereotyping of the enemy as evil, and the presence of self-appointed mind guards. Although groupthink is conceived of as being a myopic decision-making environment, Janis makes the caveat that policies emerging from such groups may in fact be appropriate and successful.

Groupthink has not escaped being the target of criticism. The primary criticism of groupthink revolves around the imprecision in the theory. Janis fails to precisely explain the relationship between the variables (the eight symptoms), and further, some of the symptoms that he ostensibly treats as independent variables can possibly be considered dependent (Longley and Pruitt 1980; Gaenslen 1992). The need to overcome the imprecision of the theory has led to a reformulation that has emphasized the need to better explain the antecedents that lead to groupthink ('t Hart 1994). First among these antecedents is the influence of the leader's point of view, which makes cohesiveness unnecessary for groupthink to occur. Second, the reformulation of groupthink posits that the inter-group context influences groupthink which can, in turn, express itself in two ways. 't Hart notes that during group conflict the group becomes hierarchically structured "increasing the potential for strong leaders to expect loyal behavior from group members" ('t Hart 1994, 120). Alternatively, groupthink can occur in groups that engage in competitive interactions among the members resulting in one or both of the groups falling victim to groupthink.

Of critical importance in this reformulation is the fact that 't Hart reintroduces a critical factor in decision making: namely, the structural relationships between leaders and their advisors and among advisors themselves. 't Hart's contribution is important because it redirects attention to the conditioning effect the leader has on the behavior of the advisors; in addition, it redirects attention back to group structure (hierarchic or competitive) and the influence on decision outcomes. However, this reformulation is not all that needs to be addressed when considering the utility of groupthink in the analysis of foreign policy. Specifically, the heterogeneity and the lack of continuity within the president's administration are argued to be the factors necessary for groupthink to occur. 't Hart (1997, 11) claims that this means groupthink should be treated "as a contingent phenomenon, rather than as a general property of foreign policy decision-making in high level groups." While this may be true, this comment presents (in addition to the other critiques of groupthink) an important point that environment and the government structure matter because they influence the decision process in groups. Small groups are not amorphous entities that are subject to any variety of social psychological processes in the course of arriving at a decision. There is a connection between the process and the structure of the decision-making group, meaning the relationship between leader(s) and subordinates. The implications of this are that there is a connection between the advisory system and groupthink can be made.

Bureaucratic politics can be thought of in two different ways. It can be thought of as a level of analysis suitable for explaining particular foreign policy decisions, thus allowing for different conceptualizations of bureaucratic politics (Welch 1998). For example, Destler's (1972) study on bureaucratic politics in US foreign policy was wide-ranging and touched on the variety of ways bureaucrats and bureaus can influence policy. This differs from Allison (1971) who constructed a useful formulation of how bureaucratic politics or governmental politics produces particular kinds of policy outcomes. It is Allison's depiction of bureaucratic politics that has had the greater impact and has influenced succeeding bureaucratic studies (Stern and Verbeek 1998).

Bureaucratic Politics or Governmental Politics Model places a greater emphasis on the structure of the decision-making unit and the kind of interaction that develops between individuals that are a part of the decision-making process, yet represent different bureaucratic organizations (Allison 1971; Halperin 1974; Vandenbrouke 1984). The Bureaucratic Politics Model maintains that decisions are made by "bureau" leadership that seek to represent and advance the interests/policies of their own departments. The bargaining among bureau heads each trying to capture the policy for themselves, results in "pulling and hauling" and consequently two different kinds of policies are produced. An individual department may have their policy prevail or alternatively a "resultant" will be produced, which is simply an aggregation of all advocated policies.

Although widely discussed, the bureaucratic politics model remains significantly under-specified. The Bureaucratic Politics Model has not explained the influence that the leader has on the formulation of policy or the politics between cabinet members. Instead of depicting a hierarchic relationship between leader and advisors, which we would expect to find in a government organization, the advisors and the leader have been treated as equals (Perelmutter 1974; Rosati 1981; Bendor and Hammond 1992). This is not meant to imply that the interactions depicted by the bureaucratic politics model do not exist, but rather that the incomplete nature of the model should give us pause before it is used as an explanation of foreign policy decision making. In order for this model, or any model, to form a strong foundation for explaining foreign policy decision making, it must first fully explain the role of the leader in relation to their advisors; it must then discuss the relationship among the advisors concerned, and finally, it must use this understanding of advisory groups to explain the nature of decision making. In addition to questioning the role of leaders in bureaucratic politics, there has been a desire to better explain the motives and actions of individual bureaucrats. The conventional wisdom is that bureaucratic actors are interested in advancing the interests of their respective agencies. The rational-actor assumption that drives the bureaucratic behavior ignores the extent that bureaucratic actors are driven by "nonrational perceptions" and the kinds of behavior that these perceptions might produce that are contrary to the conventional understanding of bureaucratic politics (Hollis and Smith 1986; 't Hart and Rosenthal 1998). Instead of focusing on conflict between representatives of bureaucracies, studies have tried to focus on the "politics" within the decision-making group specifically focusing on the series of tactics (i.e., salami tactics, leaking, agenda setting, and coercion) that can enable an advisor to influence policy (Moaz 1990; Garrison 1999).

The Organization Model, to a certain degree, focuses exclusively on the structure of the decision-making environment in a much broader sense than the bureaucratic politics model and has been used as an alternative explanation of how policy is made and how it is a determinant of outcomes (March & Simon 1958; Cyert & March 1963; Allison 1971). The Organization Model is less focused on the small group and concentrates more on the decision-making of an entire organization that is hierarchically structured and composed of small subunits, each of which is designed to carry out a specific task according to standard operating procedures (SOPs). Each subunit in the organization operates in a routine fashion, as long as a predetermined level of performance is met. However, when feedback channels indicate that the objectives are not being achieved, the organization engages in a limited search for marginally different alternatives.

While both Bureaucratic and Organization Models emphasize the influence of structure and group decision-making on foreign policy, neither attempts to take into account variations in group configurations or decision-making structures. The Bureaucratic Politics Model has ignored the influence of leadership as a conditioning factor on the behavior of the group and the organization approach emphasizes explaining behavior at a level of aggregation above the small group. The Organization Model is driven by the SOPs that guide the behavior of each unit, but, as is often the case with foreign policy, it is the non-routine phenomena that are interesting and in this respect the organization model proves inadequate. Charles Hermann (2001) has taken on this task of addressing differences between groups by looking at three different group settings and explaining the way in which these groups produce different kinds of decision outcomes. Hermann contends that there are three group models based on the management of differences found within the group. The concurrence model, rooted in groupthink, attempts to reconcile conflicting views by avoiding them. The unanimity model, with foundations in bureaucratic politics, deals with conflict by integrating views into a group policy and in the plurality model conflict can produce a range of outcomes, but is characterized by an outcome that is preferred by a subset of the group.

Other efforts have been made to identify the types of systems that presidents utilize with the intent of improving our understanding of the foreign-policy process. The most influential of these attempts to identify advisory systems was made originally by Richard Tanner Johnson (1974) and then elaborated by Alexander George (1980). The types of advisory systems created (competitive, collegial, and formalistic) have taken hold and have been used by other scholars as a means to analyze foreign policy (Haney 1997; Garrison 1999). However, the Johnson/George typology has not been systematically subjected to testing despite indications that the typology is inaccurate or possibly incomplete.

Several scholars have furthered the work begun by George and Johnson and it is important to note where this study stands in relation to these recent analyses. Margaret Hermann and Thomas Preston (1994) have constructed a typology using formal-collegial structures and centralization, but their understanding of centralization has a cognitive focus in that it asserts that presidents differ according to their focus on accomplishing a task or on managing the process. The framework presented here poses an alternative in that it argues that variations between structures can be accounted for by the structural measures the president utilizes to control the process, which in the next section is argued to be the missing piece from the George and Johnson typologies.

Preston's (2001) own work on presidential management has gone further than his research with Hermann in that he bases presidential management on the formal/collegial dichotomy established by George and Johnson, but argues that management styles result from high and low variations in sensitivity to information and desire for control. These resulting management styles can then further vary according to the degree (high or low) of a president's policy expertise. Overall these leadership characteristics result in sixteen leadership style combinations. Preston's work and the research presented here differ in that this research assumes that George is correct in his formulation of formal and collegial structures. Feelings of efficacy, attitude toward conflict and preferences for processing information, all contribute to choice of management structure. As mentioned earlier, this study does not problematize that assumption. What this research argues is that most presidents will fall into one of these two categories and that a full understanding of differences between decision-making processes in administrations is accounted for by the degree of centralization of the process. Centralization, I argue, is the key defining feature of presidential management. The main difference then between Preston's work and this research is the role of expertise in the decision-making process, which this study does not address. Expertise clearly plays a role in influencing how the president behaves during the formulation of policy, but expertise also needs to be considered with interest in the policy process, which can both vary. What this study does address is the way disagreements are resolved, which is not directly a product of presidential preferences but results from the interactions within the advisory system.

The Advisory System Framework also shares similarities with Patrick Haney's (1997) study on presidential management of the decision-making process during crises. Haney has two objectives. One is to assess whether the decision-making process conforms to the formal, collegial, and competitive models and, two, to assess how that decision-making process performs. In carrying out his study Haney relies on the George/Johnson typology as a theoretical starting point. This is problematic because George and Johnson fail to take into account control over the process, which if included more accurately represents presidential decision making. Like the work by Hermann and Preston, Haney does not account for different ways of resolving conflict, which is important for understanding the ultimate choice of policy.

On these grounds it is useful to make a re-evaluation of the advisory system typology, if it is going to be of value in the examination of presidential decision making and as a means for comprehending different foreign policy processes. In the following sections I will explain the Johnson/George typology, which is the foundation for this study; I will then raise the problems found in this typology, and then present an alternative to this typology. In the succeeding chapters the new typology is evaluated using case studies. The evaluation will test the characteristics of each system across four cases of presidential foreign policy decision making on four security issues. The cases examine the Nixon administration's deliberations on policy toward the North Vietnamese, the Carter and Reagan administrations' formulation of strategic arms control policy, and the Clinton administration's deliberations on the solution to the conflict in Bosnia.

Formal and Collegial Structures

Among scholars and practitioners alike there seems to be a consensus that advisory systems generally take on one of two forms, one composed of specialized committees that are governed by rigid rules with decisions made at the top by the president. A second structure has been identified in which decisions are made in an informal 'team-like' atmosphere. The Eisenhower administration is considered the prototype of the formal structure based on that administration's numerous committees and rigid procedures for formulating policies. The other administration pointed to as the prototype of the second form of advisory system is the Kennedy administration which, as noted earlier, was characterized as being more informal. Kennedy came to office in 1961 with an explicit commitment to change the ways in which the White House was managed and decisions were made. A Senate Subcommittee chaired by Senator Henry 'Scoop' Jackson, urged the Kennedy administration to move away from the creation of policy based on fixed committees, which was known for producing 'committee' or 'compromised' decisions (Johnson 1974; Bundy 1998; Prados 1991). Kennedy accepted the suggestions and in making these changes, 'the Kennedy Presidency was a loose, open, dynamic operating style, reflecting a desire to reach out and grab for issues and a sense that an overly formal policy machinery might victimize the President it was supposed to serve' (Destler 1972). Kennedy chose to manage his presidency by abolishing the fixed committees that characterized the Eisenhower administration; instead Kennedy often met with individuals from the cabinet to the assistant secretary level, expanding access to the president and constructing interagency committees that would 'dilute' rivalry between agencies (Destler 1972).

The deliberate effort by the Kennedy administration to change the advisory system indicates that presidents are cognizant of the systems they create and have an expectation of the type of outcomes the system might produce. This recognition is important, because it means that formal/informal distinctions made between administrations are valid and are a valuable analytic tool. These distinctions have not only been made of the Eisenhower and Kennedy administrations, but have been made of the Johnson (Destler 1972), Nixon (Bundy 1998; Lobell 2000; Brookings 2000), Carter (Destler 1972; Moens 1991), Ford (Lobell 2000), Reagan (Campbell 1986), and Bush (Lobell 2000, Brookings 2000) administrations. Thus, we can make the distinction between administrations based on the formal/informal structure, but this leaves open the question as to what are the essential features of these systems that allow us to accurately define them as one or the other.

As the Jackson committee demonstrates, practitioners have recognized the differences between types of management style, but it was not until Richard Tanner Johnson's (1974) path-breaking analysis of presidential management of the White House from Truman to Nixon that the advisory systems were enumerated and given specific characteristics. Collegial, formalistic, and competitive represent the three basic management styles. Johnson asserts that these patterns of management represent the degrees to which these structures 'resolve the four dilemmas of decision-making.' Dilemma one focuses on the need to find either the 'best' option or the most 'feasible' option. Dilemma two stresses the degree to which conflicting points of view will be made a part of the decision-making process. The third dilemma confronts the need to screen out some information that may be irrelevant while not screening out too much information so as to keep the process from degrading. The last dilemma points out the need to be responsive, while maintaining sufficient deliberation.

The competitive approach to advisor management promotes conflict among advisors who have overlapping assignments. The president in this management structure acts as the 'arbitrator' between battling advisors, allowing the president to stay fully informed and 'jolt the system' when it would be required by changing assignments or manipulating the tension between advisors. The competitive approach to management stands in contrast to both the formalistic and collegial approaches, because of the prominent roles played by conflict and presidential manipulation.

Conflict is a part of the collegial structure, but in this structure the president does not use conflict in the form of overlapping assignments as a means to generate proposals and policies. A collegial advisory system attempts to use differences in viewpoint as a means to find policy solutions that are 'substantively sound and politically doable.' Presidents use their staff as a team with advisors working in the creation of policy; from the interaction within the team divergent views arise and the vetting of different perspectives leads to a 'feasible' policy. The collegial system stands in contrast to the formal model in which conflict is discouraged by the creation of staff committees that create prepared briefs representing differing points of view. These briefs move up the hierarchy to the president who makes the ultimate decision regarding which policy is best. In this system, the intent is to find the 'best' policy, which results from weighing the advantages and disadvantages of the prepared proposals.

The features in Johnson's work are very broad and this lack of specificity results in the formulation of categories that too greatly overlap. For example, there is nothing in the description of the collegial system that causes it to stand out significantly from the competitive models. Both use conflict as a part of the decision-making process and both forego the use of highly ordered processes and procedures. Moreover, the collegial system does not rule out a president that provides overlapping assignments or uses conflict as an instrument in the process. Perhaps instead of viewing the collegial and competitive systems as being distinct, it is more productive to consider the competitive system as a variation of the collegial, whereby the use of overlapping jurisdictions is better understood as a means utilized by the president to control the collegial deliberations. A second and more important critique of Johnson's work is that although his typology is composed of ideal types, there is significant evidence that presidents do not manage their advisors in the manner that he describes. Burke (2000) has noted that Johnson's typology demonstrates a severe 'divergence between the real and ideal,' because it fails to account for advisory systems in which there can be variations in structure and the predicted effects of the advisory systems prove to be inconsistent. A final charge against the Johnson typology is that it ignores the fact that all administrations operate with some kind of informality, irrespective of the kind of structures that are put into place (Burke and Greenstein 1989; Ponder 2000). Ponder (2000) argues that it is this inherent informality in all administrations that prevents the categorization of advisory systems, because the informal relations can always 'short circuit' the structured processes that have to be instituted by the president, thus resulting in a high degree of variation. This line of argument, however takes a reasonable critique of the typology to an extreme and inadvertently indicts virtually any attempt to categorize advisory systems.

The informality that permeates all administrations does not mean that all activity within an administration is ad hoc or that policy is made by the 'seat of the pants.' The objective of a properly constructed decision making is to account for the degree of informality found within an administration and to identify the nature of the informal relationships. The assumption underlying this criticism is that the concept of 'informal' should not be taken literally and that informality can take on different forms. Informality may take place between the same set of actors, it may take place at different stages within the policy process and it may be more prevalent when an administration deals with specific issues. It is these traits that need to be captured by a typology. The problem with Johnson's typology is that it may have tried to create too great a distinction between different advisory structures leaving out certain features, such as informal processes. For this reason it is worthwhile to elaborate the Johnson typology and better specify its characteristics.

Alexander George was the next scholar to contribute to the evolution of the Johnson typology. The typology gained wider attention after George (1980; 1998) better specified the characteristics of each advisory system. George rooted these systems not in the dilemmas individuals face, but in the personal characteristics of presidents. Three personality characteristics or 'dimensions' are central to the managing of advisors—cognitive style, orientation toward conflict, and sense of efficacy. First, George (1980: 147) argues that these cognitive differences influence choice of management style because the president requires systems to suit his 'preferred ways of acquiring information.' Second, sense of efficacy relates to a president's feelings of competency in performing their tasks. These feelings of efficacy influence the president's role in the system in relation to their advisors by determining the kind of role that the president will take in the system. The third personal characteristic relates to the president's orientation toward interpersonal conflict, which influences the nature of debate. This means the president may or may not allow face-to-face confrontation as well as require consensus on solutions before decisions are made. George further argues that these personality dimensions are complemented by a president's prior experience and competency in foreign policy. Collectively, these variables (cognitive style, orientation, efficacy, experience, and competency) influence a president's choice of collegial, formalistic, or competitive structures by determining how the president will receive information, interact with advisors, and explore issues. Parenthetically it should be noted that these groups of variables are not exhaustive of the possible range of variables that could influence the formation of advisory systems.[1] Others have used different sets of variables to explain the formation of these structures, but since the emphasis of this study is on process rather than the origins of these systems this aspect will not be treated as problematic (Haney 1997; Preston 2001).

---

[1] Walcott and Hult (1995) base their study of White House governance structures on a broader set of variables than those used by Johnson and George. Walcott and Hult's study explains how governance structures emerge, remain stable, and differentiate. Thus the explanatory variables in their study focus on the environment surrounding the White House Office, which includes technology, other government actors within the US and overseas, in addition to how a president's personal characteristics play. Presidents, in choosing a structure, will take into account the salience and nature of an issue when structuring and a particular kind of strategy to address an issue. Last, preexisting organization structures will influence structure, whether it is through institutionalization of processes that are difficult to change or positive models that are worthy to emulate.

Table 1.1 George/Johnson Advisory Structures

Formalistic Structure	President at the top
	Orderly policy making with well-defined procedures
	Emphasis on hierarchy to screen information
	Specialized information and advice
	Emphasis on functional expertise
	President rarely "reaches down" for information
	Discouragement of bargaining and conflict in group
	Emphasis on finding the "best" policy
Collegial Structure	President at center
	Informal procedures
	Decision-making team led by president
	President an active member of the group
	President may assign overlapping jurisdictions
	Shared responsibility for decisions
	Advisors do not serve as information filters
	Emphasis on building consensus
	Advisors are generalists
	President "reaches down" for information
	Emphasis on finding the most "doable" policy
Competitive Structure	President at top
	Organizational ambiguity
	President may assign overlapping jurisdictions
	Multiple channels of communication to the president
	Promotion and even encouragement of debate
	President manages conflict in the group
	President may "reach down" for information

Source: Table adapted from Haney (1997).

As noted above, George provided greater specification to the characteristics of each system than Johnson. The characteristics of each structure are presented in Table 1.1. It must be emphasized that George did not see these systems as a perfect representation of the systems used by presidents during their administrations. George is well aware of the limitations of the typology when he notes, 'we should remind ourselves once again that our depiction of the communication structures associated with each of them necessarily oversimplifies the more complex reality and working of each system. To some extent, elements of two or even all three models may be present in different mixes, with each President emphasizing a different structure' (George 1980: 164).

Within George's discussion of the typology we are given a glimpse of the ways that the typologies fail to accurately represent the "real" systems. Two examples prove to be informative in demonstrating where potential problems arise. First, Franklin Roosevelt's administration is the only presidency that resembles the competitive structure. It is difficult to accept this structure as a type, since it only describes a single case. It could very well be the case that another president could come along and structure their advisors the way FDR had but the existence of a sole case should give us pause in using this in a typology. Reasonably, one can argue that this system is not a type that can be generalized across administrations, and is, rather, anomalous and specific to FDR. In short the typology might be composed only of formalistic and collegial, but there is reason to believe that these two distinctions are sufficient given the array of factors subsumed within them.

In discussing the formal system, George makes a distinction between different types of formal structures. In the Eisenhower administration's version of the formalistic model the chief of staff plays a vital role as a buffer between the president and the cabinet and is the only individual tasked with preparing recommendations. The Eisenhower formal structure contrasts the Truman administration, which had no chief of staff that functioned as a gatekeeper. George highlights the difference between these administrations, but does not then proceed to explain how this difference is significant to the functioning of the advisory systems. Does the formalistic structure with a chief of staff filter more information than the one without? What is the relationship between the chief of staff and the rest of the cabinet or advisors? Is this person an honestbroker or does this advisor take a position in the policy debate?

The last two questions are not inconsequential because depending on how these questions are answered the nature of these structures and their distinctiveness may be reevaluated. If the chief of staff is an honestbroker then the operation of the advisory system in the Eisenhower administration may not function in a manner different from the Truman administration because the chief of staff is here merely a conduit for the information prepared in the cabinet. On the other hand, if the chief of staff advocates a position in the policy debate, the kind of information that will make its way to the president's desk will be very different than if the chief of staff was policy neutral. Under these circumstances we might expect a narrowing of information presented to the president and/or the development of a collegial relationship at the top between the president and his chief of staff, but a formal relationship with all others. Either way, this simple distinction presented by George is of greater significance than his typology indicates because it calls into question the applicability of the typology. It should be remembered that these systems are ideal types, but the notion that they are ideal types should not be invoked in order to free the typology from criticism. With mounting contradictory evidence and a reasonable evaluation of the typology, it may be necessary to reconstruct the ideal types so that its characteristics better approximate those structures actually used by presidents.

The problems associated with the George and Johnson studies are sufficient to bring the typology into doubt, but the typology runs into further problems when one looks at empirical evidence. The typology needs to be questioned because, based on even casual knowledge of past and more current administrations, the typologies do not accurately describe the systems used by presidents. A brief examination of the actual decision making during Johnson's administration reveals that the Johnson/George typology quickly runs into problems. The Johnson administration is considered to have used a competitive model initially before changing to a more formal system later; but accounts of the decisions to deploy the Anti-Ballistic Missile system and to negotiate with the Soviet Union tells a different story. As Mort Halperin, then consultant at the Office of the Secretary of Defense recounts, 'the Johnson administration had no real system' when it came to these issues (National Security Council Project: Arms Control and the National Security Council 2000: 7). Halperin further relates that an ad hoc team was put together consisting of members of the NSC, State Department and the Office of Secretary of Defense and worked in an informal fashion to put a proposal together. The committee worked to generate consensus by sending drafts of their proposal to the NSC principals and the Joint Chiefs of Staff. The president was absent as a player in this process other than stating that he ultimately wanted an agreement with the Soviet Union. Thus, the system used for the formulation of a proposal to the Soviets on strategic arms talks was in part informal in that an ad hoc committee was put together with no set procedures, and was in part formal in the sense that the committee offered options to the president who remained above the deliberation process.

This hybrid formal/collegial system contrasts the formal process used to arrive at a position on eliminating biological weapons where in 1969 an interagency options paper detailing the pros and cons was presented to the President. Halperin recognizes the stark differences between the two systems when he asserts, 'that on the biggest issues it doesn't matter what the form of system is, the principals are going to find a way that works to get done what the President wants done, and that the formal system is much more important for issues that fall below that.' (National Security Council Project: Arms Control and the National Security Council 2000: 10). The account provided by Halperin contradicts George's contention that the Johnson system was first competitive and then formal. The informality that runs through the Johnson administration becomes more apparent when considering that a major feature of Johnson's decision-making was the 'Tuesday Lunch' which was an informal meeting between the President, the Secretaries of State and Defense, and the National Security Advisor. It is true that in 1966 Johnson attempted to breathe life into the committee structure by establishing management through the Senior Interdepartmental Group and numerous Interdepartmental Regional Groups, but these interagency groups gained little support from the President or the Secretary of State and as a consequence did not have a significant impact on policy (Lord 1988).

Alternatives to the Johnson/George Typology

Empirically, questions arise when examining the Johnson/George typology, but the basic structure, formal and informal, of the advisory systems holds. Other scholars have studied the kinds of management strategies employed by presidents to structure the advisory process and all loosely base their categories around the formal/informal dichotomy. Two major approaches are found in the literature that focus on presidential advisory structures, the first focuses on the collegial/formal systems (Porter 1980; Burke 2000; Walcott and Hult 2000), and the second group utilizes alternative approaches that emphasize centralization (Campbell 1986; Ponder 2000).

Porter (1980) in his study of the economic policy board identifies three kinds of management models employed by presidents which are adhocracy, centralized management, and multiple advocacy. Although demonstrating slight differences this typology, in many ways, parallels the Johnson/George typology. Similar to the formalistic model, Porter presents the centralized management model in which the White House staff acts as a gatekeeper and filters ideas and proposals that come from the cabinet departments and reconciles disputes between cabinet members.[2] This management structure is reminiscent of George's description of Eisenhower's formalistic approach in which the chief of staff stands between the president and the cabinet and acts as a filter and an honestbroker.[3] The two other structures, adhocracy and multiple

---

[2] It is interesting to note that the literature that addresses advisory structures often does not focus on foreign policy, but tends to give more attention and a greater prominence to White House staff, beyond the National Security Council staff, in the policy process. This can be explained by the fact that these authors in their discussions of policy included domestic and foreign policy. Alternatively, it may be a result of a bias amongst foreign policy analysts who pay little attention to non-foreign policy advisors who can be influential on foreign policy issues.

[3] It is curious to find that Porter treats the White House staff as essentially a unitary actor. If the interest is to understand how advisors present advice and manage the information that is seen by the president then it is necessary to open up this black box and describe the relations within the White House Staff and address the kind of relationship that exists between the president and the staff.

advocacy both parallel the collegial and competitive structures, because both are essentially variations of informal structures.

Adhocracy, the most informal of all the systems, depicts the advisory process as being composed of a series of bilateral relationships between the president and advisors. The president does not establish regular modes of interaction, but selectively doles out assignments and meets with advisors when issues need to be addressed. The advisors involved in this process often change from issue to issue, as the president seeks those individuals that he feels are suited to deal with the policy at hand. Group decision making takes place within the confines of interagency groups that are put together to deal with a specific policy issue and then are dissolved once the policy has been addressed. Burke (2000) finds that the Clinton administration's management system was an adhocracy, noting that Clinton of all the modern presidents was 'least concerned or constrained by organizational structure or ordered decision-making procedures.' Multiple advocacy on the other hand is more regularized than adhocracy and is centered on managed group decision making.[4] In this system competing views are encouraged by the president in a group setting and the president acts as a managerial custodian seeking to insure that all views are represented and considered.

Variations of formal and collegial systems are present in Burke's assessment of Jimmy Carter, Ronald Reagan, and George H. W. Bush. Reagan utilized collegial formalism, which is characterized as a system under which cabinet councils were assembled along functional lines, three interagency groups were created to support departments, and three individuals share the responsibility of chief of staff. This system is formal to the extent that the policy-making process is organized around the cabinet councils and interagency groups. However, the utility of these councils proved fleeting as they rarely dealt with issues that were considered by the president, members often worked outside of the councils to protect parochial interests and serious debate was sacrificed in the interest of preserving cordiality. With the decline of the councils came a corresponding devolution of control over the policy process to the White House staff where the process among the White House staff was collegial, principally among the *troika* of Michael Deaver, James Baker, and Ed Meese. However, this collegial relationship did not last and in Reagan's second term, control over the process was centralized around Chief of Staff Donald Regan.

Both Carter and Bush in Burke's estimation used collegial systems, but both of these structures had characteristics that set them apart from each other. In the language of Johnson and George, Burke states that, 'The spokes of the

---

[4] Multiple advocacy as discussed by George was presented as a prescribed advisory structure. Porter on the other hand treats this structure as descriptive, but his discussion does seem to suggest that this method, if properly implemented, is superior to others.

wheel would radiate from a president who would serve as its hub, not only making decisions but immersing himself in the details of policy and subjecting himself to an array of deliberations.' (Burke 2000: 118–119). Carter's system was collegial, but it was also centralized, because of Carter's need to be involved in the minutiae of the issues dealt with by the administration. It is Carter's central role in the centralized collegial system that distinguishes it from the restricted collegiality practiced by the Bush administration. Bush used a collegial process, but the number of individuals that were a part of the process was small or restricted.[5]

In both Porter's and Burke's analysis of presidential management systems, there is a basic acceptance and adherence to the elements of the Johnson/George kind of typology. Porter present's fundamentally two different kinds of structures, one formal, which he refers to as centralized management, and the other collegial, which he presents as two models that are different, but both collegial in nature.[6] The multiple advocacy and adhocracy are basically collegial processes, but operate differently. Burke on the other hand, although critical of the Johnson typology, basically accepts the collegial/formal distinction, but in his investigation of administrations from Carter to Clinton he describes aspects of each administration that make their advisory systems distinct. Burke has chosen to focus less on the interaction between advisors and presidential management and more on those aspects of the presidential institution such as the White House office that transcend administrations and can affect future administrations. The problem with this assessment is that although critical of the collegial and formal approach to analysis of the presidency, Burke still accepts these basic categorizations, despite asserting that they may not be valid.

Walcott and Hult (1995) present a typology composed of seven structures that moves toward improving the literature's ability to explain the variations among administrations that are extant in the historical records. Walcott and Hult provide an interesting contribution to the study of advisory systems due to their interest in explaining the nature of systems, how they emerge, and if they remain stable over time. These dependent variables are determined by a set of explanatory variables, which are environment, presidential choice, and organization. But there is a crucial set of intermediary

---

[5] These individuals being primarily the Secretary of State James Baker, Secretary of Defense Richard Cheney, National Security Advisor Brent Scowcroft, Vice-President Dan Quayle, Deputy National Security Advisor Robert Gates and Chief of Staff John Sununu.

[6] Both Alexander George and Porter's books appeared in 1980, so it would be a mistake to say that Porter built on George or George built on Porter without direct evidence. But it is reasonable to assume that both are working in the tradition of Richard Tanner Johnson and drew on similar literature. Thus we have the production of typologies that do not differ considerably from one another.

variables—controversy and uncertainty—and it is the extent of uncertainty and controversy within the environment and decision setting that ultimately influence 'governing structures.'

The seven categories present a variety of systems including collegial, formal, and multiple advocacy. This typology contains three different types of collegial systems (collegial-competitive, collegial-mediative, and collegial-consensual) that all share the basic aspects of collegiality, but vary according to levels of participation, expertise required, decision rules, conflict management, and uncertainty management. Also found in the typology are adjudicative and adversarial systems that are essentially both multiple advocacy structures, but they differ according to the range of advocacy that is permissible. The adjudicative system allows for advocacy from two competing points of view, while the adversarial allows for multiple advocacy. Rounding out the seven-structure typology are the hierarchy and market structures, which represent two extremes on a continuum. The hierarchy system is similar to the formalistic model, but is perhaps more formal given the emphasis on following orders and the preferences of the leader. Finally, the market model operates in a fashion similar to Porter's adhocracy in that the process lacks any coherent structure. Advisors pursue interests and the ways in which decisions are made are neither 'explicit nor consistent' (Walcott and Hult 2000: 16).

Ponder (2000) and Campbell (1986) use a different tack to address the role of advisors and the nature of management systems. Both authors address the same issues and discuss the same features found in the literature that are founded on collegial and formal structures, but they emphasize to a greater extent the degree of centralization of the policy-making process. Ponder's (2000) attention is not on the cabinet, which characterizes the analysis made by many of these authors, but on the White House staff. With a primary focus on the Domestic Policy Staff, Ponder finds that the advisors' role in the policy process can take on three different forms that are the product of cross pressure deriving from the 'character and scope of the policy, the priority level assigned by the president, the expected impacts on various constituencies and the compatibility of policy with political actors' (Ponder 2000: 176). The White House staff can be directors of policy (centralizing policy, synthesizing information, and coordinating the executive branch), policy facilitators (less control of process, managing relations between departments), and policy monitors (transferring formulation authority to departments and monitoring activity).

This is fundamentally an analysis based on the centralization of control over the process, which differentiates it from the work that focuses on collegial and formal structures. Unfortunately, this method of analysis does not fully address the dynamic between the president and the advisor to the depth of the collegial and formal frameworks. Discussing the degree to which the staff is in control of policy, permits us to understand the extent to which a president is involved in the decision-making process on a given issue, but fails to fully address the way the president is engaged in an issue and how the president manages the process when the staff acts as director and is highly engaged. Different policies create different demands on the president and the staff's time in terms of the requirements to formulate policies. Important issues will require a greater investment of time and information leading to a need for greater centralization to obtain the necessary information and to make sound policies.

Understanding the level of centralization and the imperatives behind centralization are important, but it does not take the next step and explain how policy is made within that centralized setting. It is this aspect of the decision process that needs to be better examined, because the deliberation between the president and advisors forms the fundamental decision unit in the foreign policy process. It is this relationship that determines how information is shaped, options generated, and even the degree to which the process should be centralized! Centralization is part of the decision-making environment and is one of many institutional variables that can come to bear on decision making.

Colin Campbell (1986) makes this kind of comprehensive form of evaluation of the Carter and Reagan administrations with a focus on centralization. Campbell notes the degree to which presidents since FDR increasingly centralized power over policy making within the White House. This is the question that Ponder was addressing, but instead of detailing differences between presidents, Ponder created an explanation of why centralization may differ between administrations and within them. Campbell does not provide this kind of systematic explanation, but he does take the next step previously suggested and describes the structure of the president–advisor relationship within the centralized or de-centralized context. Campbell surveys presidential literature and describes the relationship between cabinet secretaries, the structure of the cabinet, the management pattern in the White House, the relationship between advisors and the development of policy secretariats. It is interesting to note that four of the individual features that Campbell discusses are features that are addressed by the collegial and formal systems. The White House organizational pattern is described as being spokes-in-a-wheel, hierarchical, and mixed, which matches the collegial, formalistic, and competitive typology, respectively.[7] In addition, the relationship between units, the amount of countervailing views that are allowed in the process, and cabinet secretary interrelationships, are used to further describe whether the cabinet members work in collegial groups or not.

Most of the literature that addresses the relationship between advisors and president and their relationships on policy accept at their core the collegial

---

[7] The spokes-in-a-wheel and collegial systems are similar because of a reliance on informal procedures. The formalistic and hierarchical both share a common structure based on hierarchy with defined procedures, while the competitive and mixed both depict the president controlling and managing advisors with special tasks.

and formal systems as being the basic means for managing the policy process. Some have chosen to deal with this typology quite explicitly and others have used these concepts more ambiguously; for instance, Burke and many practitioners use these terms generally, often as a substitute for formal and informal processes.[8] Despite the fact that these categories arise within the literature repeatedly and are referred to by practitioners in their discussions of policy during their respective administrations, there is significant evidence that these categories, collegial and formal, are problematic. A brief overview of the historical record demonstrates that characterizations that have been made of different administrations have not held up when subjected to scrutiny.

Eisenhower's administration is formal, but it also demonstrates some collegial aspects. Likewise, Nixon also is supposed to have a formal structure, but there is evidence that his relationship with Kissinger and their joint activities on some issues reveals a process that is less formal as previously believed. Moreover, the varieties of literature that have critiqued and/or built upon the collegial/formal typology look at similar administrations, but arrive at different kinds of structures. This is exemplified by comparing the typologies created by Johnson/George, Porter, and Walcott and Hult. All make use of the collegial and formal dichotomy, but all derive different variations in terms of the number and kinds of competing systems. This is significant given the persistence and prominence given to the Johnson/George typology in foreign policy analysis. It is obvious that the collegial/formal or informal/formal distinction does describe the general nature of management styles, but the literature so far has failed to capture all the essential features. The explanations of the collegial and formal systems presented by Johnson and George as detailed above demonstrate they are less than satisfactory in describing the policy process in successive US administrations. Therefore, it is necessary to re-evaluate the nature and resulting process associated with each advisory system. A new typology needs to be reformulated to serve as a better means to describe administrations and more importantly serve as a foundation for explaining foreign policy behavior.

---

[8] The Brookings Institution Roundtables on the National Security Council are a valuable resource for examining the decision-making process and the role that the NSC plays in the process, but also for advisors in general. During these discussions, the terms collegial and formal often arise, but there is no indication that the individuals who use them have anything but a very general understanding of what these types of management style mean. Or they are simply trying to express the degree of hierarchy in the process and the role of committees in the process, which is a good understanding of these structures, but it does not present a full understanding of the complexity of the processes.

Advisory System Decision-Making Framework

The major thread running through the presidency literature is the importance of centralization within the advisory system, meaning the extent to which the president imposes and centers control over the flow of information and interaction between advisors. Porter presented a three-structure typology that can be characterized with varying levels of centralization with the 'centralized management' structure being most centralized and adhocracy having the least centralization. Centralization is found in Burke's description of the changes found in the Reagan administration, because over time Reagan shifted from the *troika* of three chiefs of staff to one, allowing greater control of information and access. The role of centralization is more evident in Burke's discussion of the Carter and Bush administrations in which both advisory systems were collegial, but it was centralization that distinguished the two systems. Ponder and Campbell more explicitly focus on the degree of centralization in the management of presidential advisors both within and between administrations.

The argument here claims that the centralization found in these different literatures accounts for the failure of the Johnson/George typology to reflect the kinds of management systems discussed previously. The differences between the formal, collegial, and competitive models implicitly contain variations in centralization, but are not sufficient to overcome the problem of overlap between types, particularly the overlap created by the competitive model. More importantly there is no consideration of variation within a type of advisory system which is a subtlety that the presidency literature has highlighted but the foreign policy has disregarded.

The inclusion of centralization within the typology overcomes some of the other problems associated with the Johnson/George typology, aside from reducing the overlap between types. If each of these categories differs according to the amount of centralization, then it is possible to take into account informality which has been widely accepted as a feature of any administration's policymaking process. What may be considered informal is better understood as a decentralization of the decision-making process within either the formal or the collegial structures. Last, by reformulating the typology based on centralization, the reformulated typology better reflects the characteristics of the advisory systems actually used by presidents.

Centralization expresses itself differently in the formal and collegial structures, but at its core centralization refers to the degree that the president places control over the management of conflict in the administration and the flow of information. Because the arrangement of the leader in relation to advisors differs between the two models, centralization will be expressed differently. Centralization in a formal system means the degree to which the president exerts control by putting in place a system in which authority and decision making occurs at the very top of the hierarchy. Typically, a gatekeeper is responsible for screening information and blocking access to the leader. This is combined with a system for which there is an established and well-defined procedure for deliberating and choosing options. This differs from the collegial system, because the collegial system has informal procedures, which means it is difficult to discuss the centralization of a system that prima facie lacks any structure. Informal procedures, however, should not be confused with an absence of any order or structure.

Centralization then forms the basis for reformulating the Johnson/George typology and with an emphasis on this factor many of the deficiencies associated with the Johnson/George typology—overlap, empirical support, and informality—are overcome and thus the typology is rendered more useful in assessing foreign policy. Previously it was argued that there is a general consensus that formal and collegial structures generally capture the fundamental differences between advisory systems. Scholars and practitioners alike use this terminology (and rightfully so) because a core set of features has been identified that makes it reasonable to make this distinction. These characteristics (Table 1.2) are not in dispute and form the basis for categorization in the following typology. For both systems the emphasis or defining features of the systems are found on the first line. Formal systems are always hierarchic and collegial systems always place the president at the center of policy making. The task in building the Advisory System Framework is to explicate how centralization and coordination create variations on these basic structures.

Table 1.2 Base Features of Formal and Collegial Structures

Formalistic Structure	Hierarchic—President at the top
	Specialized information and advice
	President rarely "reaches down" for information
Collegial Structure	President at center
	Advisors do not serve as information filters
	Advisors are generalists
	President may "reach down" for information

Centralization is treated as varying between high and low in relation to the formal and collegial systems, thus yielding four different types of advisory systems (Table 1.3). A formal system that is highly centralized (upper left cell)

Table 1.3 Advisory System Decision-Making Framework

	Formal	**Collegial**
High **Centralization**	Leader evaluates presented options Leader expresses general preference shaping consideration of options Gatekeeper acts as advocate and screens information and access Discouragement of bargaining and conflict in group; dissenting voices excluded Orderly policy-making with well-defined procedures	Leader is an active member of the group guiding and shaping deliberations Leader pushes group to assess range of options Emphasis on building consensus among core set of advisors Shared responsibility for decisions Meetings are regularized and frequent with core advisors
Low	Leader chooses between presented options Advisors compete to get preferences presented to leader Gatekeeper acts as honest-broker and presents options (opportunity for other advisors to appeal to leader) Bargaining and conflict take place at level below President Procedures may be circumvented	Willingness to delegate authority to others that have expertise Advisors instrumental in guiding policy Less emphasis on consensus building among advisors Conflict and bargaining between advisors No regular mode of interacting with advisors

results in increased control over the decision-making process at the top near the leader. This means the leader is interested in ensuring that there is an orderly process that allows them to choose the best policy. Aiding this effort, to centralize the decision-making process is a gatekeeper(s) that screens information that is irrelevant or deviates from the leader's agenda. Since the leader wants to control the process they let broad objectives or strategic goals be known so they can act as guiding principles for advisors. The gatekeeper is the means of transmitting leader preferences to advisors and blocks access to the leader, particularly dissenters who are excluded from the process. If the leader is interested in choosing among the best options then the leader coordinates the advisors to avoid dissent that results in a set of options that are unwanted. Consequently, well-defined procedures are imposed to channel and control the interaction of advisors and to avoid conflict between dissenting advisors. Advisors whose views are at odds with the leader's overall vision are excluded from the process.

Low centralization in a formal system (lower left cell) means that the leader does not maintain a high level of control at the top of the hierarchy. Low centralization permits other individuals below the president and gatekeeper to have a degree of control over the process. This kind of system possesses an honestbroker(s) that manage the process, so the distance between the leader and advisors closes and the advisors, particularly those that have differing views, have an opportunity to have their views evaluated by the leader. The 'slackening' of centralization causes a 'slackening' in the coordination of the policy process and in contrast to the highly centralized system, the low centralized system permits bargaining and conflict among the advisors. The bargaining between advisors takes place below the level of the leader and out of his view. There is less reliance on well-defined procedures; in fact advisors in this competition over policy are inclined to circumvent the system knowing that only the 'best' option will be chosen, thus placing a premium on presenting their position to the leader.

The leader in the formal system is interested in evaluating and choosing options while the leader in the collegial system stands at the center of the decision-making and interacts with advisors pursuing the most 'feasible' policy. In the collegial system that is highly centralized (upper right cell) the leader 'stands' at the center of a core group of advisors that are generalists and guides and shapes the interaction between them. The leader raises issues and questions, presses for more or different options, and the leader may assign specific tasks to different advisors. Coordination in this system requires regularity and frequent meetings allowing the leader to be updated and assist their advisors in the evaluation of new options and their attendant consequences. This kind of coordination builds consensus on the options discussed and fosters shared responsibility. Shared responsibility feeds back and encourages advisors to be critical in their evaluations knowing that they have a stake in the outcome.

A collegial system that has low centralization (lower right hand cell) means that the leader will delegate authority to advisor(s) that have a particular expertise; consequently these advisors will be influential in guiding the process, since the leader does not require a high level of control. Accordingly, coordination does not require regularity or that the leader necessarily be at the nexus of decision making, resulting in more bilateral and ad hoc meetings between leader and advisors. This kind of interaction supports an advisory system in which there is bargaining and conflict and less consensus among the leader's advisors.

Advisors System Framework and Decision Outcomes

A particular challenge in the study of foreign policymaking has been to make connections in a systematic way between the decision-making process and outcomes. Theories such as bureaucratic politics and groupthink both make general assertions about the kinds of policies that should be produced by the decision-making process. Bureaucratic politics posits that from the 'pulling and hauling' of department heads a 'resultant' is produced that is a combination of the preferences of bureaucratic actors. The implication is that this is a potentially sub-optimal outcome, because the outcome is designed to satisfy divergent preferences rather than address the problem or issue before the government. Groupthink also discusses the product of group decision making in evaluative terms; groups afflicted by groupthink fail to assess the range of options thus producing more myopic policies.

However, when it comes to discussing advisory systems the foreign policy and the presidency literatures have not fully dealt with the issue of outcomes in a systematic way. This can partially be explained by the difficulty in accounting for the myriad variables that are external to the group context or by the assertion of outcomes that are either too broad or too specific to allow generalization. It is this kind of problem that has led critics to charge that it is difficult to explain outcomes at this level of aggregation and better explanations can be derived from observing the structure of the international system or by using rational choice approaches. The greatest of all the problems when linking process and outcomes is the subjectivity that often 'creeps' into definitions of the outcome. Framing outcomes in terms of 'good' policy versus 'bad' policy or the more troublesome policy 'success' versus policy 'failure' is problematic because of the difficulty in operationalizing and measuring outcomes (Shafer and Crichlow 2002). Defining outcomes runs into the unintended problem of asserting a normatively correct policy, which undermines any attempts to approximate objectivity. However, the difficulty in discussing the connection between process and outcomes in foreign policy can be overcome by identifying dimensions of the policy process that can act as strong indicators of policy outcomes.

The advisory system literature often asserts that the formal and collegial systems are geared to find two different kinds of policy. Most often formal systems result in the search for 'best' policies while collegial systems result in the most 'feasible' options (Johnson 1974; George 1980; Hermann & Preston 1998). These are useful if the typology is limited to two broad categories of advisory systems, but with a greater number of advisory systems the utility of this simple dichotomy proves limited. Charles Hermann and colleagues (2001) have made a step toward developing the connection between process and outcomes by identifying three types of small group decision units and an associated range of process or decision outcomes. Small group decision units differ according to the way in which disagreements between members are resolved. Groups employing unanimity, concurrence, or plurality decision rules lead to three different 'unstructured solutions'. The interaction between decision rule and mediating variables create different paths toward choice of one of the four 'unstructured solutions' that are designated dominant, integrative, deadlock, and subset solutions. The solutions proposed by Hermann are useful for two reasons. One, these solutions address the *nature* of a decision outcome avoiding the difficulties associated with identifying foreign policy behavior or specific policies that are difficult to operationalize and measure. Two, the outcomes are rooted in processes that are common to group processes identified in bureaucratic, groupthink and organizational processes, but are also found in advisory systems. This last point in particular makes the use of "unstructured solutions" a good foundation for indicating the kind of outcomes that are associated with individual advisory systems.

Table 1.4 contains the decision outcomes associated with each advisory system. Like the advisory systems these process outcomes are ideal types; intervening variables arising from the systems environment or variables from within the system, such as personal characteristics of the president, can alter the kind of solutions each system produces. The decision outcome(s) in each cell are not the only outcomes to be produced by the advisory system, but they are the outcomes that have a high probability of being produced by the system and thus can be considered a key characteristic.

Table 1.4 Advisory System Decision Outcomes

	Formal	Collegial
High Centralization	Dominant Solution	Integrative Solution
Low Centralization	Dominant-Subset Solution/ Deadlock	Subset Solution/ Deadlock

In the upper left-hand cell, a formal system with high centralization leads to a dominant solution. Dominant solutions result when the advisory system chooses to adopt the main option discussed at the outset of deliberation. Hermann (2001) argues that a dominant solution would arise if 'norms prevent articulating an alternative option to an option advocated by an authoritative group member.' In a formal/highly centralized system the president expresses a preference designed to shape the formulation of policy, which is reinforced by a set of norms (excluding dissenting voices, discouragement of bargaining and conflict, and a gatekeeper that screens information). The expression of the leader's preferences with these instituted norms privileges the president's views and will gear any solutions to fit the president's preferences.

Formal systems with low centralization (lower left-hand cell) lack the controlling effect of the president's strong preferences as a guide on policy, the influence of a gatekeeper or the elimination of bargaining and conflict. Consequently, two different kinds of solutions result from this system, deadlock or dominant-subset. Deadlock 'defines a situation of stalemate in which group members reach no decision on how to resolve their differences' (Hermann 2001). The lack of control exercised over the process permits advisors to circumvent established procedures and engage in bargaining to advance their preferences. Two sides with equal influence in the process and unwilling to reconcile differences might lead to their inability to present the president with a set of satisfactory options. Of the two possible solutions a dominant-subset solution is more likely, because advisors that can better manipulate the system are able to advance their preferences. The president exercises less control over this system and unlike the highly centralized system does not express a strong preference, advisors that can appeal to certain values or presidential worldviews are better able to advance their options. For this reason, the subset solution is called a dominant subset solution and has a greater likelihood of being the decision outcome.

An integrative solution, which is produced from group interaction, partially represents the preferences of all those involved in the decision-making process. Specifically, integrative solutions 'may result from successful persuasion of some members by others to change their explicitly stated preferences, by a shift in the preference orderings of all members, perhaps as a result of the creation of a new option not initially recognized by the group, or through achieving mutually acceptable compromise' (Hermann 2001). Integrative solutions result from systems that are collegial and highly centralized (upper right-hand cell). Through group meetings that are regularized and frequent the president conducts discussion where advisors are encouraged to search for a range of options. These deliberations are guided by a shared sense of responsibility and an interest in generating consensus, thus this system is geared toward compromise among advisors and encourages advisors to be open to shifting preferences. Collegial systems that have low centralization are likely to result in the production of two different solutions, deadlock and a subset solution. Delegation by the president places greater influence in the hands of advisors, particularly experts, who bargain and compete with one another with less interest in building consensus. As a result it is very possible that advisors arrive at a stalemate, because of differently held preferences. Alternatively, one advisor or group of advisors may be more effective at getting their preferences heard by the president and their options will dominant over others resulting in a subset solution.

With the inclusion of this discussion of process outcomes the Advisory System Framework is complete. Now it is possible to have a comprehensive understanding of the process that results from a president's choice of advisory structure (formal or collegial) and the kind of centralization that they are willing to exercise over the process. The addition of process outcomes explains what kinds of solutions the advisory systems will pursue; this is significant because the solutions (deadlock, subset, dominant-subset, dominant, and integrative) present strong indicators of the kind of policy that is ultimately chosen by the advisory system. Taking this approach moves closer to linking the activities of leader-group interaction with substantive foreign policy behavior while avoiding the subjectivity and complexity associated with defining and measuring policy outcomes.

The reformulation of the Johnson/George typology overcomes the problems associated with the original typologies and presents a new framework that has greater nuance. In addition, the framework has the added benefit of functioning to help synthesize existing foreign policy decision-making models and theories. The identified decision-making processes and their associated decision outcomes are examined using five cases of decision-making on security policy drawn from the Nixon (Vietnam War), Carter (Strategic Arms Limitation Talks II), Reagan (Strategic Arms Reduction Talks), Clinton (war in Yugoslavia), and George W. Bush (pre and post 9/11) administrations. The case studies are constructed using the method of Structured-focused Comparisons, in which a set of theoretically based questions and anticipated observations to those questions are made to guide the research and allow for comparison of decision making within and between cases. In the next chapter structured-focused comparisons is explained, the questions that guide the case study inquiry are presented and explained as well as the sample observations for each of the questions.

Chapter 2

An Explanation of Method and Cases

To assess the validity of the advisory system framework, the method of structured-focused comparisons is used to construct five cases of United States foreign policy decision-making.[1] Structured-focused comparison calls for the application of a theoretically based set of standardized questions that are used to guide a researcher's examination of each case. These questions need to be specific enough to be useful in examining the cases, but not too specific so that they are relevant to only one case. The theoretically based questions deal selectively with those aspects of the case argued to be relevant to the study's objectives and data requirements, in other words they are focused by the study's theory or in this case the characteristics of the framework (George 1982). The essential purpose of this method is to allow the researcher to draw causal inferences from the explanatory variables found within each case and gain control over the subject matter. This last point is especially important because without a method that structures and focuses a case, we are left with only a rich descriptive narrative with limited ability to examine vital causal factors.

Structured-focused comparison has an intrinsic value compared to the intensively studied single-case study, because it overcomes the small 'n' problem by allowing for intensive analysis of a few cases while at the same time making systematic comparisons that permit the drawing of causal inferences similar to larger quantitative studies. This case study approach has the ability to allow the researcher to 'study a phenomenon in its real life context,' particularly when 'the boundaries between phenomenon and context are not clearly evident' (Yin, 1989: 23). Steps can be taken to increase the number of observations in each case in order to provide a better foundation for

---

[1] Coming to a common understanding of what a case study is should be straight-forward, but it is not. There is no clear consensus as to what a case is, let alone a case study (Ragin and Becker 1992; Kaarbo and Beasley 1999). Case studies have been understood to be a 'multifaceted investigation,' utilizing qualitative methods, of a single phenomenon (Feagin 1991), and a method of obtaining a 'case' through an empirical investigation of a phenomenon and its context (Kaarbo and Beasley 1999). Essentially a case study is an examination of a phenomenon – here advisory systems – within their naturally occurring context using a variety of sources. A case study that systematically compares two or more phenomenon is a comparative case study.

asserting propositions; this will be discussed further in the next section.[2] Since the same set of theoretically relevant standardized questions are applied to all the cases in the study, there is an allowance for comparison across cases that vary on the explanatory variable. The argument has been made that focused comparison has the inherent limitation of being unable to address the issue of frequency between explanatory and dependent variables, unlike statistical methods (George & Smoke 1974: 96). However, there is no reason that the values found in response to the structured questions cannot be subject to analysis like data points in a quantitative study. Nonetheless, the purpose of the focused comparison is not only to discover the frequency of causal relationships, but to provide a greater insight into the interaction between the variables under examination—in this study the presidential management structure, degree of centralization, and the resulting decision-making outcomes. For the student of history these cases may, to a certain extent, prove to be dissatisfying because they do not possess the rich description of a historical narrative (which they are not designed to provide). Further research is required to give a 'complete' description of each case because the method of structured-focused comparisons is only concerned with those aspects of the case that are relevant to the theory under investigation.

The use of case studies, as a means to study advisory systems, has been the subject of criticism, because these studies have not been comparative in nature and concentrate too much on 'turning points and the idiosyncratic' (Cronin 1969: 326). The critique is correct in arguing that scholars have not engaged in 'rigorously designed comparisons (i.e., among succeeding occupants of a particular office or role)' (Cronin 1969: 326). It is worthwhile to

---

[2] The logic of this comparative method is consistent with the logic of both statistical and experimental methods in that all three aim at making generalizations by way of controlling for a variety of variables (Lijphart 1971). However, the comparative method differentiates itself, because the number of cases it deals with is small, which presents the problem of having too many variables being applied to a limited number of cases. This 'degrees of freedom' problem makes it difficult to identify the explanatory variables that are responsible for influencing the dependent variable. Although the structured-focused comparison is a less effective method of controlling variables than statistical methods, it still permits greater confidence when making inferences compared to descriptively rich narratives where the certainty of causal relationships is opaque. Not only does a structured-focused comparison compensate for the less than high degree of verification by providing an in-depth evaluation of the relationship between variables, it also permits a ready application of its findings to other cases. George and Smoke (1974) comment that, 'variation among cases is addressed explicitly and analytically by the focused comparison method, conclusions can be drawn with this method that can assist in the diagnosis of a fresh case, historical or contemporary.'

cite Ragin and Becker (1992: 219), who have addressed this very point at length.

> Social scientists interested in testing theories that make general claims, either implicitly or explicitly, must seek to limit the uniqueness and specificity of the empirical world; it is necessary to place limits on detail and diversity. In short, the continuous web of human social life must be sliced and diced in a way compatible with the goal of testing the generality of theoretical ideas, and comparable objects of research must be established so that boundaries can be placed around measurement operations.

However, the idea that this cannot be accomplished within the confines of a case is incorrect. This study's contribution is to present a means of using the method of structured-focused comparison to systematically identify 'persisting patterns, styles and roles which characterize presidential advisory system interactions' (Cronin 1969: 326).

A final criticism of the comparative method is that the generalizations inferred from its limited number of cases can be easily invalidated by a single deviant case. To be fair, this criticism can also be leveled against statistical methods and in both instances it would be incorrect. The purpose of the comparative method is not to generate universal laws, but probabilistic ones, thus a single deviant case is not enough to invalidate the findings of a comparative case study (Lijphart 1971). The deviant case weakens the case study's hypotheses, but it is only with the mounting of deviant cases that the findings of the cases studies become invalid. Overall, this method is appropriate for this research given that the focus of this study is to test for the presence of different advisory systems in different cases and to assess the validity of their internal dynamics.

Case Study Questions

As noted earlier, the central feature of the structured-focused comparison method is the set of questions that is used to systematically structure the case study inquiry. The set of questions used in this study (Table 2.1) is designed to address the features of the advisory system framework, the system structure, and degree of centralization. More specifically, the questions are designed to address the central elements of the advisory system, which are the position of the president within the structure in relation to the advisors, the nature of control the president has over the system, the way the president coordinates activities among advisors, and the kinds of functions performed by advisors.

Table 2.1 Case Study Questions

1) What role does the leader play within the advisory system?
2) Who generates preferences in the system that will be deliberated over and finally chosen?
3) What is the nature of the decision-making process?
4) What are the procedures for managing the system?
5) What is the control mechanism employed in the management of the process?
6) What is the nature of the policy solution?

Taken as a whole the case study questions provide the researcher with the ability to assess the degree of centralization of the advisory system. Note the aims of the questions are to assess centralization within the system; they are not intended to completely reassess the nature of the advisory system. The reason for this approach is that a consensus has been built in the advisory management literature regarding the kind of system chosen by past presidents. As the preceding discussion of the various alternative typologies indicates, what is in question is not the basic structure of the formal and collegial systems, but, rather, the variations within these basic structures. There is a consensus that Reagan's system was basically formal (Johnson 1971; George 1980; Campbell 1986; Hermann and Preston 1994; Burke 2000), Carter's collegial (Johnson 1971; George 1980; Campbell 1986; Crabb and Mulcahy 1988; Hess 1988; Burke and Greenstein 1991; Hermann and Preston 1994; Burke 2000), Nixon's formal (Johnson 1971; George 1980; Light 1982; Hess 1988; Hermann and Preston 1994), Johnson's informal (Johnson 1971; George 1980; Herman and Preston 1994; Walcott and Hult 1995; Burke 2000), Eisenhower's formal (Johnson 1971; George 1980; Walcott and Hult 1995), Bush's formal (Hermann and Preston 1994; Burke 2000), and Clinton's informal (Hermann and Preston 1994; Preston 2001).[3]

It has been the practice when using the method of structured-focused comparison to simply construct the cases by asking a set of questions. However, this proves insufficient if the interest is to structure the case study and draw attention to the theoretically relevant aspects of the case because a set of structured questions necessitates that a set of expected observations be postulated (Kaarbo and Beasley 1999). Just as in a quantitative study, the values of the independent and dependent variables need to be specified before conducting a study; the same is true of structured-focused comparisons. The

---

[3] Hermann and Preston (1994) and Burke (2000) consider the Bush advisory system to possess characteristics of both formal and informal, but there seems to be a greater amount of weight given to the system's informal characteristics such as the need to build consensus. Thus, despite some formal characteristics this study treats the Bush advisory system as being informal/collegial.

structured-focused comparison is performed to 'assure the acquisition of comparable data from several cases,' but without knowledge of appropriate responses the research may be 'guided by the readily available historical data rather than by a well defined theoretical focus' (George 1979).[4]

The questions are designed to address the theoretical interest of the study, which is the nature of presidential control within the advisory system; the expected values associated with these questions are the features of the framework found in Table 1.3 (see page 23). For each question there will be a set of observations indicating high centralization and low centralization for both collegial and formal structures. The focus of this study is to assess the validity of the advisory system framework by identifying the characteristics of the advisory systems in the decision making of various administrations. This means that the response to a question asking how conflict is dealt with in the system should be 'answered' with one that matches one of the characteristics specified in the typology. The structured-focused comparison questions and examples of observations are discussed below.

Questions and Observations

What role does the leader play within the advisory system? In high and low centralized formal systems, the observations are identified by the framework: 1) a leader can evaluate presented options, 2) a leader can be an active member of group guiding and shaping deliberations, or 3) the leader delegates authority to others. When a leader evaluates presented options they will either be presented in a report or meeting. The reports can be presented in a meeting where the president listens to both sides and then decides or the president is given written reports and chooses in isolation. Presidential participation is limited in the process of generating options. For example Nixon would often receive reports from subordinates and in the evenings spend time going over the option papers noting on a pad of paper the costs and benefits of each option. Only after this isolated process would Nixon choose an option; rare was the occasion when Nixon would decide on an issue in a meeting setting. On the other hand, Preston (2001) discusses Truman's tendency to listen to advisors in meetings and then quite quickly make a decision based on their presentations.

In highly centralized collegial systems the leader participates in the formulation of options through participation in meetings or through memos redirecting or commenting on options while the advisors work on formulating options. Presidents raise questions and issues that cause advisors to rethink their options or create new options. It is also expected that presidents will be

---

[4] An implicit benefit of the structured-focused comparison method is that it provides for the ability to duplicate the research conducted on the cases and to permit the study to be checked, which is beneficial for future research or to assess the validity of the research findings.

involved and interject themselves in the formulation of options as opposed to waiting to participate in the process when the options are complete. Early in President Kennedy's tenure in office he was confronted with the possibility of a communist overthrow of the US-backed government in Laos. Kennedy was presented with a series of options by the Joint Chiefs of Staff (JCS) dealing with American use of force, but dissatisfied by the dizzying array of options, Kennedy directed the JCS to rethink and simplify the options. In addition, Kennedy established a task force, so that he had the means to be updated on the changing events in the country, thus allowing him to be more engaged in the process as more options were produced (Strong 1991).

Collegial systems with low centralization have the president making decisions on issues presented to him, not necessarily as options representing the range of opinions either in the entire administration or in all the committees, but courses of action suggested by individual advisors. In short, the leader forms the hub of the system but the interaction with advisors is desultory; essentially the leader's role is playing the 'hub' of a wheel with 'broken spokes.' This kind of role is exemplified by Bill Clinton who delegated authority, but 'failed to establish clear structures of delegation' resulting in a 'free for all' (Preston 2001: 224).

Who generates preferences in the system that the President and advisors deliberated on and finally chose? The expected observations associated with this question are 1) leader expresses a general preference, 2) the leader pushes the group to assess a range of options, 3) advisors compete to get preferences to leader, and 4) advisors are instrumental in guiding policy. Highly centralized formal systems will feature the leader expressing a strong policy preference, thereby placing parameters on the options advisors will generate. For example, Eisenhower in preparation for the four-power summit in Geneva wanted to begin the process of improving relations with the Soviet Union, thus he called on his advisors to create an arms control agreement that could be presented to the public or negotiated among the attendees (Strong 1992: 32). Within systems with low centralization, leaders or presidents will express vague or extremely broad preferences, thus less constraint is placed on advisors in conceiving options. Truman, upon becoming president, was informed of the United States' development of an atomic weapon; it was left up to Truman to decide how, if at all, to use this weapon. At this point in the war Truman's main concern was ending the war with the least loss of American lives. This broadly defined imperative permitted those who supported dropping the bomb to continue to debate the 'when and how' of the devices use, but it also opened the door for opposition to redirect policy toward a less destructive path, although their attempts ultimately failed.

The generation of preferences in high- and low-centralized collegial systems differs from the formal systems. In highly centralized collegial systems, although leaders can and will express preferences like their formal counterparts, there is significant room for preferences to bubble up from advisors as the leader pushes advisors to assess a broader range of options. Consequently, the possibility of preferences being changed or new ones arising are increased. Kennedy during the Cuban Missile Crisis was interested in bringing about a resolution of the crisis, ideally with a removal of the missiles without a confrontation. But on the issue of what would be the appropriate strategy for achieving these goals, Kennedy encouraged advisors to share all of their preferences in order to find the most practical solution. When a collegial system has low centralization, preferences are more of a reflection of advisors than those of the president. Kennedy was a part of the process of constructing preferences during the Cuban Missile Crisis resulting in his direct contribution to generating and setting preferences. Bill Clinton often delegated the formulation of policy to those in the administration that had expertise and, as a result, policy preferences tended to reflect those of expert advisors (Preston 2001).

What is the nature of the decision-making process? The observations associated with this question are: 1) discouragement of bargaining with conflict and dissenting voices being excluded, 2) bargaining and conflict take place below the level of the president, and 3) there is a shared responsibility for decisions. In highly centralized formal systems bargaining, conflict, and dissenting views will be discouraged. Presidents will try to accomplish this by clearly delineating roles among advisors, asserting strong preferences that constrain opposing voices or cut opposition out of the process. Eisenhower reduced bargaining and conflict by structuring his system so that he avoided "overlap regarding jurisdictions or responsibilities"; this was in addition to giving strict orders to individuals such as Dulles regarding his preferences (Preston 2001: 70).

In formal systems with low centralization, bargaining takes place below the level of the president, because the president is primarily concerned with evaluating options. There is no interest in hearing or participating in the wrangling between advisors. Moreover, the weak setting of preferences by the president allows advisors to push for their own preferred policies. Advisors compete to get their views expressed to the president at the expense of the policy preferences of other advisors. Alternatively, advisors in the context of committees will attempt to reconcile differences, but given the ability of advisors to advance their views without compromise, bargaining may not be productive. During deliberations over the use of the first atomic bomb, Assistant Secretary of the Navy Ralph Bard wrote to Truman urging him to reconsider dropping the bomb and instead to blockade Japan. Bard served on the Interim Committee tasked with making recommendations to the president. Instead of making his challenge in committee meetings he chose to appeal directly to the president hoping to have a better chance of making a change in policy.

Bargaining and conflict also characterize the process for low-centralized collegial systems, but in this system the bargaining and conflict takes place in front of the president in meetings and among advisors. This system is especially prone to conflict and bargaining given that the president delegates authority to policy experts. Thus, clashes between experts sharing a similar competency or area of interest should be expected. The tensions between Secretary of State Madeline Albright and Secretary of Defense William Cohen over the use of force in Bosnia are typical of the kinds of conflict that can and will arise in a collegial system with low centralization. Conflict takes place in highly centralized collegial systems, but in this type of system the leader harnesses conflict in an effort to hear the full range of options. The conflict does not come at the expense of a shared sense of responsibility for policy outcomes. This means that the president permits, or in some cases encourages, conflict among advisors by soliciting opposing points of view or by overlapping responsibility in order to bring opposing views into conflict. In the end, it is expected that even though advisors may retain opposing views they will have contributed to the process. Sharing responsibility for decisions was a feature of both the FDR and the Johnson administrations. FDR in particular is known for placing his advisors in conflict with one another in order to assess policy options with the manipulation of advisors often taking place without their knowledge (Johnson 1974).

What are the procedures for managing conflict and information in the system? The four advisory systems exhibit four different ways to manage conflict in the system 1) policy making and procedures are orderly and well defined, 2) meetings are regularized and frequent with core advisors present, 3) procedures may be circumvented, and 4) no regular mode of interacting with advisors is established. Presidents in highly centralized formal systems manage procedures by establishing an orderly and highly structured process; for these leaders there is a "proper" way to make decisions and there is a need to maintain the infrastructure created to manage the system. Although all presidents create formal committees, these committees vary according to the centrality of the committees in the decision-making process. Presidents seeking an orderly and well-defined procedure will place an emphasis on committee work that forms the foundations for formulation and deliberation of options higher up the hierarchy. Eisenhower put into place a series of committees so that policy papers could be fully vetted by staff and only issues requiring the president's attention would make their way to the top. The work done by the committees, such as the National Security Council (NSC) Planning Board, would be sent up the hierarchy to the full council for deliberation. Once a report(s) reached the NSC the issues were debated among the principals and only afterward would

Eisenhower make his final decision (Preston 2001). The Eisenhower administration did not operate based on formal structures alone; there was a degree of informality in the process, but this too was planned and functioned in a well-defined way within the system. Eisenhower would in fact consult informally with advisors. The use of informal meetings was not intended to undermine or circumvent the formal process, but instead was a deliberate means to supplement the process.

This contrasts with the formal systems that have low centralization, whereby committees are in place to manage issues, but advisors frequently operate outside of committees or use other channels to advance policy preferences. The circumvention of procedures is not a deliberate management strategy by the president, but is a product of advisors working with broad policy guidance and with no gatekeeper between themselves and the president controlling deliberations. Again, the actions of Assistant Secretary of State Bard and Admiral Grew in 1945 prove illustrative, given that this was a situation where both served on committees but appealed directly to the President outside of the process to influence policy.

Just as high and low formal systems differ in degree of control over procedures, high and low collegial systems also differ. Highly centralized collegial systems feature regularized and frequent meetings with core advisors. These meetings can be daily or weekly depending on the issue; ultimately emphasis is on coming together to deal with a specific issue. Johnson during the Vietnam War held 'Tuesday Lunches' with a core set of advisors to discuss the administration's strategy and policy toward the conflict, while Kennedy during the Cuban Missile Crisis formed the Executive Committee (EX Comm) that met daily over the course of the crisis. Low centralized collegial systems are the diametric opposite of highly centralized systems, because there is no regular mode of interacting with advisors. An administration of this kind may have committees, but their membership will fluctuate and important decisions and issues are more likely to be discussed outside these forums. Issues will be taken up by individuals who have a particular expertise or by an ad hoc grouping of advisors. Consequently, there may not be any regularity to meetings or discernable organizing principle.

What is the control mechanism employed to manage the process? Formal systems have a gatekeeper that acts as a manager of the process, but the role played by the gatekeeper differs when accounting for degree of centralization. Highly centralized formal systems possess a gatekeeper that acts as advocate and screens information and access. Contact with the president is directed through an individual(s) that allows advisors to have the discretion to alter or reinterpret information or decide who sees the president. Formal systems with low centralization have, instead of a gatekeeper, an honesty broker that impartially presents options; these individuals are designated or act as a conduit for information and advice that is transmitted up the hierarchy without alteration or re-interpretation.

The control mechanism in a highly centralized collegial system is not an individual, but the consensus a president attempts to build for any given policy. This requires that the president or trusted advisors spend time holding meetings with opposition or minority members in order to get their support and to get to an agreement on a position. Lyndon Johnson, for example, before considering a policy insisted that his advisors come to a conclusion before he would enter into a discussion on a policy issue, thus forcing advisors to interact in order to come to a common position. Low-centralized collegial systems place less emphasis on this need for consensus. Since policy is often influenced by expert advisors who have been delegated authority over formulating policy, the president meets less regularly with advisors, making the generation of consensus difficult. Consensus can arise and the president can push for consensus, but it is not critical to the president or necessary for his advisors.

What is the nature of the policy solution? It is possible to identify five different solutions in response to this question: dominant, deadlock, integrative, subset, and dominant-subset. Dominant solutions are indicated by the advisory system choosing the option that satisfies the preference expressed by the president. Eisenhower's ultimate decision not to save the French from defeat at Dien Bien Phu in 1954 demonstrates a dominant solution. Eisenhower, long before the situation at Dien Bien Phu rose to a crisis level, expressed that he did not want to deploy US ground troops to Vietnam. Eisenhower stated that this was his preference throughout this period up until the crisis. With Eisenhower's preference in mind, the National Security Council formulated a series of options that emphasized actions other than the deployment of troops, although this was admittedly one of the options. As the fall of Dien Bien Phu became more likely, discussions revolved around US air support and possible re-supply of the French garrison; by this time deployment of ground troops was no longer an option (Preston 2001). Eisenhower ultimately decided on the option not to intervene with the proviso that intervention may be necessary in the form of air power.

Dominant-subset solutions are options that are distinctly the preference of a portion of the advisory system and generally conform to a set of values or beliefs held by the president, but are not so well defined to be considered preferences. On Truman's arrival in Washington after the North Korean invasion of the South, Dean Acheson and Secretary of Defense Louis Johnson were responsible for briefing the President. At this meeting Truman exclaimed that he was "going to let them have it" and that "this was a challenge we must meet" (Preston 2001: 48). As staff and advisors began to formulate options after the North Koreans had been pushed back to the 38th parallel, disagreement arose between the staff that favored crossing the 38th parallel and those that proposed halting the advance. Bargaining ensued among advisors ultimately leading the Defense Department and the JCS to advance their preferred option of operations north of the 38th parallel which was compatible with Truman's views that the challenge must be met.

Integrative solutions are identified by options that are the product of compromise between advisors and a synthesis of the preferences of those participating in the decision making. Kennedy, confronting the possibility of the overthrow of the Laotian government by communist forces, formulated two options with his advisors, maintaining neutrality and deploying US forces. Both choices were less than optimal from Kennedy's point of view, thus he chose to combine the options, maintaining neutrality while at the same time making the necessary preparations for military intervention. The solutions found in both collegial and formal systems with low control are deadlock solutions. Deadlock solutions are indicated when a stalemate occurs and no decision can be reached on an issue resulting in retention of the existing policy or the inability to construct any new policy.

In the five case studies constructed here, each of the six questions is used. To guide the analysis those parts of the policy process focused on the formulation of strategy, thus excluding an examination of policy implementation. Each case is divided into a series decision-making episodes. Dividing the cases in this manner serves three purposes. First, it acts to increase the number of observations in the overall study, thus allowing a greater degree of certainty in the findings.[5] Increasing the number of observations, first, has the benefit of overcoming the small 'n' problem often associated with case studies. Second, it permits the researcher to track the consistency of an administration in the use of an advisory system over time. If changes do occur the researcher can isolate the change and assess the circumstances contributing to that change. There is the possibility that as the issue begins to evolve the needs of the president may change or the external environment may be altered, forcing a change. At the outset when an early position is being formulated, a president may start out with a more formal system, for example, but as events unfold and the president's attention increases and the need for quick decision-making becomes paramount, the president might change to an informal system. Only by dividing the cases into phases can one understand if these kinds of changes take place or alternatively the system used remains stable over time.

---

[5] The increasing of observations by adding cases has been criticized because (Ragin et al. 1996; Munck 1998) it can result in 'conceptual stretching.' Conceptual stretching results from taking a set of concepts and applying them to new cases when these new cases are not comparable to the original set. This concern is not a problem found in this study because the added observations are produced by parsing the existing cases that have already been determined to be appropriate to the cases.

Advisory System Case Studies

The framework is evaluated using five security negotiations from five different US administrations. The specific cases chosen are the Nixon administration's efforts to end the war in Vietnam (1969–1973), Carter's negotiations with the USSR on strategic arms limitation (SALT II) (1977–1979), Reagan's strategic arms negotiations (START I) (1982–1988), Clinton's deliberations on policy toward the war in Bosnia (1993–1995) and George W. Bush's foreign policy (pre and post-9/11). The cases were chosen according to whether they possess the appropriate advisory system characteristics, collegial/formal, and low or high centralization (Table 2.2).

Table 2.2 Presidential Advisory Systems

	Formal	Collegial
High Centralization	Richard Nixon	Jimmy Carter
Low Centralization	Ronald Reagan George W. Bush	Bill Clinton

The studies by George (1980; 1998), Burke (2000), and Johnson (1974) agree that Nixon's management structure falls into the formal category. George (1988) asserts that Nixon's management structure was essentially an elaboration of the Eisenhower chief of staff concept. The difference between the Eisenhower and Nixon structures is that Nixon centralized more decision making in the White House and it was more formal in that the number of committees was significantly increased. (The nature of the Nixon structure will be explained further in the next section.) The new structure utilized during Nixon's administration, George contends, was 'novel' and 'unconventional' in that it was superimposed on the departments and altered the traditional hierarchy that existed in the foreign policy-making process. At its core the Nixon structure is still the same as the Eisenhower model, but greater influence accrues to the advisor who serves as buffer between the president and the rest of the advisors. These characteristics dictate that Nixon's advisory system is a highly centralized formal advisory system. As such it should display the following characteristics: 1) Gatekeeper acts as advocate and screens information and access, 2) Leader expresses general preferences shaping consideration of options, 3) Orderly policy-making with well-defined procedures, 4) Leader evaluates presented options, 5) Discouragement of bargaining and conflict in group; exclusion of dissenting voices, 6) Dominant solutions should be chosen.

The features of the Carter advisory system are both collegial and highly centralized. George and Stern (1998) argue that Carter's advisory system was a mix of formalistic and collegial systems. The system structure was formalistic in that Carter initially relied on two committees, the Policy Review Committee (PRC) and Special Coordinating Committee (SCC), to deliberate and formulate options, but it is collegial in that Carter wanted advisors without the influence of a dominant figure such as a Chief of Staff to engage and coordinate with one another in a collegial manner within and across committees. In addition, Carter was involved in the process by monitoring meetings, bringing together meetings of the NSC and studying a given issue down to the smallest detail. Burke (2000) also points out that Carter used a combination of management styles; Burke refers to the Carter system as centralized collegiality. Burke, like George and Stern, notes the lack of a chief of staff, the equality among advisors, Carter's frequent involvement in deliberations, the use of committees producing written memorandum, and Carter's intense consumption of reports.

Given the characteristics highlighted by these studies, the Carter advisory is understood to fit into the highly centralized and collegial category. The Carter advisory system should thus display the following characteristics: 1) Leader is an active member of the group, guiding and shaping deliberations, 2) Leader pushes group to assess a range of options, 3) Shared responsibility for decisions, 4) Emphasis on building consensus among a core set of advisors, 5) Meetings are frequent and regularized with a core set of advisors.

Unlike the Carter and Nixon advisory systems, in which there was clear consensus among scholars on the type of structure—Nixon (formal) and Carter (collegial), the characterization of Reagan's advisory system is slightly more complex. Over the course of Reagan's two terms in office, the personnel of his staff and cabinet changed quite often, and with these changes came alterations in the advisory system. Nonetheless, in general terms, it is possible to identify Reagan's advisory system as formal. George and Stern (1998) describe Reagan as having a 'synthesis' of formal and collegial systems. Hermann and Preston (1994) on the other hand note that Reagan fits a type of president that is 'interested in institutionalizing a formal set of rules and procedures in the organization of the White House in the service of accomplishing a specific task' (Hermann & Preston 1994: 90). In addition, they cite Stephen Hess (1969) who asserts that Reagan had a formal hierarchical system.

It is clear that Reagan instituted an advisory system that had low centralization. The low centralization that characterized the Reagan administration applied to foreign affairs instead of domestic affairs which was more centralized with a greater role played by a Chief of Staff acting as a gatekeeper (Burke 2000). Reagan delegated authority and took a 'hands off' approach when dealing with advisors (George & Stern 1998). If Reagan did have an advisory system that was formal and had low centralization observations, the case study should indicate: 1) Leader chooses options, 2) Advisors compete to get preferences presented to leader, 3) Gatekeeper acts as honestbroker and presents options (opportunity for advisors to appeal to leader), 4) Bargaining and conflict take place at level below president, 5) Procedures may be circumvented.

The nature of the Clinton administration's advisory structure must be determined in light of the fact that few studies have been done with the direct purpose of understanding the structure of his advisory system. Nonetheless, with the existing literature, it is possible to assert with some confidence that the Clinton administration advisory system can be characterized as having a collegial structure with low centralization. Renshon (1996) and Campbell (1996) identify Clinton as having a spokes-in-a-wheel structure. Campbell emphasizes that this structure was loose and bottom up in nature while Renshon (1996: 186) posits that Clinton centralized power but at the same time lacked focus and had a disorganized leadership style. Burke (2000) argues that Clinton's structure and management was neither 'spokes in a wheel' nor hierarchic, 'instead, Clinton's aides moved freely from issue to issue, and Clinton spent much of his time in meetings in which participation was a function of who showed up.' What Burke (2000) identifies as a structure that is neither formal nor collegial is, in fact, collegial, but this is a collegial structure in which the president exercises low centralization over the process. From these assessments the conclusion drawn is that Clinton had a collegial structure while at the same time he maintained low centralization and, as a consequence, it should be expected that the decision-making process in his administration should have the following characteristics: 1) A willingness to delegate authority to others that have expertise, 2) Advisors are instrumental in guiding policy, 3) Less emphasis on consensus building among advisors, 4) Conflict and bargaining between advisors, and 5) No regular mode of interaction with advisors.

George W. Bush has been described as the MBA president, because aside from being the first President with a Masters in Business Administration, he has stated how his approach of managing the White House is like that of a business (Greenstein 2002). It seems clear that this is the model that Bush has pursued in managing the policy process. Bush has sought to establish early on in his administration a hierarchic structure with clearly specified responsibilities for all of his advisors (Walcott and Hult 2004). The emphasis on hierarchy and clearly delineated lines of authority indicates that Bush has adopted a formal structure. It is also clear Bush began his administration exercising low centralization over the process. Bush has approached the management of his advisors by choosing not to involve himself in the formulation of policy options, these details he leaves up to his advisors, instead he allows his advisors to develop the options from which he is to choose (Heilbrunn 1999; Greenstein 2002). Bush's belief is that this style of management allows him to focus on the big pictures. Considering these two features, hierarchy and the hands-off style of management, Bush's advisory system is formal with low centralization and should display the same set of characteristics as those of the Reagan administration.

Once again there are several objectives in the examination of these cases. The case studies serve as a means to evaluate the accuracy of the Advisory System Framework in explaining the variations in decision-making processes and decision outcomes across advisory systems. There is enough evidence within the literature on presidential management and empirical evidence that indicates that the often cited typologies (Johnson/George) are far from being accurate, despite their being ideal types. The use of cases to test the framework results in an ability to better understand the decision-making process as a whole and the interaction between leaders and advisors specifically. Chapter 8 evaluates the findings from the five case studies with an emphasis on discussing the case studies' support for the advisory system framework and any unique or unexpected findings

The examination of these cases serves to develop the Advisory System Framework which in turn provides the opportunity to develop a tool that can be useful in synthesizing existing decision-making theories and models. In short the framework functions as a basis for addressing the occurrence of bureaucratic politics, groupthink, and/or the manipulation of the decision-making process by advisors. Chapter 9 demonstrates the way in which the framework also functions as a very practical means for making recommendations for the improvement of the decision-making process. Knowing the exact nature of individual advisory systems permits a tailoring of recommendations, so they are appropriate given a president's management style and chosen system. The advisory system is the locus for the activity of the president and it is here that the president is influenced by those around him and chooses specific courses of action. Therefore, the advisory system and the variation among advisory systems are of great interest if one is to have a comprehensive understanding of the formulation of foreign policy in general and in United States foreign policy in particular.

Chapter 3

Nixon, Kissinger, and North Vietnam

Organization of Nixon's Foreign Policy Advisory System

Nixon learned from the experiences of past administrations and like many presidents before him Nixon came into office intent on avoiding the mistakes of the previous administration. Of particular concern for Nixon was the need to institute a foreign policy machinery that would allow him to have control over policy, yet enable him to achieve the ambitious goals that he had set for his administration. A primary concern for Nixon was to avoid the consensus[1] decision making that he experienced as vice-president in the Eisenhower administration (Prados 1991; Bundy 1998; Brookings 1998). Eisenhower chose to make use of a series of formal committees in which options were generated, discussed, and then offered up to the president for choice. Ideally, Nixon wanted 'a system that would provide the President with a full range of options for decision rather than a single agreed interagency view' (Lord 1988). Nixon wanted to use young, foreign policy professionals who were recruited from outside the government, thereby freeing them from the taint of the in-the-beltway bureaucracy that Nixon so much despised. The structure that Nixon ultimately wanted had the added benefit of isolating the State Department and the Central Intelligence Agency (CIA), which he believed contributed to past presidents' policy failures.

It was with these ideas in mind that Nixon charged Henry Kissinger with revamping the national security apparatus. Kissinger in turn directed Mort Halperin to prepare a memo laying out the reorganization of the national security infrastructure according to the president's broadly defined guidelines. Halperin created a hierarchic structure that placed the National Security Council in a position of prominence, followed in status by the National Review Group, a series of Inter-Agency Regional Groups, and then ad hoc working groups. Kissinger attached to Halperin's report a further set of suggestions for restructuring the National Security Council staff. The NSC would contain a group of assistants who would expedite NSC projects and focus on middle-range goals (Prados 1991). Below these assistants were the operations staff

---

[1] Nixon was noted as saying that he wanted his national security staff to function like Eisenhower, but 'without the concurrences.'

divided according to a regional focus, the planning staff that was tasked with strategic planning, and the military assistant who assembled intelligence and provided military advice.

The position of the National Security Advisor and his staff was enhanced by the fact that all the key committees were either chaired by Kissinger or by a member of his staff. The State Department was allowed to chair the Undersecretaries' Committee, which dealt with operational issues; this meant that neither the State Department nor any other major department was permitted to chair a committee that was responsible for the formulation of policy. Winston Lord highlights that 'in the government whoever chairs the committees helps run the show' and this was no less true in the Nixon administration (Brookings 1998: 7). The control of the chair positions permitted the National Security Council staff to 'slap its own views on top' of the State Department and, because all reports flowed through Kissinger, he could 'slap on his own views as it went to the President' (Brookings 1998: 7). Given this set of characteristics, the Nixon advisory system should produce a decision-making process with the following set of features:

- Leader evaluates presented options
- Leader expresses general preference shaping consideration of options
- Gatekeeper acts as advocate and screens information and access
- Discouragement of bargaining and conflict in group; dissenting voices excluded
- Orderly policy-making with well-defined procedures
- Dominant solution

By the time Nixon approved the new advisory structure on December 27, 1968, he had already selected the principals for his national security team. Individuals of particular importance in this study of Nixon's policy making during Vietnam are the Secretary of Defense, Secretary of State, National Security Advisor, and members of the National Security staff. In addition, the Chairman of the Joint Chiefs of Staff, the military commander in Vietnam and members of the White House staff all played supporting advisory roles. Filling the spot of Secretary of Defense was Melvin Laird, Republican Congressman from Wisconsin, who, prior to joining the cabinet, served on the Defense Subcommittee of the House Appropriations committee. As a result of his ties to the Congress and his knowledge of the Pentagon and its operations, Laird turned into one of Nixon's most independent cabinet members[2] (Bundy 1998).

---

[2] Laird quickly recognized the significance of the new NSC structure and the fact that all information would have to flow through Kissinger before it would reach the President. Laird objected and was given assurances by Kissinger that the Pentagon would not be cut out of the loop. Laird's willingness to challenge Kissinger and the

Traditionally, the most important player on the National Security Council is the Secretary of State, but this was not the case during Nixon's years in office. William Rogers, former Attorney General in the Eisenhower administration and Nixon's personal friend, was chosen to head the State Department despite having no foreign policy experience. Nixon's interest in controlling and conducting foreign policy and his distrust of the State Department led him to choose someone whom he felt would be loyal and unlikely to object to being excluded from participating in activities traditionally within the Secretary of State's purview.

Nixon's activity in foreign policy not only undermined the role of the Secretary of State, but also, as a result, it ensured that his National Security Advisor would not be making policy on his own. Nixon was more familiar with Henry Kissinger's writings than with Kissinger personally, having only met him once before he selected Kissinger to be Special Assistant for National Security Affairs. Both Kissinger and Nixon shared a common 'realist' orientation to foreign policy and Kissinger's style of decision making fit well into Nixon's plans to centralize decision making within the White House (Hersh 1983; Bundy 1998). Kissinger, in addition to participating in the restructuring of the NSC staff, expanded the size of the staff to 114 persons, which was larger than both the Kennedy and Johnson staffs (Prados 1991). Among these staff members several of the assistants played important roles in the formulation and operation of the policy on Vietnam, most notably, Alexander Haig, Anthony Lake, Roger Morris, William Watts, Bill Smyser, and Winston Lord.

Individuals other than the president's principal advisors and the NSC staff contributed significantly to policy formulation. Nixon retained the services of several individuals who held posts in the Johnson administration; Ellsworth Bunker, for example, was kept in his position as US Ambassador to South Vietnam. While on the military side, Nixon kept Creighton Abrams as commander of US forces in Vietnam, Earle Wheeler as Chairman of the Joint Chiefs of Staff and Admiral Thomas Moorer as Chief of Naval Operations who would occasional fill the role of Chairman of the JCS. Aside from these individuals, domestic policy advisors, such as H.R. Haldeman, Secretary of Treasury John Connally, and Spiro Agnew occasionally contributed to the formulation of foreign policy.

The following section presents a description of the international and domestic environment surrounding Nixon and his advisors' attempts to arrive at a favorable settlement with the North Vietnamese. This environment serves as both a source of opportunities as well as constraints for Nixon and his advisors

---

president increased his ability to influence decision making on negotiations with North Vietnam, though his primary focus was on the military aspects of negotiations.

during the attempts to negotiate and is important to present this before moving on to analyze the actual decision-making process.

US and North Vietnam Negotiations: Policy Environment Overview

Throughout the 1968 campaign, Nixon publicly alluded to his plans to bring an end to war in Vietnam. Although not specific, Nixon indicated on the campaign trail that he wanted a settlement to the war that would not be seen as a defeat; to bring this about Nixon wanted to 'mobilize economic and political leadership' (Bundy 1998). In private Nixon intimated that he wanted to bring to bear, in a 'carrot and stick fashion,' economic, political, diplomatic, and military pressure on the North Vietnamese (Bundy 1998; Kimball 1998). However, even by late 1968, negotiations with the North Vietnamese barely got off the ground. After having begun the process of seriously negotiating in May, no progress was made on the substantive issues confronting the participants in the war in Southeast Asia.

Negotiations begun by the Johnson administration became bogged down in a myriad of procedural issues. Discussions carried out by Cyrus Vance and Averell Harriman concerned the participation of the National Liberation Front (NLF)—the organizational name for the Vietcong guerilla forces in South Vietnam—in negotiations. The South Vietnamese government objected to the participation of the NLF in any talks, fearing their participation was tacit recognition of their legitimacy. A compromise formula was eventually constructed that allowed NLF participation, but avoided the need for South Vietnam to recognize the NLF. Throughout the summer, North Vietnam objected to this compromise formula and refused to begin negotiations until October when they finally relented. With this concession, Johnson fulfilled his promise of halting the bombing of the north. Despite Johnson's efforts to jump-start the talks, negotiations could not begin because the South Vietnamese President Nguyen Van Thieu, after winning his presidential election, refused to attend negotiations until the South Vietnamese government was given higher status than the NLF. Thus, Nixon entered office with the Paris negotiations stalled in their most nascent stage.

Domestically, a subtle but pronounced shift was taking place within the body politic away from supporting the war efforts and toward a withdrawal of US forces in Vietnam. As Kimball (1998: 42) maintains, 'Despite their flaws, polls provided persuasive evidence in early 1968 of a citizenry uneasy about the war and growing more weary of it, with a majority turning against its prosecution.' At the time of Nixon's election victory a majority favored a withdrawal of troops whether that be by negotiations or 'Vietnamization.' Overlaying the general public sentiment were the very public activities of the anti-war movement, the demonstrations at the 1968 Democratic National

Convention and civil strife over issues of race that took place around the country. Nixon believed he was confronted with resolving the war in Vietnam in a manner that suited US interests (which in his view was an 'honorable' peace) while at the same time resisting the pressure coming from changing public sentiment and protesters.

On the ground in South Vietnam, the military situation began to change in the months that followed the Tet Offensive. The North Vietnamese after Johnson's bombing-halt announcement reduced the number of regiments operating south of the demilitarized zone (DMZ) from 25 to 22. US military commanders took advantage of the reduction in NVA regular forces by diverting the newly freed South Vietnamese forces to offensive operations further south. Consequently, joint US and South Vietnamese army (ARVN) operations increased by a third during November and December, with small-unit actions doubling between November and March (Kahin & Lewis 1969). The big-unit sweeps conducted by US forces, combined with pacification and small-unit operations, were effective in bringing about the short-term attrition of North Vietnam's order of battle. However, these operations created long-term problems politically, because relocation, search and destroy missions, indiscriminate bombing, and the purposeful destruction of villages alienated the same population that the war effort was supposed to help (Hersh 1983). By the time of Nixon's inauguration the military situation on the ground could best be described as stabilized, if not favoring the US/ARVN.[3]

Overall, Nixon and his advisors faced numerous constraints as Nixon's first term in office began. Domestically, pressure was building for a rapid resolution of the conflict, preferably with an American withdrawal. Public sentiment created an even greater sense of urgency in restarting the diplomatic efforts, which had stalled due to the recalcitrance of the governments of North and South Vietnam. Militarily, the situation in the South appeared to have stabilized, but the combination of uncertainty about the North's intentions and the public's aversion to the mounting casualties, made the situation in actuality tenuous at best. Under these conditions, Nixon attempted to extricate the US from South Vietnam while maintaining US credibility internationally. It is in this context that the Nixon advisory system and its attempts to bring an end to the conflict in Vietnam are evaluated.

---

[3] An issue that would early on preoccupy the NSC meeting was the capability of the NLF and North Vietnamese. The administration was particularly concerned with the lull in fighting. Kissinger (1979) notes three different strands of thought on this issue. The lull could have been the result of a new North Vietnamese negotiation strategy, a decline in capability to fight, an attempt to achieve de-escalation or success of US strategy. Kissinger seems to indicate that he believed the latter, but unanimity formed around the notion that this was an attempt at de-escalation and the US should reciprocate.

Pressuring the DRV and Operation Menu (February 1969 – March 1969)

On February 22, 1969, the North Vietnamese initiated an offensive across the
DMZ into South Vietnam; for the Nixon administration this was a clear
violation of the understanding between the United States and North Vietnam
created by Johnson's bombing halt. Nixon's reaction to the news of the
offensive was to call for bombing against North Vietnamese supply lines and
bases of operations in Cambodia. Nixon's decision to bomb Cambodia was not
random, rather, the planning for possible air strikes against NVA positions had
been going on since early January. It is worthwhile to detail the process that
created this option, because it both reveals aspects of the decision-making
process in the Nixon administration and provides a background for the
decisions that would be made after the February 22, 1969 offensive.

The idea of bombing NVA infrastructure in Cambodia preceded the
Nixon administration and had for some time been advocated by individuals
inside and outside the government (Kimball 1998, 124–125). Nixon entered
office with an interest in rooting out and destroying the capability of the North
Vietnamese to operate from Cambodia and engage in offensives across the
DMZ. Of particular interest to the administration was the destruction of what
was known as the Central Offices for South Vietnam (COSVN), which was the
appellation given to the NVA's headquarters in Cambodia. On January 8,
1969, Nixon ordered Henry Kissinger to develop a report on North Vietnamese
capabilities and options for striking NVA forces and infrastructure. Kissinger
in turn contacted Colonel Ray Sitton, at the Pentagon, to develop a list of
bombing options. The options for bombing the NVA were further discussed in
a January 25 NSC meeting and in a meeting between Laird, Wheeler, and
Kissinger on January 30. In this second meeting Laird expressed concern about
the implications of the bombing of the North on the American public, while
Wheeler suggested striking bases in Cambodia. In subsequent exchanges
between the US military commander in Vietnam General Creighton Abrams
and Wheeler it was decided that it was possible to find COSVN and that this
was the best way to degrade NVA abilities to initiate an offensive into the
South. The judgments of the JCS were then passed to Kissinger who in turn
passed the recommendations on to Nixon in whom they found a willing
recipient.

The process of formulating options and passing them to the President
did not take place within the formal channels for decision making. The process
was restricted to military planners with the specialized expertise to make
judgments on the best targets and in the process excluded the views from the
State Department and Central Intelligence Agency. Perhaps most importantly,
the planning did not make use of the elaborate committee structure that had
been put in place by Nixon upon entering office.

It is with this background that Nixon chose on February 24 to give the order to begin the bombing of Cambodia, which would ultimately become known as 'Operation Menu.' After initially learning the news of the offensive, Nixon's reaction was to immediately call for air strikes, but he held off on the decision knowing that bombing could negatively impact the trip he was about to make to Europe. Still feeling a need to act, Nixon decided on his flight to Europe to begin bombing, but Kissinger advised Nixon to hold off on his order for forty-eight hours until other 'relevant officials' could be consulted and a plan for dealing with consequences could be formulated. Kissinger then held a meeting with Alexander Haig and Sitton in which they conceived of a plan to alter the official reporting of the bombing raids with the intended purpose of keeping the bombing secret from Congress and the public. Until this point neither Rogers nor Laird had been consulted, but upon returning to the United States, Nixon informed Laird who agreed with the decision, but Laird was concerned about public reaction despite administration attempts at secrecy. Haig informed Rogers and Rogers, on the other hand, opposed the operation because he felt this would undermine the Paris peace talks.

Nixon was now receiving conflicting advice from his advisors. The Secretary of State opposed the bombing; the Secretary of Defense supported it but questioned the political implications; the Joint Chiefs of Staff advocated both bombing the North and Cambodia and Kissinger supported a Cambodia-only option (Nixon 1978). Given the divergent views among the president's principal advisors he continued to postpone ordering the bombing, this was despite his growing feeling that the public supported retaliation for the offensive and feelings of impotence on his part. The president ultimately decided to go ahead with the bombing after a rocket attack on Saigon on March 14. In his instructions, Nixon urged Kissinger not to consult the State department until it was too late.[4]

Nixon's decision-making process closely conforms to the hypothesized decision-making process in the framework. As indicated in Table 3.1, throughout this episode, Nixon was presented with options from Kissinger regarding offensive operations against COSVN in Cambodia. Nixon was presented with different and opposing views when he had to decide whether or not to proceed with Operation Menu. At the outset, he stated that he had an interest in stopping incursions across the DMZ coming from Cambodia and, with this direction, the NSC and military leadership set out to find options to stop the North Vietnamese offensive. As military options were being

---

[4] An NSC meeting was held on March 16 to further discuss the idea of bombing, even though the order had been given. Kimball (1998) argues that this meeting with Laird, Rogers, Wheeler, and the President was designed for the principals to state their views 'if only to protect themselves from public uproar.' He further argues that Kissinger wanted to use this meeting to expose those on the NSC—namely Rogers—that did not share the president's views on the war effort.

developed, Kissinger sought to exclude the Secretary of State and the Secretary of Defense, because he knew they would be voices of dissent. Kissinger's exclusion of the other principals was even more evident after Nixon decided to carry out bombing in Cambodia and with the instructions that Kissinger avoid notifying other departments. The process was orderly in that those who were allowed to participate operated in an organized, coordinated way, but the process was not well-defined, since interagency and principals were left out from parts of the process.

Table 3.1 Operation Menu

Process	Characteristics
• Leader evaluates presented options	Yes
• Leader expresses general preference shaping consideration of options	Yes
• Gatekeeper acts as advocate and screens information and access	Yes
• Discouragement of bargaining and conflict in group; dissenting voices excluded	Yes
• Orderly policy-making with well-defined procedures	No
• Dominant Solution	Yes

Paris and Opening Moves (April 1969 – November 1969)

By bombing Cambodia, Nixon demonstrated his willingness to use force against the DRV and that negotiations were not the only option he had in dealing with the DRV. In April the administration became more active on the diplomatic front and for public consumption attempted to restart the formal talks in Paris, in addition to beginning secret talks with the DRV. But like many of the strategies conceived during the Nixon administration, there was nothing simple about Nixon's diplomatic strategy. Nixon and Kissinger were mainly responsible for cobbling together a strategy that combined a direct diplomatic approach to the DRV, but also an indirect diplomatic approach through the Soviet Union, that was intended to isolate the DRV from one of its chief allies. Diplomatic efforts were complemented by a military strategy that signified that during this period the administration would give serious consideration to a massive air campaign.

　　Both Kissinger and Nixon wanted to engage the Soviet Union diplomatically by indicating that US-Soviet relations would be linked to the willingness of the Vietnamese to negotiate[5] (Nixon 1978). Nixon and Kissinger both contributed to the development of this option. However, Kissinger claims that in March he consulted with Cyrus Vance who would ultimately be responsible for traveling to the Soviet Union to present the US position. This stratagem took place outside the regular diplomatic channels; specifically, the Secretaries of State and Defense were not consulted, nor was the committee system utilized to vet Nixon and Kissinger's decision. Kissinger by this time was especially concerned that Rogers was trying to undermine his influence on foreign policy; in response Kissinger chose to exclude voices, like Rogers's, from the process. Nixon and Kissinger had arrived at a strategy they thought to be the best given the situation and proceeded without searching for alternatives or even entertaining different options that may have existed within the administration.

In his mission to Moscow, Vance, as planned, linked strategic arms talks and issues involving the Middle East to the amount of pressure the Soviet Union placed on Vietnam. Vance also presented a set of proposals that were to be transmitted to the North Vietnamese that included a cease-fire combined with mutual withdrawal, the participation of the NLF in the government, and an independent South Vietnam for five years (Kissinger 1979). Unfortunately for Nixon and Kissinger, in mid-April the Soviet Union refused to meet, because of its objection to the linkage of issues. Consequently Vance never went to the Soviet Union. Later, on May 14 in response to the North Vietnamese public announcement of a peace proposal, Nixon responded with his own eight-point proposal, which was essentially the same plan that Vance would have proposed in Moscow.

The rebuff by the Soviet Union and the distraction of the North Korean shoot-down of a US EC-121 caused the administration to reformulate its approach to the DRV. On July 7, Nixon met with Kissinger, Rogers, Laird, Wheeler, Attorney General Mitchell, and CIA Deputy Director Cushman to discuss strategy options and resolve differences over preferences within the administration. The military and diplomatic aspects of the administration's efforts needed to be resolved. Laird and Rogers advocated and gained the support for increasing the assistance to South Vietnam, for pacification, for greater efforts to reduce the flow of enemy supplies, and, most importantly, a stepped up withdrawal of US troops. These changes in policy were essentially designed to appease Laird and Rogers, because Kissinger and Nixon in this

---

[5] There are discrepancies between Nixon's and Kissinger's memoirs, because both claim to have come up with the idea of linking issues between the US and Soviet Union to Vietnam negotiations. Kissinger claims that the president was skeptical of this approach and favored more of a military solution. However, as early as March Nixon indicated to Premier Kosygin the linkage of the issues. It is possible that both president and advisor contributed to the overall strategy or that it was Nixon's original preference, but Kissinger developed it into a fully evolved plan.

meeting decided to begin to move forward on a strategy that would be far more forceful. With this compromised decision the administration began planning 'Operation Duck Hook,' a massive air offensive that included attacks on targets far in the north including the bombing of Hanoi and the mining of Haiphong. This campaign would be implemented on November 1 in the event that the DRV were unwilling to begin serious negotiations. Kissinger proposed that the president employ the services of Jean Sainteny a long-time friend of the National Security Advisor who had been a French colonial delegate-general in Vietnam. Sainteny would deliver to Mai Van Bo, the DRV representative in Paris, a message that stated that the president wanted a quick resolution to the war, but if a breakthrough could not be found he would have to resort to force.

The DRV did not respond to the content of Nixon's message, but they did call for a meeting between Kissinger and Xuan Thuy, DRV representative to the Paris peace talks. In the secret meeting that eventually took place on August 4 between Xuan Thuy and Kissinger, Kissinger argued for a reconciliation of the DRV and US proposals, but he reiterated that if this did not occur there would be consequences for the North. Kissinger had a similar encounter with Soviet Ambassador to the United States Anatoly Dobrynin, except in this interaction Kissinger emphasized that US-Soviet relations were explicitly linked to Vietnamese willingness to negotiate. Once again the decision to take the approach of contacting the DRV through an intermediary—Sainteny (the approach through the USSR)—and linking a breakthrough with a threat of force was devised between Nixon and Kissinger. The committee system was by-passed and the other principals on the NSC were excluded, thereby eliminating opposition and the need to bargain within the administration.

This closed deliberation on the diplomatic aspects of the Nixon strategy was not true of the military planning in general and the decision to proceed with the Duck Hook operation in particular because of its size and the need and greater support. Operation Duck Hook was in the planning stages as early as April—without the knowledge of Laird—but was put aside when the downing of the EC-121 took place (Berman 2001: 57). Berman asserts that 'in July, when they decided to "go for broke" and Nixon issued the November deadline ultimatum, it was probably this April program that was revived and expanded upon...' It was not until September when Kissinger became frustrated with the progress of the negotiations, and with mounting pressure on the administration for the withdrawal of troops, that the plan resurfaced and was debated among the members of the NSC (Kissinger 1979; Hersh 1983; Kimball 1998; Berman 2001).

At this time, Kissinger brought together a select group drawn from his staff that pursued an extensive study of a military strategy, of which Duck Hook was a part. This group included Anthony Lake, Winston Lord, Laurence Lynn, Roger Morris, Peter Rodman, Helmut Sonnenfeldt, William Watts,

Alexander Haig, Colonel William Lemnitzer, and Captain Rembrandt C. Robinson. This group worked from September through November developing and evaluating the military plan that Nixon would have to decide on for his November 1 deadline. At this point Kissinger, Nixon, and Haig supported a vigorous military response but it was not long before that Nixon began to vacillate and ultimately decided against the Duck Hook option; the role of NSC staff and Laird's and Rogers's positions were instrumental in shaping this decision.

Lake, Lynn, Morris, and Watts began writing reports critical of the success of the Duck Hook option on military and political grounds. The general consensus among the staff was that air raids and the mining of harbors would not sufficiently degrade the North's ability to carry on the war, because there were few industrial targets to strike and China and the USSR could circumvent the proposed blockade (Kimball 1998; Hersh 1983). In return the US would suffer significantly high B-52 losses, as well as inflict high North Vietnamese civilian casualties, which would be seen as an expansion of the war (Kimball 1998; Hersh 1983). In short the offensive would result in no military advantage and would cause an increase in public protest and demonstrations. But despite the revolt of Kissinger's staff to an option that he wholeheartedly supported, Kissinger continued to advocate to the president the most vigorous military strategy, which meant that the president was not hearing the voices of dissent within the group formulating the administration's strategy. This situation changed once Laird and Rogers were made aware of the consideration of the Duck Hook option.

In early October both Laird and Rogers learned of the military strategy being considered and immediately sought to stop the president from going on the offensive. Laird, using reports written by Lake, Lynn, Morris, and Watts, made the case that military strikes and mining would be ineffective and that the military and political costs would be detrimental to the administration's long-term goals (Kimball 1998). This pressure coming from within the NSC and the concern among White House staff about the growing anti-war movement that was now more mobilized than ever before proved too much for the arguments put forth by Kissinger and Haig; Nixon ultimately decided not to go ahead with his November 1 ultimatum. Nixon confided to Haldeman before dropping the military option that he did 'not yet rule out K's Plan as a possibility, but [he] does now feel [the] Laird-Rogers plan is a possibility, when he did not think so a month ago' (Kimball 1998: 170). Nixon abandoned Duck Hook and chose to weather the protests and make a public statement to the public on November 3 (later to be known as the 'Silent Majority' speech), stating the administration's current position on the war and calling for public support. During these months Nixon hoped that the ultimatum that he had given to the North Vietnamese directly and through the Soviet Union would have produced some movement, but it did not. Yet, Nixon did not drop this strategy of mixing willingness to negotiate with the threat of force, because in late October, after having already given up on the Duck Hook option, Nixon met with Dobrynin and reiterated the linkage of the Vietnam issue to the Strategic Arms Limitation Talks and the possibility of escalation if no breakthrough was made.

Nixon chose to pursue a dual military and diplomatic strategy. The process that developed during this particular episode is consistent with the hypothesized description of a formal and highly centralized policy-making process. In only two instances were there deviations from the hypothesized process (Table 3.2). During this episode, Nixon made decisions by choosing from presented options, as well as by making decisions in group settings with a select few advisors. When deliberating on diplomatic approaches to the North Vietnamese, Nixon consulted mainly with Kissinger who briefly consulted with Cyrus Vance. But Nixon followed a different pattern when deliberating military action; initially Nixon met with his principal advisors and the military leadership. In these decisions, Nixon compromised and accepted suggestions from Laird and Rogers and at the same time supported Kissinger's position for forceful action. When Nixon was deciding to carry out Operation Duck Hook he heard from Kissinger who supported the operation and from Laird and Rogers who used NSC staff reports to argue against an offensive.

Table 3.2 Paris and Opening Moves

Process	Characteristics
• Leader evaluates presented options	Yes/No
• Leader expresses general preference shaping consideration of options	Yes
• Gatekeeper acts as advocate and screens information and access	Yes
• Discouragement of bargaining and conflict in group; dissenting voices excluded	Yes
• Orderly policy-making with well-defined procedures	No
• Dominant Solution	Yes/No

The decision making on diplomatic efforts was confined primarily to Nixon and Kissinger, with Kissinger again playing the role of gatekeeper excluding dissenting views. Like the previous episode decision making was orderly, but did not follow well-defined procedures because different procedures were followed for the military and diplomatic aspects of Nixon's strategy. For the most part all decisions had a dominant solution with Nixon strongly supported by Kissinger when making final decisions. The only exceptions were the deliberations on a military approach where Nixon did not compromise, but cobbled together recommendations made by Kissinger, Laird, and Rogers.

Secret Negotiations and Cambodia (February 1970 – October 1970)

In January 1970, Kissinger suggested to Nixon that the administration should attempt to reopen the secret Paris talks with the North Vietnamese. Knowledge of these talks would be withheld from the Secretary of State, Secretary of Defense, the Joint Chiefs of Staff, and most of the major players in Nixon's White House. Nixon and Kissinger decided between themselves that in the negotiations the administration should propose a mutual withdrawal, raise the issue of prisoners of war (POWs), and ensure that a political solution was found that would keep South Vietnamese President Thieu in place (Kimball 1998: 188). Nixon and Kissinger hoped that if the Vietnamese responded to the POW issue by demanding the release of their own POWs, Kissinger could exploit the fact that the DRV were recognizing the presence of DRV troops in the south (the DRV had always denied such a presence). The recognition by the DRV of DRV forces in the south would then give Kissinger a stronger hand in making an argument for a mutual withdrawal of US and DRV forces (Berman 2001; Kimball 1998; Kissinger 1979). In the three meetings held on February 21, March 16, and April 4 the North Vietnamese did not move from their position, which was the unilateral withdrawal of US troops and bases within six months, in addition to the removal of Thieu from power. The other principals in the NSC, notably Rogers and Laird, were not aware of Kissinger's secret meetings at this point in the negotiations—both would learn of his activities later in 1971.

In May, Kissinger directed the NSC staff to formulate a set of reports on the diplomatic options available to the administration that could break the deadlocked negotiations. Interagency committees and the NSC would spend the balance of the summer assessing these reports and a consensus developed that a 'stand-still' ceasefire was the best option given the change in combat activity on the ground in South Vietnam (Hersh 1983; Kissinger 1979). The Vietnam Special Studies Group (VSSG) was tasked with conducting a study on pacification in the South and the group, led by Charles Cooke, revealed that the ARVN had made progress in the pacification of the countryside, by making a 300 percent gain compared to 1968 (Hersh 1983: 298). However the Cook/VSSG study also indicated that the gains may have been a product of reduced Vietcong activity and that the ARVN might control the ground militarily, but the Vietcong was in control politically in many rural areas. The Cooke study asserted that a ceasefire was possible as long as military control was the issue and not political control.[6] The Cooke findings were supported by two other studies carried out by members of the NSC staff. One study by Laurence Lynn agreed that the attrition of Vietcong forces in the South had been successful and that the call for a ceasefire would work. A second study conducted by Wayne K. Smith found that the Cambodia operations 'Fishhook' and 'Parrot's Beak' had given the US more time to enhance the Vietnamization program.

Nixon, thus, was presented with the option of a cease-fire from Kissinger as the best strategy to pursue in moving the stalled negotiations forward. Nixon did not participate in this planning, which took place within the confines of interagency committee meetings. There was little disagreement over options, and individuals were chosen for their knowledge of the area and the military situation as it existed on the ground in South Vietnam. Kissinger claims that in August Nixon, based on these reports, decided to go forward with negotiations where a 'stand-still' ceasefire would be proposed, but this would only be put forward after David Bruce had established himself in his new position as chief negotiator in the public talks. The impact of this decision on the negotiations was enormous in that with a cease-fire in place the US would be accepting the fact that DRV forces would remain in the South (Kissinger 1979; Kimball 1998). At the same time the administration was examining options, Kissinger in July approached the North Vietnamese for another round of secret talks.

In the meetings with Xuan Thuy in September, the issue of a 'stand-still' cease-fire was not raised. In the first meeting, Kissinger proposed a complete withdrawal with no residual forces in a twelve-month period followed by elections with a mixed party election committee. Kissinger added that no date for the withdrawal of troops could be set until guarantees were given that US POWs would be released in exchange. In response, Xuan Thuy refused to accept any of these proposals and reiterated the DRV position that Thieu be excluded from any future political settlement (Kissinger 1979). Thuy's recalcitrance meant nothing of significance took place at this meeting besides an agreement to hold another meeting on September 27. In between, Nixon and Kissinger exchanged memos on the strategy for the next meeting with Nixon suggesting that Kissinger propose that the POW issue be settled separately from other political and military issues. But this modification of the proposal made no difference because Thuy refused to concede the points dealing with the removal of Thieu or a six-month withdrawal.

---

[6] The VSSG study was circulated in the US embassy in Saigon as well as among other agencies and these agencies argued that the study's interpretation of the ARVN strength in the South was excessively pessimistic. The study, these branches of the government argued, did not take into account the attrition of the Vietcong by the Cambodia offensive and the assassination of Vietcong cadre (Hersh 1983).

With talks once again stalled, at an October 4 meeting with Kissinger, David Bruce, Philip Habib, and William Rogers, Nixon decided to announce publicly a new peace initiative. The proposal called for a comprehensive peace conference, a negotiated timetable for withdrawal, the release of POWs and a post-agreement political solution including Thieu. The centerpiece of the proposal was the 'stand-still' cease-fire that Nixon chose as an option back in August. All agreed that this would be a useful strategy because it would put the responsibility for action in 'Hanoi's court' and perhaps more importantly it would defuse the pressure coming from administration critics (Kimball 1998). This decision was then in part the product of a semi-structured committee process that produced the ceasefire option and a small informal group process that dealt with the decision to go ahead with the option. The resort to a formal structure stands in contrast to the informal give and take between the president and Kissinger on the kinds of proposals to make toward the DRV in the Paris secret talks.

The administration's deliberations on the reopening of the Paris Peace talks was dominated by Nixon and Kissinger, but it is clear that it is following the pattern set by an administration with a formal structure and high centralization (Table 3.3). Kissinger approached the president and suggested that the president secretly renew the Paris Peace Talks and together they decided on the kind of issues that Kissinger would raise in talks with the DRV.

Table 3.3 Secret Negotiations and Cambodia

Process	Characteristics
• Leader evaluates presented options	Yes
• Leader expresses general preference shaping consideration of options	Yes
• Gatekeeper acts as advocate and screens information and access	Yes
• Discouragement of bargaining and conflict in group; dissenting voices excluded	Yes
• Orderly policy-making with well-defined procedures	No
• Dominant Solution	Yes

Interagency committees were then tasked to formulate an option the president could choose to create the conditions to restart the negotiations. The interagency committee presented Kissinger with a proposed cease-fire option that Nixon finally chose. During this process Kissinger acted as a gatekeeper and participated in excluding Laird and Rogers, both potential dissenters. The process was orderly in that Kissinger had the NSC staff and interagency committees examine a range of options for the president, but the procedures were not well-defined and took place outside of established decision-making channels. The solution produced during this decision-making process was a dominant one with Nixon choosing from the options presented to him.

More Force (November 1970 – February 1971)

A new consensus began to develop between Kissinger and Nixon in late 1970 that the administration might need to initiate a military offensive in the dry-season to increase their diplomatic leverage (Kimball 1998; Kissinger 1979).[7] Originally, Kissinger favored another incursion into Cambodia similar to that of early 1970. However, upon returning from a trip to Vietnam, Haig presented a plan proposed by Bunker, Abrams, and Thieu. The plan, to be known as Lam Son 719, required a two-phase attack into Laos by ARVN forces to cut the Ho Chi Minh Trail, thereby degrading the ability of the DRV to engage in large-scale operations in the South. South Vietnamese forces would be tasked with invading Laos, with the US only providing close-air and artillery support. On December 18, Nixon and Kissinger discussed the Abrams plan and both were basically convinced of its utility. However, they both believed that it was necessary to have all the principals on board before proceeding (Kimball 1998).

In order to build a consensus, Haig and Moorer, who supported the operation met with Laird and laid out the plan, which resulted in Laird's support. Nixon decided that he would approve the operation in principle but would review it further after Laird returned from Vietnam. A second meeting on January 5 that included Haig, Moorer, Laird, Helms, and Rogers surprisingly convinced Rogers that the operation should proceed. But Rogers's support quickly changed after being influenced by Under Secretary M. Alexis Johnson who made the argument that the enemy had learned of the plan and that the force was inadequate to achieve its objectives (Bundy 1998). These objections resulted in Kissinger questioning the prudence of proceeding and the objections were the cause of a call for another meeting on January 27. But before this larger meeting could be held, Kissinger, Haig, Moorer, and the president met again to reexamine the military plan and the political implications, notably the affect on the summit to be held between Nixon and Brezhnev. Among the group it was believed that the operation would in fact be decisive and that this would put the administration in a good position for preparing for the 1972 elections.

The January 27 meeting included the president, Kissinger, Rogers, Packard, Haig, and Moorer. Again Rogers presented his arguments in

---

[7] Kimball (1998: 241) notes that the origins of the invasion of Laos 'remain obscure' and he relies on Kissinger's memoirs to explain that Kissinger and Nixon had decided on a military offensive in November 1970.

opposition, highlighting that this offensive could risk Thieu's position if it failed. Undeterred by Rogers's arguments, the president decided to go ahead with the operation with Kissinger supporting the decision. But as Kimball (1998) argues, the plan did not go through unmodified because Nixon only ordered Phase I of the operation, which was done in order to avoid having to confront Rogers in the meeting; however, this would not end the issue because a leak to the press of the operation caused another round of deliberations.

The difference between these meetings and those after the leak are that the advisors in the meetings are domestic advisors. Kissinger on the day of the leak, February 1, met with Agnew, Connally, and Mitchell, who were generally supportive of going ahead. On February 2, Nixon brought together the whole cabinet and their discussion revolved around the impact of the polls on public opinion and the possibility of the operation violating the Cooper-Church Amendment and the McGovern-Hatfield Act that place restrictions on the administration's ability to deploy troops and provide assistance to the South. That evening Kissinger expressed to the president that he thought the plans for initiating Phase I should be canceled. Moreover, Kissinger has stated that the president was also having second thoughts (Kimball 1998: 245). The president put off making a final decision until the next day after again meeting with Kissinger, Connally, Mitchell, and Haldeman, which turned out to be the decisive meeting. The three domestic advisors argued, convincingly, that this operation was necessary on the grounds that it would help safeguard withdrawing troops and the domestic consequences would not be as severe as Nixon and Kissinger were making them out to be. Later in the day, in one last review of the argument's pros and cons, Nixon made the decision to go ahead with Lam Son 719.

The decision-making process for Lam Son 719 was a deviation from prior episodes of decision making within the Nixon administration (Table 3.4). Nixon, on this occasion, decided to engage in an offensive that was presented to him as a recommendation from Kissinger who received a report from Alexander Haig on a plan constructed by Bunker and Abrams. Prior to this Nixon had expressed a preference for an offensive in the dry season. Thus, the president shaped the kind of plans that Kissinger sought. Kissinger plays less of a gatekeeper's role during this episode compared to others, which is a result of Nixon's interest in getting the input of other advisors before taking action. Unlike other occasions, dissenting voices are not included, rather, potential dissenting voices are systematically consulted. Because Nixon had decided that a military engagement in the dry season was necessary, his preference shaped deliberations and, as a result, the unstructured solution in this episode was dominant.

Table 3.4 More Force

Process	Characteristics
• Leader evaluates presented options	Yes
• Leader expresses general preference shaping consideration of options	Yes
• Gatekeeper acts as advocate and screens information and access	No
• Discouragement of bargaining and conflict in group; dissenting voices excluded	No
• Orderly policy-making with well-defined procedures	Yes
• Dominant Solution	Yes

Kissinger, Nixon, and Secret Talks—Round I (June 1971 – April 1972)

Lam Son 719 turned out to be an utter disaster for the Nixon administration because not only did it fail miserably militarily, demonstrating the ineptness of the ARVN without the support of US troops, it also piqued domestic opposition at a time when Nixon was preparing for an election campaign. In this atmosphere Nixon and Kissinger agreed that it was necessary to head back to the negotiating table, but this time with a willingness to make concessions. The essential elements of the latest proposal were produced by discussions held between Kissinger and Nixon between May 24 and May 29 in a series of memos sent back and forth between the two.[8] The seven-point proposal that Nixon agreed on contained the most significant and perhaps the most important concession the US would make to that date. The new proposal did not include a requirement for mutual withdrawal. Thus, the North Vietnamese could keep troops in the South but they had to end further infiltration. In addition to this concession, a ceasefire would take place when the US withdrew, Laos and Cambodia would remain neutral and the release of POWs was connected to the US withdrawal timetable (Kissinger 1983). At a meeting in Paris on May 31, the DRV delegation was willing to consider and discuss the proposal but they were still unwilling to give up on the demand for Thieu's removal from power. Again this meeting resulted only in a call for a future meeting on June 26 in which Le Duc Tho (DRV 'special advisor') put forth a counter-proposal that

---

[8] In his memoirs, Kissinger claims that he, Winston Lord, and Richard Smyser worked out the proposal. It is Kimball's contention that this was not the case based on memos sent back and forth between the president and Kissinger. It is reasonable to argue that Kissinger's contributions to the proposal could have been the product of deliberations between the National Security Advisor and his assistants.

included some of the same points as the US proposal but still contained the condition that Thieu must be removed from power.

Over the next series of meetings there would be little movement in the positions of the two sides, although the DRV did accept a stand-still ceasefire with international supervision, a position they had previously rejected. Thus the negotiations proceeded based on the proposal worked out between Nixon and Kissinger and changed little except for Nixon's direction that ordered Kissinger in the July 12 meeting to link progress in the negotiations with use of force (Kimball 1998). In fact this back and forth between the president and his advisor continued throughout the negotiations well into the fall when Kissinger presented the president with a reformulation of the US proposal. Kissinger believed that it was imperative to reach an agreement before US assets were depleted and domestic pressure became too great. On this basis he proposed new presidential elections in South Vietnam six months from the signing an agreement, an electoral commission that would be internationally supervised, the resignation of Thieu one month before these elections, and withdrawal within seven months from the signing of the agreement.

The creation of the proposal was not so much designed to achieve a breakthrough with the North Vietnamese as it was constructed to allow the president to fend off domestic criticism, which in turn would make Nixon's negotiating hand stronger vis-à-vis the DRV (Berman 2001). Nixon was certain that the DRV would reject the provision of Thieu's remaining in power prior to the election despite the US concession of an electoral commission. When the DRV did reject the proposal, Nixon made public the provisions of the proposal and the whole public record of the secret talks. The purpose was to put the DRV in a position to be seen publicly as being the obstacle toward peace and not Thieu or Nixon because both had conceded to elections held by a coalition commission combined with Thieu's resignation (Berman 2001). On October 11, the North Vietnamese were sent the text of the proposal and an offer for a November 20 meeting. However, the DRV rejected the proposal as being insolent, but agreed to another meeting. But this time, the meeting would be with Xuan Thuy and not Le Duc Tho who was supposedly ill. The US was unwilling to meet with Xuan Thuy, who did not have the negotiating power of Le Duc Tho and called off the meeting. At the same time, Nixon and Kissinger decided to increase bombing raids over North Vietnam as punishment for DRV intractability at the negotiating table. With mounting domestic pressure and the debates in Congress concerning legislation that would cut off funding for the war effort, Nixon carried out his plan and went public with the administration's proposal and the existence of the secret talks on February 25.

The day after Nixon's public announcement, Kissinger requested that the president agree to allow Kissinger to contact the North Vietnamese for another meeting. In attempting to set up the meeting Kissinger negotiated over the date, essentially agreeing to hold the talks on April 24 after a restart of the public talks two weeks before. As the negotiations become more intense and more frequent, the pattern of deliberation over strategy took on the form that would characterize the period between June 1971 and January 1972. Deliberation and formulation of strategy would take place between Kissinger and Nixon; this is particularly true of the period of negotiations that took place after the Easter Offensive. It is important to note that Kissinger and Nixon differed over the mixture of negotiation and force. Kissinger comments that he believed Nixon wanted to place greater emphasis on bombing and the use of force to coerce the DRV, while he himself had greater faith in diplomacy and its ability to provide a solution most beneficial to the US and the South Vietnamese.

As the secret talks with the DRV deepened, Nixon and Kissinger isolated themselves and shut out the rest of the administration from the decision-making process. Consequently, the decision-making process differs from earlier episodes (Table 3.5) but is similar in that Kissinger plays the role of gatekeeper excluding dissenting voices in the administration.

Table 3.5 Secret Talks—Round I

Process	Characteristics
• Leader evaluates presented options	No
• Leader expresses general preference shaping consideration of options	Yes
• Gatekeeper acts as advocate and screens information and access	Yes
• Discouragement of bargaining and conflict in group; dissenting voices excluded	Yes
• Orderly policy-making with well-defined procedures	No
• Dominant Solution	Yes

Nixon continued to express general preferences and shape the consideration of options although this took place in the interactions and memos between Kissinger and Nixon. As a result, the solution in this episode is a dominant one. This episode deviates from the others in that Nixon was now presented with fewer options because of his interaction with Kissinger. In prior episodes, the process was orderly but lacked a set of well-defined procedures since Kissinger and Nixon were working outside of the committee system and selectively including other principal advisors. But in this episode the process is not particularly orderly or well-defined as Nixon and Kissinger consulted with one another as the need arose.

Easter Offensive and Faltering Negotiations (April 1972 – May 1972)

Three days after the DRV agreed to meet Kissinger once again in Paris, the DRV initiated another offensive across the DMZ into South Vietnam. Like many of the decisions to use force during Nixon's tenure in office, the decision to use force to turn back the DRV offensive was tightly bound to diplomatic negotiations. Nixon's immediate response to the DRV assault was to begin air strikes within 25 miles of the DMZ, which would be later changed to air strikes up to the 20th parallel. Nixon had been waiting for this opportunity because now he would have the ability to engage in unrestrained bombing that he believed would be more effective in bringing a rapid end to the Vietnam conflict rather than a reliance on negotiations. Berman (2001: 124) cites Haldeman who claimed that 'he [Nixon] feels that this will give us a fairly good change of negotiations, which he has never really felt we've had up to now, but thinks they're doing this as a desperation move and then will have to negotiate. Henry has the same view.'

Nixon was predisposed to using an overwhelming amount of force to improve the administration's negotiating position. Nixon directed Kissinger who then tasked Haig with preparing a planning paper that called for a massive bombing of the maximum number of military targets throughout North Vietnam in addition to the mining of Haiphong harbor. Nixon's predisposition meant that Laird who forwarded a similar plan, but smaller in scale and with his reservations would have no impact on the nature of the counter-offensive. Not only did the Secretary of Defense think that a massive bombing raid and mining operation would be a mistake so did the State Department as well as analysts on the NSC staff (Kissinger 1979). The consensus among these players was that the US should increase the capacity of the South Vietnamese to defend themselves instead of increasing the US effort. But no one among the three key players, Kissinger, the president, and Haig, who was becoming a greater influence on policy as the relationship between the president and Kissinger deteriorated, thought doing nothing was an option. They all believed that a forceful response was necessary for the battlefield, and, most important for their efforts in Paris.

There were three different prongs to the Nixon approach to negotiating with North Vietnam; there was the consideration of the bombing of Hanoi and the mining of Haiphong, diplomatic pressure through the Soviet Union and attempts to continue secret talks directly with the North Vietnamese. After the invasion, Kissinger and Nixon decided to once again use pressure on the Soviet Union as leverage over the DRV. This was communicated to Leonid Brezhnev by way of discussions between Kissinger and Ambassador Dobrynin. Kissinger then decided to task Hal Sonnenfeldt to devise a series of options that would allow the US to threaten to slow negotiations with the Soviets in exchange for their cooperation on Vietnam. In response, Sonnenfeldt created a series of options and was directed by Kissinger to make use of all of them except one (Kissinger 1979: 1118). In this case the president was not consulted as Kissinger used his discretion with the knowledge that the president had generally approved the use of linkage as a means for achieving administration objectives.

On April 20, Kissinger traveled to Moscow with two purposes. One was to lay the groundwork for Nixon's upcoming summit with Leonid Brezhnev and to enlist the Soviets to pressure the DRV to halt their offensive and return to the negotiating table. The decision to use this venue was an idea that was shared between Nixon and Kissinger although Nixon was more willing to take a tougher line with the Soviets and wanted this issue to take precedence over summit discussions. Before Kissinger left, Nixon approved a memo that laid out the strategy Kissinger would employ in Moscow; Kissinger claimed that the Vietnam issue would have to be discussed before any other issue and that the Soviets needed to pressure the North Vietnamese or future relations would be jeopardized (Kissinger 1979). Kissinger was partially successful in that before leaving Moscow, Kissinger was told by Foreign Minister Andrei Gromyko that they would try to influence the government in Hanoi and bring an end to the war.

Nixon and Kissinger were not relying on Soviet pressure to be sufficient to bring a halt to the offensive or to get the DRV to compromise at the negotiating table. Despite the offensive and the US bombing, both sides throughout April tried to restart the plenary and secret negotiations. Kissinger and the North Vietnamese went back and forth proposing dates for a meeting until May 2 was set for a meeting between Kissinger and Le Duc Tho. Two times before the meeting Nixon threatened to cancel and proceed directly to heavy bombing of North Vietnam, but in both instances Kissinger, recognizing that these were decisions made out of fits of frustration, convinced the president not to make this decision until the diplomatic avenue had been exhausted first (Kissinger 1979). In a meeting on May 1, before Kissinger was to meet with Le Duc Tho, Nixon directed Kissinger to engage in 'no nonsense,' 'no niceness,' and 'no accommodations' (Hersh 1983). Nixon had just learned from Abrams that it was possible that the ARVN had lost the will to fight and wanted to give no ground to the DRV, so this meant that Kissinger was forced to go to the meeting in Paris with no new proposals and thus lacking leverage. The North Vietnamese were also not in the mood to make any concessions to the US, thus the meeting ended without any movement and failure at the negotiation table meant the Nixon administration was to initiate the third prong of its strategy toward the North, which was the use of force—specifically widespread bombing of the North including Hanoi and the mining of Haiphong harbor.

Upon returning from Paris, Kissinger met with Nixon and Haig late in the evening on the presidential yacht *Sequoia* and, here, the trio discussed the options for using force, which included invasion of the north, bombing the Red River dikes, and the use of nuclear weapons. Nixon quickly rejected these options and settled on mining and an expansion of bombing above the 20th parallel. Both Haig and Kissinger were in agreement that this was the best option, but Kissinger argued that if the US goes through with the escalation, the upcoming summit between Nixon and Brezhnev should be postponed. Kissinger's reasoning was that the president would look weak going to a summit while Soviet weapons used by the DRV were advancing on the South. Moreover, the bombing could and would send a strong psychological message to the North and the Soviets (Kimball 1998; Kissinger 1979). Nixon was convinced that the escalation was necessary, but he was unsure about the idea of canceling the summit, because polling data indicated that the public wanted the summit to take place. With this in mind, Nixon did not make a final decision, but put it off until he could have others, notably Connally and Haldeman, voice their opinions.

Nixon asked both Kissinger and Haldeman, who supported the bombing and summit, to meet with Secretary of the Treasury John Connally (whom the president trusted and felt would probably fill the position of Secretary of State after the election) and present him with the set of options. Connally was convinced that the best option was to escalate and to go ahead with the summit. Berman (2001) cites Connally as saying, 'Most important – the President must not lose the war! And he should not cancel the summit. He's got to show his guts and leadership on this one. Caution be damned – if they cancel, and I don't think they will, we'll ram it down their throats.'

The following day, the president met with Kissinger, Haig, Haldeman, and Connally, where he was presented with Connally's arguments for going ahead with the offensive and this was enough to convince the president that the proper strategy was to begin bombing and to proceed with the summit. At this point, Kissinger argues, he too shifted his position and realized that the proper strategy was to do both. Finally, on May 8, Nixon held a meeting with the entire National Security Council and, as Kissinger argues, the president by this time had made up his mind, but he wanted to give the principals the opportunity to stake out their positions on the issue. Predictably, Laird and Rogers objected to an escalation, but at this point it was of no consequence. Nixon, on May 8, decided to give the go ahead for 'Operation Linebacker.'

Nixon's move to a three-pronged approach to negotiations with the DRV, made the decision-making process more complex, but for the most part it followed a pattern consistent with the hypothesized decision-making process (Table 3.6). The diplomatic front continued to be dominated by deliberations between Nixon and Kissinger. Nixon and Kissinger discussed between themselves the approach to pressure North Vietnam by way of the Soviet Union and they both deliberated on the proposals to be made.

Table 3.6 Easter Offensive

Process	Characteristics
• Leader evaluates presented options	Yes
• Leader expresses general preference shaping consideration of options	Yes
• Gatekeeper acts as advocate and screens information and access	Yes
• Discouragement of bargaining and conflict in group; dissenting voices excluded	Yes
• Orderly policy-making with well-defined procedures	No
• Dominant Solution	Yes

Nixon was presented with a memo on the strategy Kissinger would take when dealing with the Soviets. In short, Nixon was able to express his preferences and shape the considerations of options and he was in a position to evaluate options. This situation also meant that solutions were inherently dominant. The diplomatic efforts continued to be controlled by Kissinger and potential dissenters were not allowed to participate in the process.

The military prong in Nixon's strategy followed a slightly different process in that more individuals were involved in the process and to a certain extent the process was more open. Nixon was presented with options in response to the DRV offensive. The secretary of defense, as well as secretary of state and members of the NSC staff, objected to a massive bombing, while Kissinger passed to the President a planning paper created by Haig. When talks in Paris failed, the president evaluated options presented to him by Haig and Kissinger. Prior to this the president had long expressed an interest in initiating massive bombing and the defeat of the ARVN presented such an opportunity. More importantly, options that conformed to Nixon's preference were more successful in gaining approval. Kissinger as always was a gatekeeper and opponents to the use of massive bombing against the North were excluded from most of the process particularly after May 1. Only after Nixon made up his mind were other members of the NSC allowed to have an opportunity to voice their opinions. This episode differs in that Nixon sought the opinion of Connally and Haldeman, whereas when making previous decisions, Nixon did not hold off until he could get a consensus. This broadening of those in the deliberation process—although selective—is similar to the decision-making process that took place leading up to the decision to go ahead with Lam Son 719. The differences between Nixon's diplomatic and military prongs is that the diplomatic prong was exclusively dominated by Nixon and Kissinger and the military prong was more inclusive, indicating that the administration was not following an orderly and well-defined set of procedures for both. This does not mean that Nixon was not in control, but he was altering the decision-making process to meet his needs.

Toward a Final Settlement (June 1972 – January 1973)

It was only days after Operation Linebacker had begun that Kissinger and Nixon again tried to restart negotiations with the North Vietnamese. Aside from differing over the ratio of negotiation to force, Nixon and Kissinger differed over when they should press hardest for a settlement. Nixon was concerned that the Paris negotiations might detrimentally affect the November elections; primarily, he was concerned that if he pursued a final settlement before the election it might fail and ruin his electoral bid (Kimball 1998). Kissinger on the other hand felt that a settlement before the election was the most propitious time to push the DRV to settle because he believed that the DRV was ready to negotiate prior to the election, as opposed to afterward when they would have to deal with a Nixon with a new mandate on his policies and four more years (Hersh 1998). Despite these differences, Nixon was willing to allow Kissinger to restart the negotiations. As had been the norm for the direct negotiations with the DRV, Nixon and Kissinger set the negotiation strategy between themselves. However, as Kissinger claims, Nixon set general guidelines and it was up to Kissinger to do the rest during the negotiating process (Kissinger 1979: 1361).

In late summer, Kissinger met with Le Duc Tho in Paris for another round of talks that culminated in early October with a major breakthrough. In the first meeting on August 1, Kissinger presented a new plan that contained only cosmetic modifications; the provisions included a complete withdrawal of all US forces and bases, a withdrawal timeframe of four months, and the provision that the US would respect any result of the political process, which meant recognition of any new government (Berman 2001). Le Duc Tho, in response, presented a proposal that most importantly called for a tripartite government that could include Thieu and recommended talks between Saigon and the PRG, which was the political organization that represented the Vietcong in the south. Just like Kissinger, Tho presented a proposal that only had minor modifications, but the modifications by both sides were significant because they indicated to each other a willingness to make concessions.

Kissinger reported to Nixon that no new progress had been made, but that he did believe that the North Vietnamese were close to making major concessions. Nixon asserted that he did not think it was best to make more concessions, because he did not want the talks to jeopardize the elections; Kissinger and Nixon agreed, but for different reasons, that they should not go to the next meeting with any concessions. Kissinger, as previously mentioned, thought that the DRV would make concessions in September when they had a better sense of Nixon's election victory. In the meantime Kissinger wanted to make minor concessions and adjustments that would keep the North Vietnamese negotiating and prevent them from going public in order to 'trigger domestic controversy' (Kissinger 1979: 1316). Over the next series of meetings Kissinger and Le Duc Tho presented each other with various proposals that moved closer toward a final agreement; the North Vietnamese, in each meeting, moved their position closer to the US proposal. The North Vietnamese at the October 8 meeting presented changes to their proposal that resulted in the breakthrough that had eluded Lyndon Johnson.

The ability to get a final settlement turned on the willingness of Thieu to accept the proposal developed between Kissinger and Tho. But to Kissinger's and to the president's consternation, Thieu did not accept the proposal; instead he returned the proposal with 69 modifications. In the round of talks held from November 20 to 23, Kissinger presented Thieu's changes, but, over the course of the meeting he dropped most of them. The reintroduction of issues the North Vietnamese believed to be settled led to the breakdown of the talks and caused Kissinger to send a message to Nixon laying out the options given the new turn of events. After the last meeting, Kissinger cabled Nixon laying out the options as he saw them at this stage of the negotiations: (1) break off the negotiations and resume bombing above the 20th parallel or (2) get more concessions and leave the rest of the provisions as they were written in the October breakthrough.

At first Nixon decided on option two, arguing that the resumption of bombing was not a viable option and that the October 8 agreement was in US interest, but only hours later Nixon, reversed his decision and decided that a massive bombing strike was the best option and that he did not need to concern himself with domestic support, because the elections were over. In his next meeting with Tho , Kissinger showed him Nixon's telegrams that stated that Kissinger was not to accept anything less than the provisions already published, which were the October 8 provisions. This meeting resulted in a recess and a date for a new meeting on December 4. In between meetings Nixon, in consultation with Kissinger, devised a strategy that included encouraging Thieu to accept the peace agreement, because Nixon would promise that any violation of the agreement—which he expected from the North—would be met with intense US bombing raids. Nixon had support from Kissinger and Haig for this strategy, but in an effort to build consensus within the administration, on November 30 Nixon held a meeting with the Joint Chiefs of Staff where he sought and gained their support.

In the talks on December 4, Kissinger presented a new plan with a schedule to conclude an agreement by the evening of December 5, but this amounted to nothing because Le Duc Tho rejected all proposals and withdrew nine changes that he had previously accepted. After the meeting, Kissinger reported to Nixon that he believed that he could not accept any of the changes the North proposed and he could not accept the October 8 agreement that did not have any of the changes demanded by the South. Based on this assessment he suggested two options to Nixon that he had discussed with Winston Lord and Haig. The president could both drop new demands and accept the agreement that the DRV agreed to in November that was a modification of the October 8 proposal, or, he could try and push for two additional changes that would satisfy Thieu, changing some language and denying the DRV legal right to intervene in the South. In the event this did not work, Kissinger argued, there would be no real choice but to resort to force. Kissinger stated that he thought option two was best and Nixon concurred because Nixon, as Kissinger argues, was influenced by Haig who was fully behind ending the negotiations (Kissinger 1979). Further, Nixon believed that he needed to get something signed soon before Congress reconvened and forced the president to fully withdraw (Kimball 1998; Kissinger 1979). On December 6 neither side made any changes in their positions causing Kissinger to suggest that they return the next day with their minimum positions. The next day Le Duc Tho made some concessions, notably a change in the timing of ceasefires in Laos and Cambodia and on the release of civilian prisoners, but these were not the concessions Kissinger wanted to hear.[9]

Kissinger again cabled Nixon with a set of options. Nixon could either make one of two choices; he could make a minimum demand on the DRV and if accepted break with Thieu, or, he could make an unacceptable demand and if rejected call for a recess. Nixon choose to keep the talks going because he felt at this point the public support was no longer there and that he should get an agreement that improved on October 8. Kissinger and Tho went back and forth with Tho making concessions but unwilling to give up on the phrasing of a provision calling for North and South to respect the DMZ. By October 13, the talks completely broke down and Kissinger cabled Nixon stating that he again only saw two alternatives. One, the President could, '...turn hard on Hanoi and increase [pressure] enormously through bombing and other means.' Two, the President could hold back on bombing, resume talks in January and in the meantime try to get Thieu aboard for an agreement. Nixon without hesitation decided on the first option, believing that this was necessary to force a conclusion (Kissinger 1979; Nixon 1978).

The decision to proceed with Operation Linebacker II was a result of a decision-making process in which Nixon's preferences shaped the consideration of options. Two preferences shaped the administration's approach to the North Vietnamese. Nixon throughout his presidency was inclined to use a simultaneous combination of force and diplomacy and Nixon

---

[9] Kissinger was looking for a three-month demobilization of forces, the withdrawal of North Vietnamese troops, changes in language that would maintain a distinction between the North and South and a strengthening of the status of the demilitarized zone.

did not want the negotiations to damage his chances at the polls. In addition, Kissinger notes that Nixon set the guidelines for Kissinger's talks with Le Duc Tho in Paris. As indicated in Table 3.7, the other features of formal/high centralization advisory systems are also present. As Kissinger negotiated with Le Duc Tho and movement began in the talks, Kissinger contacted the president and presented him with the state of negotiations and the options that were available to the administration. The deliberations were usually restricted to Nixon and Kissinger with Haig occasionally giving the president advice on which options to choose. Although the policy-making was orderly in that Kissinger consistently consulted with the president, it cannot be considered well defined. As usual, the solution in this episode was dominant as Nixon's stated preferences influenced the kind of options with which he was presented.

Table 3.7 Toward a Final Settlement

Process	Characteristics
• Leader evaluates presented options	Yes
• Leader expresses general preference shaping consideration of options	Yes
• Gatekeeper acts as advocate and screens information and access	Yes
• Discouragement of bargaining and conflict in group; dissenting voices excluded	Yes
• Orderly policy-making with well-defined procedures	Yes/No
• Dominant Solution	Yes

Denouement (December 1972 – January 1973)

When Nixon ordered the continuation of bombing on the North (code named Linebacker II) his objective was to force the DRV back to the table and to force an end to the war. The resort to the use of force had the added benefit of demonstrating to Thieu that the US was sincere in its promises to severely punish DRV violations of any final agreement through renewed bombing. Kissinger advised the president to contact the DRV and propose a return to talks. Nixon's effort was rebuffed and the two sides went back and forth until December 26. Kissinger suggested to Nixon that the president offer the North Vietnamese the December 18 proposal and insist on a three- to four-day meeting. The meeting between Kissinger and Tho would be preceded by a resumption of the plenary talks and bombing would continue. Nixon agreed to this plan and the DRV ultimately agreed on a January 8 meeting after Nixon agreed to stop bombing on the day the meeting was announced to the public.

Nixon and Kissinger met one more time before Kissinger left for Paris, which turned out to be the last round of negotiations of the war. At a meeting held at Camp David, Nixon and Kissinger discussed two options: (1) agree to a settlement on the best terms that could be negotiated or (2) break with Thieu and resume bombing until the North Vietnamese return US POWs in exchange for a complete withdrawal (Nixon 1978). Nixon chose to go with option one, which meant accepting the October proposal if necessary, despite Kissinger's reservation that 'they would lead to Saigon's collapse' (Kissinger 1979: 1462). With this final decision by Nixon, Kissinger left for Paris to work out a final agreement that was finished on January 13.

The Nixon administration decision-making is consistent with previous episodes of decision-making found in the case (Table 3.8). Kissinger presented the president with options that were designed to bring about a final settlement and were shaped by Nixon's preferences which Kissinger was well aware of. Advisors other than Kissinger were kept from participating in the process; particularly all those who would advocate options that were at odds with Nixon's preferences. The interactions between Nixon and Kissinger were orderly, but no well-defined procedure was ever produced. Consistent with the other aspects of the decision-making process the unstructured solution to decisions were dominant in nature.

Table 3.8 Denouement

Process	Characteristics
• Leader evaluates presented options	Yes
• Leader expresses general preference shaping consideration of options	Yes
• Gatekeeper acts as advocate and screens information and access	Yes
• Discouragement of bargaining and conflict in group; dissenting voices excluded	Yes
• Orderly policy-making with well-defined procedures	Yes/No
• Dominant Solution	Yes

Assessing Nixon's Decision-Making Process

The decision-making process during the Nixon administration is the result of Nixon's choice of a formal structure and the desire to maintain a high degree of centralization over the deliberations and the flow of information. It is hypothesized that these two factors produce a decision-making process that results in the president expressing general preferences that shape options and him choosing between options. An advisor acts as a gatekeeper controlling access and information. In addition there is discouragement of conflict and bargaining; orderly and well-defined procedures; and the choice of dominant unstructured solutions. This hypothesized process has been evaluated by examining the negotiations between the Nixon administration and the North Vietnamese and the analysis demonstrates that the case does conform to the proposed hypothesis found in the framework (Table 3.9).

The two features of the decision-making process that arise consistently in each episode are the president's expression of general preferences that shape options and the presentation of options to the president for choice. When he first came into office, Nixon expressed his willingness and desire to use force, particularly bombing to get the DRV to the negotiating table. Nixon also wanted to combine the use of force with diplomatic initiatives and throughout the process he reiterated his preferences as circumstances changed. Nixon's willingness to assert his preferences influenced the kind of options that his advisors, notably Kissinger and Alexander Haig, pursued. Part of Kissinger's ability to play a central role in the policy process was his ability to understand what the president's preferences were and to give him policy options that fit those preferences; this was the case for the decision to proceed with "Operation Menu" or the generation of the stand-still ceasefire. The fact that the policy options chosen always reflected Nixon's general preferences means that the unstructured solution in each occasion for decision was dominant. A dominant solution was found in seven of the episodes with the one exception being Nixon's attempts to compromise with Laird and Rogers on "Duck Hook" when he cobbled together proposals by Laird, Rogers, and Kissinger.

It should be noted that Nixon occasionally deviated from this pattern and actively participated in the generation of options and policy. Nixon and Kissinger developed options between themselves or Nixon set general guidelines and Kissinger conducted the secret talks based on these guidelines. This was true of Nixon's decision in the period of April 1969 – November 1969 when Nixon decided to pressure the North Vietnamese using the Soviet Union as a third party. Nixon's participation in generating options is also evident in late 1970 when the administration shifted toward the use of force and decided to initiate a South Vietnamese offensive into Laos. Most Importantly, this characterized part of the formulation of options during 1972 in relation to the secret talks.

Table 3.9 Nixon's Advisory System: Formal System/ High Centralization

	Pressuring the DRV	Opening Moves	Secret Nego-tiations	More Force	Secret Talks Round I	Easter Offensive	Toward a Settlement	Dénoue-ment	%
Leader evaluates presented options	Yes	Yes/No	Yes	Yes	No	Yes	Yes	Yes	75
Leader expresses general preference shaping consideration of options	Yes	Yes	Yes	Yes	Yes	Yes	Yes	Yes	100
Gatekeeper acts as advocate and screens information and access	Yes	Yes	Yes	No	Yes	Yes	Yes	Yes	87
Discouragement of bargaining and conflict in group; dissenting voices excluded	Yes	Yes	Yes	No	Yes	Yes	Yes	Yes	87
Orderly policy-making with well-defined procedures	No	No	No	Yes	No	No	Yes/No	Yes/No	37
Dominant Solution	Yes	Yes/No	Yes	Yes	Yes	Yes	Yes	Yes	87

Present in seven out of eight episodes in the case study was a gatekeeper that was controlling access and screening information. Discouragement of bargaining and conflict primarily by the exclusion of dissenting voices was also found in seven out of eight episodes. Kissinger and Nixon deliberately avoided informing Secretaries Rogers and Laird about the opening of secret talks with the DRV, the kinds of options and proposals being formulated, and occasionally they were excluded from deliberations on the use of force. Kissinger's role as a gatekeeper was designed to ensure that the president was not exposed to internal disagreements, which he was not comfortable with. But not all dissenting voices and discouragement of bargaining and conflict were eliminated. Although Henry Kissinger played a gatekeeper's role, his ability to screen and block access was not absolute.

On crucial issues, for which failure could have a severe negative impact on overall policy, advisors that held differing views could made their voices heard within the administration. Most importantly, these conflicting points of view were resolved out of the view of the president. Nixon heard these views within the context of meetings, exemplified by Nixon's decision not to proceed with 'Duck Hook' or delaying the Lam Son 719 operation after hearing arguments presented by Laird and Rogers. Inclusion of differing points of view was often an effort to build consensus on a policy direction that the president was favoring. When Nixon felt unsure about taking a particular option (and this was the case on two occasions), he sought the advice of Connally, Mitchell, and Haldeman before he made a final decision increasing the use of force. This was true in Nixon's inclusion of the Joint Chiefs of Staff in order to support his decision to begin the 'Christmas Bombing' and the decision to go ahead with the Laotian offensive.

Nixon's advisory system should operate according to well-defined procedures, but it clearly did not. Well-defined procedures characterize only three episodes. Nixon came into office with the intent of altering the way decisions were made in the White House and at the center of this effort was the creation of an elaborate committee system divided between functional and geographic interest. Nixon in the case of Vietnam did not rely on these committees for the formulation of policy. Rather, the task of formulating policy was mostly carried out within the National Security staff or with the assistance of individuals, such as Bunker, Abrams, and Haig. The choice of procedure for constructing policy was dictated not by the committee structure but by the demands of the President and his interest in controlling the conduct of policy, which meant avoiding leaks, involving individuals with sympathetic views, and/or building consensus. The failure to use the established committee system is at odds with George and Stern (1998) who argue that the committee system was designed to 'protect his [Nixon's] personal control over high policy'. The system may have been designed for this purpose, but it did not in practice function in this manner, thus the Nixon system described by George and Stern in fact conceals more than it reveals about the operation of the Nixon advisory system, at least on the issue of Vietnam.[10] The structure and procedures exist but they are more informal than an organizational flow chart of the Nixon system would indicate.

Nixon's formally structured and highly controlled advisory system displays characteristics consistent with those found in the framework. There were only few exceptions and these differences are not significant enough to bring the process described by the framework into doubt. However, Nixon's shift toward a system that is more inclusive is revealing because it means that consensus on issues of great enough magnitude—in this case use of force—is important. Those individuals Nixon sought out to build his consensus were a select few, who in all likelihood were predisposed to support the president. By doing so Nixon could still exclude views that were fundamentally at odds with his own and ensure he maintained control over the process.

---

[10] The George and Stern description of the Nixon advisory system departs from the broad schematic used earlier by George, which was very simple in design. George's earlier depictions do not include the formal committees, but simply explained the relationships between leader and advisors. In the later study of advisory systems, George and Stern place the President at the top of the system followed by the National Security Advisor that serves as chairman of a series of committees; one of which, the Senior Review group, composed of principals, oversees the activities of interdepartmental groups chaired by assistant secretaries. The problem with this description is that it does not account for the influence of the Secretary of Defense or State, both of whom had the ability to influence policy. In the account provided by George and Stern, the National Security advisor dominates the whole process completely, which was not the case.

Chapter 4

Negotiating Strategic Arms Limitations

> A lot has been written by political analysts about how Presidents should deal with top staff and executive officers. I found through experience that a collegial approach – with a group discussing issues as equals – is good, provided the gathering includes primarily those who will be directly involved in carrying out the decision or explaining it to the public. (Carter 1982: 59)

Organization of Carter's Foreign Policy Advisory System

Like Nixon, Carter came into office with a clear sense of how he wanted to manage the policy process while in office. Carter placed an emphasis on building a collegial structure in which the president was required to be an active, hands-on participant, which fit Carter's needs and operating style. Within this structure Carter wanted to shift the focus of US foreign policy toward a focus on human rights, arms control, and global environment. Although Carter was not well steeped in the intricacies of foreign policy when he came into office he felt personally responsible for advancing this agenda (Thompson 1994: 54). Thus Carter's personal commitment to a set of valued issues was combined with the need to be informed and involved in the minutiae of any issue. As Talbott acknowledges, Carter immersed himself in the details of important issues, constantly ask for briefings and background information until he had mastered the issue (Talbott 1980: 2).[1]

Thus with the need to place his personal stamp on policy and to be active in policy formulation, Carter desired an advisory system to obtain both of these objectives (McClellan 1985: 28).[2] Before being inaugurated Carter directed Zbigniew Brzezinski, against advice, to restructure the series of policy committees that the president would rely on to formulate policy; specifically Carter wanted to move away from the complex series of committees that

---

[1] Barry Blechman, assistant director of the Arms Control and Disarmament Agency, has commented that the tendency of the President to immerse himself in the minutiae of issues resulted in a failure to understand the 'overall posture' of the administration or 'strategy' (Thompson 1997: 111).

[2] Brzezinski has recounted that as he and Carter searched for a Secretary of State, Carter's reaction to candidates who could be described as wanting to 'run American foreign policy' was that 'he's not my type' (Brzezinski 1982).

characterized the Nixon administration toward a system that was simpler and would foster a collegial relationship among advisors (Brzezinski 1983). The new system revolved around the Policy Review Committee (PRC) and the Special Coordinating Committee (SCC), which were alone responsible for dealing with the bulk of the work of the National Security Council. Ideally the majority of the administration's work was to be conducted in these two committees, thereby allowing the NSC to meet less frequently (Prados 1991: 388). To ensure collegiality, cabinet members were encouraged when appropriate to participate in either committee in order to 'accustom Cabinet members to working as a team under each other's chairmanship' (Brzezinski 1983: 60).

The prime responsibility of the PRC, chaired by Secretary of State Cyrus Vance, was to deliberate and make recommendations on diplomatic, defense, and international economic issues. Aside from Vance, Secretary of Defense Harold Brown, and, on occasion, the Secretary of the Treasury and Director of Central Intelligence also chaired the PRC. National Security Advisor Zbigniew Brzezinski chaired the SCC that was responsible for issues that were 'cross-cutting' and required 'coordination in the development of options and the implementation of Presidential decisions,' specifically arms control, intelligence policy issues, and crisis management (Vance 1983: 36; Brzezinski 1983: 59).

Associated with the bipartite committee system was a well-specified procedure for the formulation and presentation of reports and options to the president (Brzezinski 1983: 61). Before a PRC or SCC meeting, the department that holds the chairmanship would be responsible for preparing a Presidential Review Memorandum or an options paper. The prepared documents would be discussed in the following PRC or SCC meeting and at that time, if there was consensus, a report would be sent to the president containing minutes of the meeting as well as options or recommendations. However, if there was disagreement, a report would be prepared for the full NSC, where the issue(s) could be resolved. No matter what the outcome of the committee process, the NSC staff produced the final report that landed on the president's desk, ostensibly giving the National Security Advisor an ability to influence the final product read by the president (Vance 1983; McLellan 1985).

On paper, the Carter advisory system appears to be quite formal in nature, particularly in terms of its structure, but for two reasons it would be incorrect to believe that this description captures the extent of the advisory structure and process. First, this committee system did not always function as planned. According to Vance, this simple structure and fairly simple process did not remain effective for the duration of the administration because, as disagreements arose between principal advisors, it was easier to deal directly with the president or other advisors (Vance 1983: 38). Second, Carter and his advisors met frequently in more informal settings to deliberate on issues. In

March of 1977, Vance, Brzezinski, and Harold Brown began meeting weekly for lunch (known as the VBB Luncheon) to discuss issues and policy differences unencumbered by set agendas or department constraints. The advantage of these informal lunches was that it allowed for quick decisions and the ability to bridge differences and build consensus (Vance 1983: 39). These meetings were extremely important because, although options were generated in the SCC or the PRC, the VBB luncheons functioned as a forum where the three advisors discussed issues until they built a consensus critical for a decision (Aaron 2002). Because the president wanted to be connected to the policy process, Brzezinski sent the president a memo noting decisions or recommendations. Over time, these meetings became more formal in the sense that agenda were negotiated among the principal's respective staffs before each meeting, consequently often making the agenda 'too long' and 'complex' (Vance 1983:39). Nonetheless, this forum presented an opportunity for advisors to engage in open debate and resolve differences on policy issues.

Another informal mechanism was initiated in June 1977, when Carter began to hold weekly Friday breakfasts. The intended purpose of the Friday Presidential Breakfast was to give Vance greater opportunity to discuss issues with the president. Originally, these meetings were attended by the president, Vance, Brzezinski, Brown, and Vice President Mondale, but eventually more domestic policy staff were invited to participate in the meetings. No formal agenda was supposed to be set for these meetings, although Brzezinski who met with the president earlier in the morning was able to make suggestions (Andrianopolous 1991: 143). At the breakfast the president was presented a list of agenda items and his advisors could add to them during the meeting. Carter asserts that these meetings were important because he could make 'a final decision, and ordinarily, the decision would be implemented' (Carter 1982: 32). These meetings also served the same function as the VBB Luncheon which was, in Vance's words, a 'frank discussion,' a forum where issues were 'aired thoroughly,' and a discussion on the 'interaction between domestic and foreign policy matters' (Vance 1983: 39).

Carter relied predominantly on Zbigneiw Brzezinski, Cyrus Vance, and Harold Brown for policy advice. Carter came to know his principle advisors while serving as a member of the Tri-lateral Commission. Brzezinski and Vance were suitable choices because they shared with the president a belief that the realization of independence by Third World countries expanded the interdependence and stability already achieved by the United States, Europe, and Japan. However, Brzezinski and Vance differed on a range of other issues, primarily on US-USSR relations, with Brzezinski being an advocate of challenging Soviet military buildup. During the campaign, Brzezinski was Carter's principle foreign policy advisor and was a logical choice for National Security Advisor once elected to office. Carter wanted a National Security Advisor who could give him a variety of ideas and then let him (Carter) 'sift through them to see if they were good or bad' (Carter 1982: 40). Vance too from Carter's perspective was the obvious choice for a position in the Carter administration because Carter held a personal affinity for Vance, an appreciation of his legal skills and ability to solve problems (Clifford 1994: 7). Secretary of Defense Harold Brown, also a member of the Trilateral Commission, served as Deputy Secretary of Defense in the Kennedy and Johnson administrations and was an expert on nuclear weapons. Other individuals such as Deputy National Security Advisor David Aaron, Arms Control Negotiator James Goodby, and Director of Central Intelligence Stansfield Turner also contributed to the process.

Drawing on the findings of the advisory system literature and the presidency literature discussed in Chapter 2 and the above discussion, the Carter advisory system is characterized as having a collegial structure with high centralization. These two factors result in a hypothesized decision-making process with the following features:

- Leader is an active member of the group guiding and shaping deliberations
- Leader pushes the group to assess range of options
- Emphasis on building consensus among core set of advisors
- Shared responsibility for decisions
- Meetings are regularized and frequent with core advisors
- Integrative Solution

Whether or not the Carter decision-making process does in fact operate in the above manner is evaluated by examining the decision-making process during the SALT II negotiations held between the Soviet Union and the United States between February 1977 and May 1979.

SALT II: Policy Environment

Jimmy Carter did not enter office in what could be described as the best of domestic and international circumstances. Domestically the country was still grappling with what was putatively a military defeat in Vietnam and its domestic consequences; in addition, Watergate and Richard Nixon's resignation stoked public disillusionment in government. While the domestic scene was grim, the international scene was truly bleak. The period of détente between the US and USSR, begun during the Nixon administration, was under severe pressure as the Soviet Union exploited conflicts in places such as Ethiopia and Angola. Of particular concern was the increase in the sale of arms by the Soviets to underdeveloped and developing countries. The breakdown in détente occurred at the same time that the US and developed countries were being pressured by the dramatic increase in oil prices brought on by the organized action of OPEC as a consequence of the progress of the Arab-Israeli conflict that had been stalled since the end of the Yom Kippur War.

Nonetheless, from an arms control perspective, the prospects for continued limitations or even reductions by the Soviet Union and United States seemed promising. Upon arriving in office, Carter was confronted with restarting negotiations with the Soviet Union regarding the limitation of strategic weapons that had first begun with Nixon's signing of the first Strategic Arms Limitation Talks treaty (SALT I) in 1972 and further advanced under President Ford and Secretary of State Henry Kissinger. During the Ford administration, Kissinger agreed at Vladivostok that in the next round of negotiations an equal ceiling of 2,400 launchers would be applied to strategic launchers on both sides.[3] A sub-ceiling was created under the 2,400 limit that limited either side to 1,320 MIRVed launchers (multiple independent targeted re-entry vehicles).

In order to arrive at an agreement on both the US and USSR made concessions on major systems and these concessions resurfaced as critical issues during the SALT II talks. In exchange for the Soviets' acquiescence on the placement of forward-based systems (forward positioned nuclear weapons) in Europe, the United States agreed to drop its demand that Soviet heavy missiles be reduced. Both sides also agreed to restrictions on cruise missiles and the Soviet 'Backfire' bomber. US cruise missile carrying bombers were to be counted against the 1,320 MIRV sub-ceiling and in return the Soviets were to accept a numerical limitation on the number of 'Backfire' bombers that were produced.

However, Ford and Kissinger were not able to get much further than laying the groundwork for the follow-on to SALT I before the 1976 elections diverted the administration's attention and ended any momentum toward an agreement. But the presidential election only interrupted the arms control process; it did not end permanently, and, in fact, the work of the two previous administrations created an expectation among the public that Carter would continue the progress started by his two predecessors (Gaddis 1986). The new

---

[3] SALT I (also known as the 'Interim Agreement between the United States of America and the Union of Soviet Socialist Republics on Certain Measures with Respect to the limitation of Strategic Offensive Arms') placed different caps on the number of strategic launchers that the United States and Soviet Union could possess for a five year period. The limitation for the Soviet Union was set high enough that it permitted the Soviet Union to continue to build more launchers. The different limitations were a product of different characteristics of Soviet and US nuclear arms, principally, their quality and dispersal among delivery systems. The Soviet Union up until the early 1970s produced ballistic missiles with a high throw-weight, but poor accuracy while the US made smaller missiles with greater accuracy (thus making US missiles a greater counterforce weapon). For a comprehensive explanation of the reasons for the differences in number of launchers see Talbott (1980).

administration's attempts to build an agreement with the Soviet Union would not go unopposed because, within a segment of Congress, and among some of the foreign policy elite, a consensus was developing that was in opposition to both détente with the Soviets and the construction of a SALT II agreement on anything other than deep reductions in the Soviet arsenal. The détente/SALT II opposition came from Congress in the form of Senator Henry Jackson who was both vocal and influential on arms control issues and from the 'Committee on the Present Danger' whose members included Dean Rusk, Eugene Rostow, Admiral Elmo Zumwalt, Richard Allen, and most importantly, because of his experience with arms control talks, Paul Nitze.

Carter was presented with a situation where the public and the Soviets expected renewed efforts on arms control (for the Soviets this had to take place within the established limits agreed on at Vladivostok), but at the same time domestic opposition was already well in place and prepared to challenge the president. All of this was to take place within the confines of the larger US-Soviet strategic relationship that was at best stalled and at worst quickly deteriorating. For Carter, though, the primary interest was not satisfying the interest of the elite, but reducing the nuclear arsenals of both superpowers, which for him was not just a security issue, but also a moral one (Aaron 2002).

First Proposal (February 1977 – March 1977)

Carter initiated efforts on arms control early in his administration. From the beginning Carter played a hands-on role in shaping and defining the discussion on the kind of proposal to prevent the Soviets. In February, deliberations took place at an SCC meeting that eventually culminated in a series of meetings in March in which Carter played a significant role in evaluating options and integrating differing views. It is important to keep in mind that the structure of the Carter committee system was designed to create collegiality and a give and take between advisors. Prior to the meetings of February and March, Carter, along with Brzezinski and Vance, worked to formulate a series of letters that would be sent to Brezhnev explaining the administration's position on US-Soviet relations and on a range of other issues. Among the issues discussed, arms control and Carter's interest in finding an agreement were prominent. But it is not until late January that Carter began this process of mobilizing his advisors and staff to focus on creating SALT proposals. Carter began the process by directing the NSC on January 24 to create a negotiating position that Cyrus Vance could take to Moscow in March.

At an SCC meeting on February 3, Carter let it be known that he wanted to make substantial reductions in US and USSR arsenals based on the Vladivostok Agreement (Brzezinski 1983; Garrisson 1999). Carter called for 'profound' reductions in strategic arsenals that were favorable to both sides.

The president also requested information on US anti-submarine warfare capability and prior notification agreements with the United Kingdom and Germany. Brzezinski suggested that the SCC examine a range of options based on Vladivostok levels and options based on 'significant reductions' (Memo, Brzezinski 2/4/77). The participants in the meeting agreed to inform the president that the SCC believed it is not clear if an agreement that excluded the Backfire bomber and cruise missiles was either 'negotiable or desirable'. Despite the consensus that formed around building on the Vladivostok agreement, it was agreed that the SCC should develop a range of options around deep cuts and the Vladivostok agreement (Brzezinski 1983; Memo, Brzezinski 2/4/77). Between this SCC meeting and the next SCC on SALT, Carter met with Senator Henry Jackson who was identified as a critical key to ratification of any final agreement because of his knowledge of arms control issues. On February 4, Carter met one on one with Senator Jackson and both agreed at the end of the meeting that a SALT II agreement needed to contain substantial cuts in strategic forces. Eleven days later, Jackson provided Carter with a detailed SALT II proposal and he recommended that the administration move beyond the levels agreed on at Vladivostok (National Security Archive Chronology 1994).

The Special Coordinating Committee continued to meet and work on different specific SALT packages. On February 25, the SCC considered three SALT proposals that were closely tied to Vladivostok. One option was essentially the Vladivostok agreement without major changes. The second option called 'Vladivostok-plus' that was Vladivostok with special provisions for the Soviet Backfire bomber. A third option separated the cruise missile and Backfire bomber from the negotiations. At the outset of the meeting, Brzezinski indicated that the President wanted the SCC to look seriously at reductions to 1500 as one of the proposals to be put to the Soviets (Memo, Brzezinski 3/8/77). However, the meeting primarily focused on the treatment of the Backfire bomber and Cruise missiles. Secretary of Defense Harold Brown felt that the latter two options needed to be studied in greater detail, which the group agreed to do. Further, Brown said that he preferred strict limits on the Backfire bomber and that he would accept loose limits on cruise missiles but added that he objected to a 1500-kilometer range limit on all cruise missiles. Representing the Joint Chiefs of Staff, Admiral James Holloway stated that the Joint Chiefs of Staff were concerned with the Backfire bomber, but at the same time, they also believed that it could easily be countered with air defenses. Acting in the place of Cyrus Vance, Deputy Secretary Warren Christopher argued that the Backfire bomber should not be counted and a 300-kilometer limit should be put on all cruise missiles. Leslie Gelb, Assistant Secretary of State pointed out that if the US pushed for restrictions on the Backfire the Soviets might link this to US forward-based systems in Europe. The issues raised by Christopher and Gelb put the State Department's views at odds with those of the Secretary of Defense. The members at the SCC meeting went on to discuss cruise missile definitions and its implications for verification.

Before ending the meeting, Brzezinski circulated a table outlining the possible options and it was agreed by all members that the SCC continue to study the options and at the next meeting the group would discuss reductions to about 2000 and the possible combination of Backfire and cruise missile reductions. Paul Warnke, representing the Arms Control and Disarmament Agency, encouraged the group to give consideration to the priorities in US negotiating positions. The issues remained unresolved at the end of the meeting because none of these options achieved the substantial reductions called for the by the president.

The SCC convened again on March 2 and Brzezinski began the meeting by reasserting that the purpose of the meeting was to discuss Backfire and Cruise missile reductions in combination with a reduction to 2000 ICBMs (Memo, Brzezinski 3/2/77). The discussion was dominated by the issue of cruise missiles and the limitation of missile ranges. Paul Warnke advocated a 300-kilometer limit on all cruise missiles, arguing that to accept this low limit would be advantageous in later stages of the negotiations. Leon Sloss, who also represented the Arms Control and Disarmament Agency, defended a 1500 limit arguing that, although this range brought a cut, it allowed the US to retain cruise missiles designed for specific roles. The Defense Department wanted to maintain longer ranges (2500 km) on cruise missiles because of the decision made that cruise missiles would be used to strike medium and intermediate range ballistic missiles in the western part of the Soviet Union. Again at the end of the meeting, Brzezinski summarized the discussion and noted that preferences seemed to be coalescing around Vladivostok reductions with a variety of options on cruise missiles and Backfire still remaining unresolved.

It was not until the March 10 SCC meeting that two clear options were provided, but they divided Carter's advisors. Brzezinski, Brown, and Deputy National Security Advisor David Aaron were in favor of a proposal calling for deep cuts; specifically Aaron argued for deep cuts in ICBM (2,400 to 2,000) and MIRVs (1,320 to 1,200). Brown supported the deep cuts proposal and he called for a freeze in the testing of ICBMs. Both Vance and Warnke accepted the deep cuts but they believed that this deviation from the Vladivostok agreement needed to include a concession to the Soviets, which led Warnke to suggest that the US exempt the Backfire and place limits on cruise missiles.

The next day, Brzezinski sent Carter a memo outlining the options that the SCC had arrived at so far and the positions of his advisors (Brzezinski 1983). Carter was made aware of the nature of the debate in the SCC and was put in a position to monitor the progress of the SCC. Two days later, Carter joined a meeting of the SCC (Vance, Brown, Brzezinski, Warnke, Aaron, Chairman of the Joint Chiefs of Staff George Brown, Vice President Walter

Mondale, and DCI Stansfield Turner) where he commented on and raised questions on a range of issues in addition to restating his interest in deep cuts (Talbott 1980: 58). After hearing the argument for deep cuts once again, Carter made the decision to support the Brown, Vance, and Aaron proposal, which most closely fit his own. In a meeting on March 19, Carter, Vance, Mondale, Brzezinski, and Brown reviewed the draft Presidential Directive. Carter determined that in the directive the deep cuts proposal should be the preferred option, but he also made the decision to integrate the Vance/Warnke position and make the 'Vladivostok-minus' proposal the fall back position. Finally, Carter decided to amend the reduction numbers and chose to reduce the number of ICBMs from 2,000 to 1,800 and 1,200 to 1,000. On March 22, Carter met with the Joint Chiefs of Staffs in a meeting during which he sought and obtained their support (Brzezinski 1983 and Garrison 1999).

The decision-making process that led to a proposal at the end of March resembles the process expected to be produced from a collegial structure with high centralization (Table 4.1). Carter became an active member of the group, guiding and shaping deliberations when he attended the February 3 and March 19 SCC meetings. Carter was also active in drafting the early letters sent to Brezhnev, setting out the administration's general position on a range of issues including arms control. As expected, Carter requested a range of options on a SALT II proposal. However, there was no explicit attempt by the president to foster consensus among his advisors with the exception of Carter's efforts to gain the support of the Joint Chiefs of Staff at the end of March. Any consensus that was built was created by the efforts of the advisors in the SCC. Like consensus, there was no explicit indication of shared responsibility. However, meetings throughout the process were frequent and regularized in the SCC and Carter was constantly made aware of the progress at each meeting. Last, the decision process did produce an integrative solution of the different perspectives in the administration. Advisors throughout the process sought integrative solutions in the SCC and the final proposal decided on by Carter was also integrative.

Table 4.1 First Proposal

Process	Characteristics
• Leader guiding and shaping deliberations	Yes
• Group to assess range of options	Yes
• Emphasis on building consensus among	No Indication
• Shared responsibility	No Indication
• Meetings are regularized and frequent	Yes
• Integrative Solution	Yes

Working Toward a New Proposal (April 1977 – May 1977)

The proposal presented to Brezhnev at the end of March by Vance was rejected by the Soviets as too much of a deviation from Vladivostok and as an attempt to get the USSR to make disproportionately larger cuts. Brezhnev's rejection forced the administration to rethink its approach and construct a new proposal that better interested the Soviets. Brzezinski states that from April onward Carter fully participated in the efforts to restart negotiations.

> From April on, Carter came to commit an inordinate amount of time to the SALT effort. He would meet frequently with his key advisors on a Saturday morning, in sessions lasting sometimes as much as two or three hours. He carefully monitored the work of the SCC, which met with increasing frequency, and on which I would report to him the same day a given meeting was held. (Brzezinski 1983: 166)

During this process the president let it be known that he was willing to change the 'style of his approach to a SALT II Treaty' and that he wanted to maintain the commitment to obtaining the main goals of the comprehensive proposal presented to the Soviets in March (Talbott 1980: 83). This imperative shaped the discussions of an April 7 SCC meeting in which the committee decided that the administration should emphasize privately Carter's preference for a comprehensive proposal. The group also concluded that there should be an effort to examine how the comprehensive proposal and deferral proposal could be combined into one package (Memo, Carter 4/11/77).

Essentially, the administration set out to construct a proposal on which all in the administration could agree and that would be acceptable to the Soviets (Talbott 1980: 1982–1983). David Aaron and William Hyland were tasked with blending the president's preferred comprehensive proposal, the Vance deferral proposal, and the Soviet counter-proposal into a three-tiered proposal. The plan called for a treaty lasting until 1985, a weapons ceiling reduced from Vladivostok, the creation of an interim agreement on contentious issues, such as cruise missiles, and an agreement of limitation on weapons development. On April 23, the president deliberated over these ideas proposed by Aaron and Hyland with Vice President Mondale, Vance, Brown, Arms Control and Disarmament Agency Director Warnke, and Brzezinski (Memo, Brzezinski 4/26/1977). On April 25, Carter decided to have Vance present the Soviets with a new US position that was a combination of the comprehensive and deferral positions. Dobrynin responded positively to Vance's proposal and afterward Vance sent a memo to Carter detailing the major points discussed. Carter responded to the memo by indicating that the administration should not make any more proposals and that 'it is time for inflexibility' (Memo, Carter 4/29/1977).

This episode reveals for the most part that the Carter administration followed a collegial/highly controlled decision-making process (Table 4.2). Carter was an active participant in guiding and shaping deliberations, for example when he told his advisors that he wanted a new style of approach to the negotiations; which was further evident from his deliberations on the Aaron-Hyland plan. The advisory system contained a search for a range of options with efforts to combine and consider the comprehensive and deferral proposals. Like the first episode for decision there is not an explicit indication of attempts to build consensus by the president or any identifiable sense of shared responsibility. Based on comments by Brzezinski, meetings between the president and his advisors were frequent and regular and the product of these deliberations was an agreement that was integrative.

Table 4.2 Second Proposal

Process	Characteristics
• Leader guiding and shaping deliberations	Yes
• Group to assess range of options	Yes
• Emphasis on building consensus among	No Indication
• Shared responsibility	No Indication
• Meetings are regularized and frequent	Yes
• Integrative	Yes

Carter and Gromyko (June 1977 – September 1977)

In Vance's meeting with Gromyko in Geneva, the Soviets agreed to the three-tier formula with the adjustment that the interim agreement be constructed as a protocol. Aside from this overall framework there was no movement on specific aspects or details. Cruise missiles and bombers in particular continued to be a major sticking point between the two sides. Brzezinski asked Carter whether he wanted to make an intermediate proposal to the Soviets or should the administration inform the Soviets that the US will not make any more proposals and that the onus was now on the Soviets to devise a plan since the US had proposed the three-tier framework (Memo, Brzezinski 6/3/1977). Carter's response to Brzezinski was that he wanted an analysis of what the difference between the two approaches would be.[4]

---

[4] For the most part, the administration turned its attention to other issues during the summer. Aside from deciding to let the Soviets make the next move, the administration also decided that since it was canceling the B-1 bomber, the Soviets had to allow the US under SALT to deploy bombers armed with ALCMs without reducing the number of MIRVs.

Carter finally decided that the administration should not make any new proposals to the Soviets but should continue to work on the technical issues that were discussed during the Vance and Gromyko meeting. In meetings held in June and July, the SCC continued to discuss issues such as definition of cruise missiles, cruise missile ranges, verification, reductions in aggregate, and MIRV levels as well as a range of other issues (Memo, Brzezinski 6/7/1977; Memo, Brzezinski 6/28/1977; Memo, Brzezinski 7/7/1977; Memo, Brzezinski 7/22/1977). Divisions arose between members of the administration on many of these issues. When these disagreements arose, the issues were either put aside to be further studied by a working group for further consideration within the SCC, or they were offered to the president for a decision. It was at this time that Harold Brown split with Vance and Warnke over the issue of cruise missile range. Brown argued that the limitation of cruise missiles should apply to those missiles that are armed with nuclear warheads; Vance and Warnke thought that limitations should be applied to all armed cruise missiles (Memo, Brzezinski 6/28/1977). The same divisions arose over MIRV reductions and heavy bomber limits (Memo, Brzezinski 7/22/1977).

By the end of August the administration was preparing for another meeting between Vance and Gromyko and a series of issues had to be decided on before the end of September. The SCC met on August 30 with the intent of considering ways of repackaging the administration's existing proposal, so that a final decision could be made at a National Security Council meeting on September 6 (Memo, Brzezinski 8/31/1977). Carter had to make decisions on five issues at the NSC meeting that could not be resolved between the agencies. The most important issue Carter had to deal with at that meeting was whether or not to count air-launched cruise missile-carrying heavy bombers in the 1,320 delivery system total in return for a raised MIRV limit (Brzezinski 1983: 169). On September 9 the administration communicated to the Soviets, through Ambassador Dobrynin, that the US expected the Soviets to address three issues: reducing the numerical ceilings set at Vladivostok, limits on heavy ICBMs and a sub-ceiling on MIRVed ICBMs.

On September 22, Vance met with Gromyko and in the second session of talks Gromyko presented the Soviet proposal, which included a willingness to reduce MIRVed ICBMs to 820, if the US were to drop demands for reductions in heavy ICBMs. In addition, the Soviets agreed to publicly declare that the Backfire bomber did not have intercontinental capability and that they would not increase the aircraft's production rate. Carter believed that Gromyko had made serious concessions but he also thought that politically it would be difficult to drop US insistence on heavy ICBM reductions. That evening, Carter, Vance, Brown, and Brzezinski began working to put together a counter-proposal. Two issues confronted Carter and company: first, whether or not to accept Gromyko's proposal, and second, how could the Gromyko proposal be fit into the US position. The group concluded by accepting the offer, but realized that it would be necessary to make a concession and include ALCMs in the 1,320 ceiling. To help construct a proposal package, Brzezinski sought the help of both members of the NSC staff working on SALT, David Aaron and William Hyland.

The Aaron and Hyland solution to the problems was based on 'allowance' for cruise missile carrying bombers (Talbott 1980: 125). The allowance solution permitted the US and USSR to have a set number of ALCM bombers, but every additional ALCM meant that one MIRVed missile had to be eliminated, in addition attached to the proposal was a new MIRV subceiling that was lower than the 1,320 already put forward. Brzezinski advocated a 1,100 to 1,150 subceiling, while the Joint Chiefs wanted 1,250. Ultimately the president chose 1,200 as the new aggregate level of MIRVed missiles. The next day Carter presented the US counter-proposal to Gromyko. Gromyko reacted positively to the counting of ALCM bombers under the 1,320 ceiling, but was less than enthusiastic about making concessions on the proposed MIRV sub-ceiling. Gromyko told the president that he would communicate his proposal to Moscow (Talbott 1980: 127–128).

During this episode the process begins to change in part as a result of the changes in the negotiations (Table 4.3). As major issues and the broad outlines of the negotiations begin to develop, more work is done in the SCC, as decisions needed to be made on specific issues. Carter is noticeably less active in guiding discussions and as the negotiations proceed more work is being done by the SCC and options are being offered to the president. This does not include the meeting held during Gromyko's visit where Carter was active in constructing a counter-proposal, nor does it include Carter's request for an analysis of the differences between not offering a new proposal and making an intermediate proposal. During this episode, the president largely is given options from the SCC that are a product of consensus among his advisors. The consensus is built among advisors within the SCC, before they go to the president. Once again, responsibility for the decision is not explicit in the events leading up to the Gromyko meeting in September. During this part of the negotiations meetings are less frequent, which can be attributed to the more work is being done by the SCC and options are being offered to the president. This does not include the meeting held during Gromyko's visit where Carter was active in constructing a counter-proposal, nor does it include Carter's request for an analysis of the differences between not offering a new proposal and making an intermediate proposal. During this episode, the president largely is given options from the SCC that are a product of consensus among his advisors. The consensus is built among advisors within the SCC, before they go to the president. Once again, responsibility for the decision is not explicit in the events leading up to the Gromyko meeting in September. During this part of the negotiations meetings are less frequent, which can be attributed to the changing of priorities in the administration. Solutions to disagreements are not integrative during this episode either. The SCC reaches a deadlock and offers Carter options, thus producing a subset solution. During the deliberations on a counter-proposal, Carter chooses the Aaron-Hyland plan that can be thought of as another subset solution.

Table 4.3 Carter and Gromyko Counter-Proposal

Process	Characteristics
• Leader guiding and shaping deliberations	Yes
• Group to assess range of options	Yes
• Emphasis on building consensus among	Within SCC
• Shared responsibility	No Indication
• Meetings are regularized and frequent	No
• Integrative	No

Breaking the Impasse (February 1978 – July 1978)

In the early part of 1978, the US-USSR relationship deteriorated as a result of tension over Soviet and Cuban support for the Ethiopian government which was in the midst of fighting a secessionist movement in the Ogaden. During this period Vance met with Gromyko several times on technical issues in an effort to move the SALT negotiations forward, but these discussions often focused on the greater US-USSR relationship than on SALT II. The preoccupation with the strategic relationship between the US and USSR also came to color discussions within the administration on SALT II. Brzezinski, at a February 21 SCC meeting, argued that Soviet actions in Africa ought to be linked to SALT II (NSA Chronology 5/6/1994). Vance and Brown opposed, arguing that there was no need to create this kind of linkage since it would impede progress with the Soviet Union.

The issue arose once again during another March 2 SCC meeting where again Brzezinski insisted that 'the Soviets needed to be made aware of the fact that they are poisoning the atmosphere' and 'What we are saying is that if there is an aggravation of tensions because of what the Soviets are doing in the Horn, there is going to be linkage. That is a statement of fact' (Meeting Transcript 5/2/1978).[5] Vance's position was that the US would lose the ability

---

[5] On the morning of March 2 the President gave a speech at the National Press Club where he alluded to a connection between Soviet actions in Africa and the future of a SALT II agreement. Carter stated: 'The Soviets' violating of these principles would be

to conclude a SALT agreement if this linkage was made and the resulting failure would be a blot on the President's record. Harold Brown agreed with Brzezinski that linkage may form between issues, but the administration should not encourage it and instead find 'something else to beat the Soviets with' (Meeting Transcript 5/2/1978). The SCC agreed to suggest to the president (and he accepted) that the US suspend talks on space, the US consult with the Chinese, and that serious engagement be made with the Soviets regarding the situation in the Horn of Africa (Meeting Transcript 5/2/1978).

Aside from debating the merits of linking Soviet-US relations to SALT the administration deliberated whether it was prudent to toughen the US negotiating position on SALT. In January, Vance and Warnke sent a report to the president proposing that the US move quickly to resolve all outstanding issues with the Soviet Union by the spring of 1978 and conclude SALT II. They also sought Carter's approval on plans to begin negotiations with the Soviet Union on the cutoff of fissionable materials. This latter issue was quickly dealt with by Brzezinski who sent the plan to Secretary of Energy James Schlesinger, who condemned it because the plan, in his opinion, lacked the proper analysis and gave the impression that the US lacked 'stability and resolve' (Brzezinski 1983: 316–317; NSA Chronology I-22). Given the counter-arguments presented by Brzezinski and Schlesinger, Carter decided to not to approach the Soviet Union for negotiations.

On the issue of softening the US position on SALT, Brown, with Brzezinski's support, opposed Vance and Warnke in SCC meetings on this approach arguing that it would make it difficult for the US to halt the Soviet strategic buildup. An agreement full of concessions, in their view, was difficult to ratify. Brzezinski was able to advance his preferences by making these arguments in the weekly reports that he submitted to the president in April. He further followed up by meeting with the president to discuss the contents of his reports and was able to convince the president of a tough position. As a result of these discussions, the president in a subsequent cabinet meeting stated that in the next meeting between Vance and Gromyko, Vance should discuss

---

a cause of concern to me, would lessen the confidence of the American people in the world and peaceful intentions of the Soviet Union, would make it more difficult to ratify a SALT agreement or comprehensive test ban agreement if concluded, and therefore the two are linked because of actions by the Soviets. We didn't initate the linkage' (Brzezinski 1983: 185). Brzezinski, prior to this speech, had made his feelings known about Soviet actions and linkage to SALT. However, it is not entirely clear whether the President's statements were arrived at on his own or if they were a result of prompting by Brzezinski. Given the perceived seriousness of Soviet actions, Carter's involvement in policy and Brzezinski's access to the President, it is likely that Carter came to the decision on his own, but he probably seriously considered Brzezinski's views before doing so. Nonetheless, the linkage between the two was only alluded to in speech and never became a policy priority for the administration.

SALT, but also discuss the US-Soviet relationship. With this support, Brzezinski was allowed to draft the instructions for Vance's meeting. Brzezinski claimed that he continued to influence the president's thinking through the weekly reports and conversations (Brzezinski 1983: 317–318).

The decision-making process during this episode changes when compared to the others because of the change in administration priorities, which in turn is the result of the breakdown of the US-Soviet relationship (Table 4.4). Thus, during this episode the major issues (tougher stance on SALT and linkage) are discussed in the SCC and options are offered to the president as options for choice. The administration built a consensus in the March 2 meeting on the issue of linkage between SALT and US-Soviet relations, but consensus was not sought on toughening the administration's approach to SALT as Brzezinski and Brown opposed Vance and Warnke. Because of the change of priorities within the administration, meetings become infrequent. Also, there is no explicit indication of shared responsibility and there are mixed findings on the presence of integrative solutions. The March 2 meeting, in which the issue of linkage is taken up, results in an integrative solution. But, later, Brzezinski ensures a subset solution by way of immediate access and the weekly reports that allow him to influence the president.

Table 4.4 Breaking the Impasse

Process	Characteristics
• Leader guiding and shaping deliberations	Yes
• Group to assess range of options	Yes in SCC
• Emphasis on building consensus	Yes/No
• Shared responsibility	No Indication
• Meetings are regularized and frequent	No
• Integrative Solution	Yes/No

Getting Back on Track (July 1978 – September 1978)

SCC meetings during this period increased to three to four a month out of recognition that the Soviets wanted to conclude an agreement (Brzezinski 1983: 316, 326). During a July meeting with Vance, Gromyko proposed that during the life of the treaty both sides should be able to introduce one new MIRVed or non-MIRVed ICBM. Despite being overshadowed by the overall tension in US-Soviet relations this proved to be a significant concession.

The SCC chaired by Brzezinski met on September 1 and at that meeting the committee worked to formulate a series of proposals that resolved all outstanding issues between the United States and the Soviet Union

(Thornton 1991; Brzezinski 1983). The committee came to a consensus and decided to propose that SLBM reentry vehicles be limited to fourteen warheads, SLBM depressed trajectory testing be banned and they agreed on a range of other positions including: ALCM limits, cruise missile range definition, dismantling excess missiles, and an expiration protocol (Brzezinski 1983: 326–327). However, building a consensus on how to treat the Backfire bomber proved difficult. Chairman of the Joint Chiefs, General David Jones proposed that the US should tell the Soviets that the Backfire should be counted in the overall ceiling or the US would radically improve its air defenses. David Aaron countered and took the position that instead of responding with an upgrade of air defenses, the US would increase the numbers of the F-111 medium-range bombers, an aircraft that like the Backfire would not be considered strategic and therefore would not be subject to production restraints. To resolve this issue, Brzezinski brought the president into the SCC meeting to help decide on an agreed position. The president ultimately supported the idea put forth by Aaron. The president attended an NSC meeting held the next day to further discuss these issues. Brzezinski disagreed with the president on the strategy for dealing with the Backfire question. However, the president decided that Vance at his September 27–28 meeting with Gromyko would go with the F-111 counter-option.

For the earlier part of these deliberations, policy was formulated in the SCC, but when deadlock arose over the backfire bomber, the president involved himself in the process and actively engaged in deliberations. The operation of the advisory system during this episode is similar to that of previous episodes (Table 4.5). The president was an active member in an SCC meeting and the main NSC meeting when deciding the disposition of the F-111. However, the ranges of options are reduced because of the work of the SCC. Brzezinski, as on previous occasions, sought consensus on the issues being discussed in the SCC and those issues that did not have a consensus were offered to the president as options. Shared responsibility is not readily apparent, but meetings are frequent and regularized. The decision, in this occasion, is a subset produced by the president in choosing his preferred option on the issue of the F-111.

Table 4.5 Getting Back on Track

Process	Characteristics
• Leader guiding and shaping deliberations	Yes
• Group to assess range of options	Yes
• Emphasis on building consensus among	Yes in SCC
• Shared responsibility	No Indication
• Meetings are regularized and frequent	Yes
• Integrative	No

Deliberating Cruise Missiles (October 1978 – December 1978)

Vance's meeting at the end of September proved to be an exercise in futility. The Soviets conceded that they would notify the US of extraterritorial missile tests, a concession the administration desired since early 1977 (Talbott 1980: 218). The Soviets further agreed to accept the US position on the number of ALCMs permitted on bombers, but the Soviets argued that this had always been tied to a warhead freeze on existing types of ICBMs. The Soviets withdrew their commitment to limit the number of MIRVs by asserting that the MX, the SS-17, and the SS-19 would be permitted to carry ten warheads as opposed to only four. The two sides disagreed on a range of other issues, most notably the encryption of telemetry during missile tests and the definition of cruise missiles.

The SCC and NSC met throughout this period in order to bring about a consensus within the administration on the remaining issues before Vance met with Gromyko again at the end of December (Talbott 1980: 223). At an informal meeting on October 13, Brzezinski, Vance, and Paul Warnke met with the president to discuss whether or not the administration should be willing to make concessions on the remaining issues in order to rapidly conclude SALT II. Warnke and Vance proposed the US should not insist that the Soviets confirm in writing their promise to limit production of the Backfire bomber. The president pushed Vance and Warnke to reconsider this position because he believed that in the long run this would not be in the best interest of the country.

Both Vance and Warnke attempted to defend their positions by arguing that if the US states that the Soviets should not produce more than 30 bombers a year and the Soviets do not reject this statement then the US would have tacit confirmation. Brzezinski intervened and argued that in the future the US would have a difficult time proving that the Soviets accepted the stated limit. The president further argued that this 'unspoken' confirmation would prove problematic when it came to getting the treaty ratified. Warnke came up with a compromise position whereby the US would send a message requesting the Soviets assert the '30 a year limit' and have them respond to this position in writing. Both the president and Brzezinski were willing to accept this compromise. Vance and Brzezinski further worked together to construct the instructions that Vance carried with him to the next meeting with Gromyko.

The administration held a series of meetings in November to put together positions on the remaining issues. Particular attention during this period was given to determining a cruise missile definition. Divisions existed within the administration over whether or not the US cruise missile definition was an impediment to the negotiations. The Soviets wanted to treat equally conventional cruise missiles and nuclear cruise missiles. It was Brown's and Carter's position that conventionally armed cruise missiles should be exempted from the Treaty, while Vance, Mondale, and eventually Brzezinski, believed that the US did not need to make an exemption and that it was only getting in the way. Carter first held a meeting with Brzezinski and Mondale; each argued that a concession was necessary to move the negotiations forward and that under the US proposal the Soviets were permitted to cheat in the future (Talbott 1980: 224). Later, Carter held meetings with the JCS, who argued that it was a mistake to accept limitations on cruise missiles, specifically ground and sea-launched cruise missiles. Through his discussions with others, Harold Brown slowly changed his position and accepted that the US position was not the best choice (Talbott 1980). In late November, just before Vance left for his meeting, Carter met with Mondale, Vance, Brown, Brzezinski, and Hamilton Jordan and decided after hearing their views that he would change his original position and accept that the conventional cruise missile exception was untenable because it was unverifiable (Talbott 1980: 225).

This episode sees Carter very active in shaping and guiding deliberations and in assessing a range of options (Table 4.6). Evidence for both the former and latter are present in the October 13 meeting and in the discussions held in November on the approach toward cruise missiles. It is also evident from the November meetings that a consensus was built among Carter's advisors and, finally, the President himself agreed to not exempt conventionally armed cruise missiles. The meetings held in November were frequent in order to meet the December deadline and on the issue of the Backfire bomber the administration produced an integrative solution. Shared responsibility during this period can possibly be inferred from the actions of Carter's advisors in and after the October 13 meeting because of their willingness to compromise and their support for the policy.

Table 4.6 Deliberating Cruise Missiles

Process	Characteristics
• Leader guiding and shaping deliberations	Yes
• Group to assess range of options	Yes
• Emphasis on building consensus among	Yes
• Shared responsibility	No Indication
• Meetings are regularized and frequent	Yes
• Integrative Solutions	Yes

Reaching an Agreement (January 1979 – May 1979)

Vance met with Gromyko at the end of December to discuss some of the same issues that they discussed at their meeting in Geneva earlier in December.

Little was resolved and the negotiations slowed dramatically as US-Soviet relations began to deteriorate over a range of other geo-political issues. It was not until February that negotiations were restarted with increased discussions between Vance and Soviet Ambassador Anatoly Dobrynin and between the formal delegations in Geneva.

Much of the deliberations within the administration on the remaining issues took place within the SCC with the president signing off on the SCC's collectively agreed upon position. The resolution of two major issues taken up by the SCC, telemetry encryption and modernization of existing ICBMs, moved the negotiations toward completion. During January and February, the SCC discussed the definition of 'new types' of ICBMs. The first meeting held by the SCC on this issue resulted in the group constructing a set of negotiating parameters that ensured that the delegation in Geneva did not deviate from the five percent rule. The administration position was that any changes greater than five percent on any existing missile meant that it was a new type. On February 12, the SCC met to figure out a proposal that Vance could present to the Soviets that would maintain the five percent parameter. In this meeting the SCC agreed that Vance should propose to Dobrynin that the US would ban testing of MIRVed ALCMs and in return the Soviets would concede to the US position on the 'new types' definition.

The SCC held a series of meetings during March in an effort to resolve the telemetry issue. The Soviets had not, to the Carter administration's satisfaction, clearly stated its position on the verification of missile telemetry. On March 5, the SCC met and Stansfield Turner stated that all encryption of telemetry should be banned; Brown and Brzezinski argued that this was an unreasonable position and that the Soviets would not accept. However, it was agreed that it was necessary to get the Soviets to explicitly state that there are some instances when verification necessitates access to telemetry (Talbott 1980). The SCC thus drafted a letter that Carter sent to Brezhnev that would elicit a commitment to a shared understanding of telemetry encryption. The response from Brezhnev was unequivocal and negative. The administration was forced to continue to find a formula acceptable to the Soviets.

Starting the week of March 19, the 'mini-SCC' (cabinet-level SCC member's deputies) held a series of meetings that resulted in a second Carter letter to Brezhnev. The 'mini-SCC' in the letter proposed to the Soviets that 'some encryption as practiced impedes verification' (Talbott 1980: 259). In addition they made no references to two missile tests that the administration had previously argued were violations of SALT. However, at a March SCC principals-only meeting, Brown, Brzezinski, and Turner objected to the idea of removing the reference to the missile tests. Consequently, they felt that a note should be added to the letter from Vance to Dobrynin that clarified the US position on the two Soviet tests. Carter agreed to send both the letter and the note but before doing so he wanted to ensure that the Joint Chiefs of Staff supported the administration's position. Carter subsequently held a meeting with Brown and the JCS where they discussed encryption and other issues; the President was able to obtain their support. With this final agreement and Soviet concessions on other issues, the Carter Administration and the Soviets' negotiations came to an end (with the exception of some technical issues) in early May. Both sides agreed to a spring summit between Brezhnev and Carter to sign the SALT II agreement.

This last episode reveals that Carter became less involved in the guiding and shaping of deliberations as the remaining issues focused on technical issues (Table 4.7). At this stage, the SCC was formulating proposals and offering them to Carter for approval. Any options that were considered were primarily confined to the SCC meetings and not presented to the president. Consensus was generally formed in the SCC on issues and no strong indication of shared responsibility existed beyond the ability of the advisory system to create and present proposals to the president. Meetings held by the SCC are frequent and regularized and integrated solutions are arrived at, evidenced by Carter's sending of a note clarifying the US position on Soviet missile tests.

Table 4.7 Reaching an Agreement

Process	Characteristics
• Leader guiding and shaping deliberations	No
• Group to assess range of options	Yes in SCC
• Emphasis on building consensus among	Yes in SCC
• Shared responsibility	No Indication
• Meetings are regularized and frequent	Yes
• Integrative Solution	Yes

Conclusion

The examination of the Carter administration's decision-making during the Strategic Arms Limitation Talks supports the hypothesized decision-making process in the Advisory System Framework. However, not all of the characteristics of the process were present during every episode and for some decisions the administration behaved in ways that were not fully expected. Table 4.8 shows the characteristics of the decision-making process and how each characteristic faired across all episodes. Carter was an active participant, in over half of the episodes, guiding and shaping the deliberations on strategy in dealing with the Soviets and in constructing the administration's proposals. He accomplished this by attending meetings, participating in constructing and deliberating on options, and making his preferences known to his advisers. When negotiations ran into problems in mid-1977, Carter ordered that his advisors rethink the 'style' of approach toward the Soviet Union. Brzezinski highlighted that Carter was constantly informed of SCC findings and that in key periods Carter worked closely with his advisors to create administration policy.

During two episodes, Carter played less of a role in shaping and guiding deliberations. The reason for the decline in Carter's participation can be explained by the fact that as the relationship between the United States and the Soviet Union deteriorated, as a consequence, the administration spent less time deliberating on SALT. Thus, there was less of a reason for Carter to be involved. The issues that they did discuss often revolved around small technical issues that would not have commanded a high priority, given the other issues confronting the administration. The other instance of decline in Carter's contribution to the process came as a result of the evolving nature of the negotiations. At the beginning of negotiations more work is required to establish the parameters of a government's negotiating position, such as goals, objectives, and strategy. As the negotiations progress many of these larger issues are resolved and more technical issues come to the fore and require less active involvement by the president. In all of the cases the group was encouraged and sought a range of options. Despite differences of opinion held by many of Carter's closest advisors there was a willingness by all those involved to entertain and consider differing points of view. Options were developed in two ways, first by Carter directing members of the administration (SCC) to establish or evaluate alternative proposals (found in five out of seven episodes). This was demonstrated, for example, when Carter directed Brzezinski to provide the president with an analysis evaluating benefits of remaining firm on the administration's position or constructing an intermediate proposal. Alternatively, options were developed within the SCC itself by advisors. The willingness by the SCC to actively create options was a product of the structure put in place by Carter and his advisors understanding that the president wanted to be exposed to a range of views (Aaron2002). Finding evidence of an emphasis on consensus during this case was difficult and where it does seem to exist it does not seem to be emphasized by the president. In two of the seven episodes there is no indication that the president or his advisors sought or placed an importance on consensus.

In the other episodes, advisors working within the SCC built consensus on issues before sending their suggestions to the president. Only in the deliberations over exemption of cruise missiles from any agreement is there evidence that the administration was seeking a consensus. Carter, who held a view in opposition to some of his advisors, held a series of meetings during which a consensus developed around the idea of rejecting exemption. Carter

Table 4.8 Carter Advisory System: Collegial / High Centralization System

	First Proposal	New Proposal	Carter and Gromyko	Breaking the Impasse	Getting on Track	Cruise Missiles	An Agreement	%
Leader guiding and shaping deliberations	Yes	Yes	Yes	Some	Some	Yes	No	57
Group to assess range of options	Yes	Yes	Yes	Yes in SCC	Yes	Yes	Yes in SCC	71
Emphasis on building consensus among	No indication	No indication	Yes in SCC	Yes in SCC	Yes in SCC	Yes	Yes in SCC	71
Shared responsibility	No indication	No indication	No indication	No indication	No indication	No indication	No indication	—
Meetings are regularized and frequent	Yes	Yes	No	No	Yes	Yes	Yes	71
Integrative Solution	Yes	Yes	No	Yes/No	No	Yes	Yes	71

and Brown through this process gave up their views and joined with Brzezinski, Vance, and the Joint Chiefs of Staff. These findings question whether there is an emphasis on consensus in advisory systems with collegial structures and high centralization. David Aaron has argued that President Carter did not feel the need to build consensus on issues because Carter was comfortable with his advisors holding different views on a given issue (Aaron 2002). Carter wanted his advisors to hold differing views because it improved the decision-making process. But the reason for this comfort was Carter's understanding that individuals see situations differently and that this resulted in different recommendations; however, Carter also knew that he would make the final decision, which meant that his opinion was what mattered most, and, therefore, alternative views were not a concern.

If Carter did not place an emphasis on building consensus, why is it that the SCC often discussed issues until they reached a consensus? One explanation is that as chair of the SCC, Brzezinski often sought to build a consensus on an issue before sending it to the president. The alternative explanation for the emphasis on consensus in the SCC is the same as the explanation for the creation of options on the part of advisors within the SCC. Just as the SCC was deliberately designed as a forum for creating and evaluating options, the SCC was also a forum deliberately designed for building consensus. The SCC either generated options which then could be further discussed by the president and the rest of the National Security Council or, as the SALT II case demonstrates, the SCC built a consensus on an option or two. In short, the members of the SCC operated according to the president's original intent when he constructed his decision-making infrastructure, because he wanted decisions to be made based on collegiality. Thus, the consensus that did occur in the administration was a result of the structure created by Carter and the efforts of Brzezinski and other advisors to create consensus on certain issues.

Surprisingly, there is no indication in the case of the SALT II negotiations of a sense of shared responsibility among the president's advisors. Again, two reasons present themselves as possible explanations for this outcome. First, a sense of shared responsibility is a feature that is not verbally expressed, which makes it difficult to find evidence of it in secondary sources or primary documents. Perhaps a better way to look at responsibility is to understand it in terms of loyalty and with this understanding it is possible to argue that there was a shared responsibility because their existed a high level of loyalty at the cabinet and sub-cabinet level to President Carter (Aaron 2002). Loyalty at these levels contrasts the lower degree of loyalty among the bureaucracy where greater loyalty lies with the department or agency. Second, shared responsibility can be found in those instances where Carter's advisors working within the SCC were willing to come to a consensus and integrate their ideas based on a belief that they all had a stake in the administration's policy. The second of these two explanations better explains why shared responsibility although present does not explicitly manifests itself; shared responsibility is a part of the system if all members can contribute to the policy.

The last two characteristics of highly centralized and collegial advisory systems—frequent and regularized meetings (five out of seven episodes) and integrative solutions (five out of seven episodes)—are both present in the SALT II negotiations. Frequent and regularized meetings took place during all episodes except two and these two episodes coincided with the decline of Soviet-US relations and the change in the administration's priorities. Similarly, integrative solutions were found in all the episodes except two, and in those two instances the outcomes were subset solutions for which the president was presented with a set of options for choice. Even in those instances where there were subset solutions, integrative solutions were often chosen among Carter's advisors to limit the amount of options and decisions required by the president. Overall, the Carter administration's negotiations with the Soviet Union regarding strategic arms limitations conforms to the process predicted by a system that is highly centralized and collegial in structure. The only aspects of the hypothesized process that are not fully supported are: emphasis on consensus and shared responsibility. However, there is evidence that these characteristics are embedded in other characteristics such as the assessment of a range of options, and the choice of integrative solutions, and the general desire of the president set at the outset of the process. So, although these features are not explicitly present they can be inferred from other aspects of the process.

Chapter 5

Strategic Arms Reduction Talks

The chief executive should set broad policy and general ground rules, tell people what he or she wants them to do, then let them do it; he should make himself (or herself) available, so that the members of his team can come to him if there is a problem... But I don't think a chief executive should peer constantly over the shoulders of the people who are in charge of a project and tell them every few minutes what to do. (Reagan 1990: 161)

Organization of Ronald Reagan's Foreign Policy System

Reagan's delegation of responsibility, as well as his desire to have issues resolved among his cabinet and then presented to him as options, indicates that his advisory system can be characterized as being formal, with Reagan exercising a low centralization (George & Stern 1998; Burke 2000). Reagan sought two identifiable goals in constructing his advisory system. First, Reagan wanted to add greater coherence to the foreign policy-making process by making the Secretary of State the president's principal spokesman and advisor, while restoring the National Security Advisor and National Security Council staff to the role of policy coordinator (Shoemaker 1991: 57). Reagan believed that under Carter the decision-making process in the NSC became unruly and was undermined by the actions of advisors such as Zbigniew Brzezinski, who acted without fully consulting with the NSC. By changing advisor roles Reagan wanted to downplay the role of National Security Advisor, which characterized of previous administrations. Reagan sought a cabinet style of policy-making in which cabinet members would come together to address a specific issue, and after the advisors had discussed the issue, the president would decide on a course of action (Fischer 1997: 71).

The other goals Reagan had for his advisory system were to delegate and maintain a 'hands off' style of management. As the quotation at the beginning of the chapter indicates, Reagan wanted to surround himself with competent individuals to whom he could then delegate responsibility and be assured that the job was done. Reagan did not want to be a part of the process of working through problems; rather he wanted to be presented with solutions, ideally those that had been reached through consensus (Sloan 1997: 561–562). Reagan believed that he did not need to be a hands-on manager, and that all he needed to do was focus on the big picture and give general direction to his administration (Kengor 1998). Overall, this system allowed Reagan to focus on issues that he felt were important and when an issue of particular magnitude did arise he could hear what the solutions were and come to a quick decision.

An advisory system based on cabinet style decision-making with responsibilities delegated to the president's principal advisors is the kind of system Reagan wanted. However, this does not exactly reflect the system that the administration adopted when Reagan came into office. Unlike Carter and Nixon, Reagan did not, at the time of coming into office, issue a presidential directive (National Security Decision Directive – 2) that formally stated the administration's foreign policy decision-making infrastructure. After meeting with the president on January 6, 1981, newly appointed Secretary of State Alexander Haig began to work in coordination with the Department of Defense, National Security Council staff, and Central Intelligence Agency to construct the national security structure. In their meeting, both Haig and Reagan agreed on relegating the National Security Advisor and staff to a coordinating role, while the Secretary of State would be the president's sole advisor and spokesperson on foreign affairs (Haig 1984: 74; Henderson 1988: 149).

The document that eventually emerged from the joint interagency effort was one that gave the Secretary of State the responsibility for 'formulation of foreign policy and for the execution of approved policy' (Shoemaker 1991: 59). In fact, the proposed directive placed all authority for formulating national security policy with the Secretaries of State and Defense as well as the Director of Central Intelligence. In a notable break with the past the National Security Advisor was removed as a member of the NSC and was not permitted to chair any committees. The National Security Advisor could, in principle, participate and serve on Interagency Group committees, although assistant and sub-assistant members of the major departments chaired the committees (Shoemaker 1991: 60). Interagency groups were tasked with constructing policy reviews known as National Security Study Directives and any decisions arrived at by the administration were to be formally written in National Security Decision Directives (NSDD). Despite having formulated this first directive on the structure of the national security system with the assistance of other departments and agencies, Haig's proposal ran into difficulty when presented to Reagan's White House staff, specifically Ed Meese, Reagan's Chief of Staff. Early in the administration, Meese positioned himself as Reagan's gatekeeper and it was Meese's belief that the draft NSDD-1 had to be cleared by him first. This soured initial relation's in the White House, but Meese's relationship with the cabinet members would improve, yet the relationship with the National Security Advisor remained tense well into the president's first term. Not until 1982, with the removal of Richard Allen and the arrival of William Clark as Reagan's new National Security Advisor was Meese's position in the foreign policy-making process diminished (Fischer 1997: 87).

With the arrival of a new National Security Advisor in 1972 came the signature of Haig's proposed NSDD-1 and the formal imposition of the national security committee system. However, before Reagan signed NSDD-1 the administration extemporaneously put in place a structure to add coherence to the decision-making process. In the summer of 1981, the National Security Planning Group (NSPG) was put in place to deal with a range of issues including US-Soviet relations, crisis management, intelligence, and covert operations. The NSPG was chaired by Vice-President George Bush and included the NSC principals as well as members of White House Staff such as Ed Meese (Prados 1991: 456; Fischer 1997: 82). In 1987, Reagan's fifth National Security Advisor Frank Carlucci created two new committees, the Senior Review Group (SRG) and the Policy Review Group (PRG). Each group was tasked with reviewing policy on issues that cut across department expertise and required coordination for formulation and implementation of policy (Shoemaker 1991: 62).

In short, Reagan's national security infrastructure evolved slowly over time, but it was still guided by Reagan's need to delegate responsibility to close advisors and the desire to establish a cabinet style decision-making process. The apparent consequence of the intersection of Reagan's hands-off style with the slow establishment of an official management structure was that individual advisors took the initiative in carrying out what they believed to be Reagan's will (Sloan 1997: 562). Different advisors who were rigidly ideological began to compete to advance their policy preferences and gain Reagan's approval (Sloan 1997: 562–563). Alexander Haig has commented that he often felt 'there was no description of duty, no rules, no expression of the essential authority of the president to guide his subordinates in their task' (Shoemaker 1997: 72). Caspar Weinberger has pointed out, on the issue of arms control, that it was not an orderly process and that a variety of means were used to create policy (Weinberger 2002). Thus, the evolution of the advisory system combined with Reagan's chosen management style indicates that the policy-making process during the START negotiations with the Soviet Union should have the following characteristics:

- Leader chooses between presented options
- Advisors compete to get preferences presented to leader
- Gatekeeper acts as honest-broker and presents options (opportunity for other advisors to appeal to leader)
- Bargaining and conflict take place at level below president
- Procedures may be circumvented
- Disagreement leads to dominant-Subset Solution or deadlock

Because of Reagan's need to delegate, it was important that he bring into his administration individuals that he could trust to carry out tasks in his best interest. To a certain extent this required finding advisors that held similar ideological views on world politics. Members of the White House Staff in particular were chosen for their strong commitment to both conservative issues and to Reagan personally; this also held true for Reagan's foreign policy advisors (Sloan 1997). The need for ideological compatibility led Reagan to choose a group of advisors with anti-communist credentials who believed that the Soviet Union was the source of evil and had 'aggressive impulses' (Scott 1996). Forming the core of Reagan's foreign policy advisors during the Strategic Arms Reduction Talks were Secretary of Defense Caspar Weinberger; Secretary of State George Shultz; National Security Advisors Robert McFarlane; William Clark and Admiral John Poindexter; Assistant Secretary of Defense Richard Perle; Assistant Secretary of State Richard Burt; Secretary of State Alexander Haig Jr.; chief arms control negotiator Edward Rowny; and NSC arms control specialist Ronald Lehman.

Two unexpected figures came to dominate the deliberations over the Reagan administration's position on the reduction of strategic arms. Richard Perle and Richard Burt set the tone for deliberations and embodied the differing approaches to arms control found in the administration. Assistant Secretary of State Richard Burt, a former *New York Times* reporter and defense intellectual, was asked to head the State Department's Bureau of Political-Military Affairs where he was charged with formulating policy on arms control. Burt took the lead in this effort for the State Department because of the Secretary of State's lack of expertise on arms control and his interest in other issues (Talbott 1984: 12). Opposite Burt, in the Defense Department, was his counterpart the Assistant Secretary of Defense for International Security Affairs Richard Perle. Perle cut his teeth on arms control issues as an aide to Senator Henry Jackson where he was instrumental in generating opposition to the SALT II treaty. Like Burt, Perle was allowed to play a prominent role in forming the Defense Department's position on arms control. Perle acted as Secretary of Defense Weinberger's representative and went to meetings with the purpose of securing the adoption of the Department of Defense's policies (Weinberger 2002). Perle served with Burt on the Special Arms Control Policy Group (SACPG) later to be known as the Senior Arms Control Group. The Special Arms Control Policy Group was tasked with constructing the administration's policy toward the Soviet Union on all arms control reductions.

Despite the prominence of these two Assistant Secretaries, the Secretaries still played important roles in the struggle that emerged over the direction of administration policy. Secretary of State Alexander Haig, although delegating a considerable amount of responsibility and authority to Burt, was still responsible for approving Burt's proposals and promoting them for acceptance by the president. As was previously discussed, Reagan looked for

the Secretary of State to be his main advisor and Haig believed that he should
be the administration's 'vicar' on foreign policy. Haig's efforts to advance his
preferred policy options were hampered by Caspar Weinberger, a personal
friend, political associate, and ideological bedfellow to the president (Fisher
1997: 85). These factors provided Weinberger with an advantage because it
assured him access to the president and an ability to influence Reagan's
thinking on issues.

The tension between the State and Defense Departments was
perpetuated with the arrival of George Shultz as the new Secretary of State.
Shultz, president of the Bechtel Corporation and Secretary of the Treasury
during the Nixon administration had only limited interactions with Reagan
before the president asked him to take over for Haig. Inexperienced in foreign
affairs, Shultz did not rush to dominate the policy process on arms control
reductions; instead he allowed Burt to take the lead and took the time to
improve his knowledge of arms control before assuming full control. When
Shultz did increase his involvement in arms reduction he found himself at odds
with both Perle and Weinberger.

Shultz often found support for his policy positions from Reagan's third
National Security Advisor Robert C. McFarlane. Reagan wanted his National
Security Advisor (NSA) to play a coordinating role and nothing more. During
Richard Allen's tenure this was the case, but beginning with Judge William
Clark, the NSA's role shifted away from this marginalized position. Clark,
McFarlane, Admiral John Poindexter, Frank Carlucci, and Colin Powell acted
as honest-brokers on the issue of arms reductions, attempting to mediate the
conflict between State and Defense. The exception to this rule was McFarlane
who often sought a compromise solution between State and Defense positions,
even though McFarlane frequently sided with Shultz and often advocated for
his own policies (Weinberger 2002). Shultz had another strong ally, when it
came to arms control, in Paul Nitze who was appointed as the Secretary of
State's advisor on arms control. Prior to his appointment, Nitze served as chief
negotiator in Geneva on medium range ballistic missiles in Europe and more
recently had been assisting Shultz in learning the minutiae of arms control.
Nitze's status meant that Shultz would be able to make the most convincing
arguments when it came to debating proposals. Other advisors exerted their
influence at various points in time, but not as consistently as those presented
above: Deputy National Arms Control Advisory Ronald Lehman, Lieutenant
General Edward Rowny, assistant Secretary of State James Goodby, Director
of Central Intelligence William Casey, and Chairmen of the Joint Chiefs of
Staff William Crowe and David Jones.

The following case study examines the Reagan administration's efforts
to reach an agreement with the Soviet Union on the reduction of strategic arms,
from April 1982 – May 1988. The actual decision-making process is divided
into eight episodes and each episode will be examined to assess the strength of

the hypothesized decision-making process. Reagan's choice of system was formally structured and where the president exercises low centralization.

START: Policy Environment

US – Soviet relations at the beginning of the Reagan administration were at one of their lowest points in the history of the Cold War. The rapid decline began in the Carter administration with increasing Soviet support for insurgent movements around the world culminating in the 1979 invasion of Afghanistan. Soviet aggression in addition to other US policy failures contributed to a perception of a weakening US foreign and defense policy on a global scale. The failed attempt by the Carter administration to use Special Forces to free American hostages, held in Iran by Iranian students in particular, fostered a belief that US foreign policy had become indecisive and ineffective. Conservatives capitalized on this perception and during the election campaign made an issue out of 'American military inferiority' and the gap that was developing between the US and the Soviets. The conservative argument was that arms control agreements signed by previous administrations, such as SALT II, had created this inferiority and encouraged Soviet expansion (Talbott 1984: 6–7).

Domestically, the US economy had been in decline and contributed to a growing unease about the US position internationally. Inflation doubled during Carter's term in office, rising from six percent to more than 12 percent by 1980; while unemployment and interest rates both increased during the four years prior to Reagan's election. Unemployment constantly hovered around 7.6 percent and interest rates twice peaked at 20 percent. Much of the economic difficulty was brought on by the energy crisis and the United States dependence on foreign oil, both of which were long-term problems that did not lend themselves to easy solutions. The problems found in the domestic economy in conjunction with an unstable and threatening international environment instilled a desire for change in the American public. Thus, Ronald Reagan was elected running on a platform that promised to revitalize the economy and reverse the downward decline in the US's international position.

Shortly after being elected, Reagan made it publicly known that the United States would start a "get-tough" policy with the Soviet Union, because it was Reagan's belief that the Soviets were evil and that they sought to dominate the world. The mission for Reagan and his administration was to shift away from détente, which was the source of US problems, and confront the Soviet Union. Confrontation had two requirements: first, the United States had to resist the spread of Soviet influence by supporting political forces that were anti-communist; by providing financial and military aid for both governments and insurgent movements. Second, the US military needed to be revitalized by engaging in a build-up of nuclear weapons with the ability to fight and win a nuclear exchange.

Initially the public supported this reinvigorated defense policy following the events surrounding the end of the Carter administration. But enthusiasm soon waned and the percentage of Americans that believed the United States should 'get tough' with the Soviet Union fell from 74 to 40 percent between January 1980 and May 1982 (Knopf 1998: 209–221). Decline in support expressed itself in the form of grassroots mobilization and Congressional activism in support of a nuclear weapons freeze, thus forcing arms control onto the president's agenda, thereby causing the president to change his 'get-tough' policy and move toward adopting an arms control policy. Reagan refused to participate in the creation of arms control agreements that would result in either side increasing their weapons; instead, he wanted an agreement that resulted in real reductions in nuclear arsenals. This position was an explicit rejection of the strategic arms limitation agreements that had been concluded in the 1970s under Nixon and Carter (Weinberger 2002). With these perspectives as the cornerstone of his foreign policy, Reagan began to take on the task of strategic nuclear arms reduction.

The War of the Richards (April 1982 – May 1982)

The formulation of an administration position on arms control that served as the basis for an initial proposal to the Soviet Union began in earnest in the spring of 1982 after National Security Advisor William Clark and Deputy National Security Advisor Robert McFarlane were given a directive that called for the Interagency Group (IG) to develop a proposal. At this stage in the process Reagan did not play a role, instead, the issues that he was presented with in April were first deliberated on solely in the Interagency Group. Two sets of positions quickly emerged from these discussions, one was represented by Richard Burt, Assistant Secretary for European Affairs, and the other by Richard Perle, Assistant Secretary of Defense for International Security Policy (Talbott 1984: 234–240). Burt and the State Department proposed that the US make the reduction in launchers and warheads the basis for an arms control agreement because of the ease of verifiability.[1] Perle and the Office of the Secretary of Defense (OSD) believed that the destructive capability of missiles was important and Soviet heavy ICBMs posed the greatest danger to the United States, therefore reduction needed to be based on ballistic missile

---

[1] In mid-spring 1982, the State Department had developed a proposal that called for an overall ceiling on delivery vehicles with sub-ceilings on ICBM silos and SLBM launch tubes as well as heavy ICBMs. Burt proposed that the US and Soviet Union reduce the number of silos and tubes to 1,200 and 1,100 respectively. Warheads would be reduced to 5,000 with a 2,500 limit on ICBM warheads.

throw-weight.[2] The proposal offered by Perle and the OSD, Burt argued, required disproportionate cuts by the Soviets, and thus was unacceptable and in fact not comprehensive enough. The Burt and Perle approaches both required deep cuts in the Soviet ICBM force which was the centerpiece of Soviet nuclear deterrence; but they differed mainly on the means for cuts and on the crucial issue of bombers and cruise missiles.

Burt wanted to continue the tradition begun in the SALT II treaty and consider bombers under the ballistic missile ceiling with sub-ceilings for the number of bombers that could carry air-launched cruise missiles (ALCM) and the number of ALCMs that they could carry. Perle took the position that if bombers were limited they had to be in a separate category. If not, the Soviet Union would be able to give up some of their bombers, of which they had fewer, to acquire more ICBMs.

In early April, the Interagency Group debated the different proposals back and forth with the OSD and the Arms Control and Disarmament Agency with Edward Rowny supporting cuts based on throw-weight. The opposing proposals presented by the State Department had Robert McFarlane's support, but Burt sought further support in the government for his launcher proposal by holding meetings with the Joint Chiefs of Staff outside of the IG without the knowledge of Richard Perle (Talbott 1984: 260–261). The chiefs were not completely sold on all aspects of Burt's plan, but they did fundamentally agree that reductions based on launchers made more sense than throw-weight, which was from their perspective 'overrated as an index of Soviet power and non-negotiable for arms control' (Talbott 1984: 261).[3] The plan formulated by the JCS did not have the support of all the chiefs—which meant according to the rules governing policy proposals—Perle was able to ensure that the proposed plan was not circulated to the full NSC.

The president finally heard the views of his advisors at an April 21 meeting of the NSC. In attendance at the meeting were the major players in the debate on START, with the only exception being Perle who was absent. Haig (Secretary of State), Weinberger (Secretary of Defense), Burt (Assistant Secretary of State for European Affairs), Fred Ikle (Defense Department Under Secretary for Policy), David Jones (Chairmen of the Joint Chiefs of Staff), Clark (National Security Advisor), and Eugene Rostow (Director of the Arms

---

[2] Throw-weight is defined as the total weight a missile can carry over a given range. The weight refers to the part of a missile that falls back to earth after reaching the mid-course stage of a rocket's travel. This part of the missile includes the warhead(s), dispensing and releasing mechanisms (bus), guidance systems, propulsion devices, and penetrations aid (Talbott 1984: 215).

[3] At the April 19 meeting, Admiral William Williams, the Joint Chiefs of Staff START delegate, presented a JCS proposal that called for a limit of 850 launchers and 5,000 to 6,000 warheads with a separate ceiling for bombers including the Soviet 'Backfire' bomber.

Control and Disarmament Agency) all attended what was meant to be an informational meeting during which the president and his advisors would become acquainted with the issues. The meeting turned from an informational meeting, however, to one where each of the opposing camps argued for their preferred plan. Reagan spent part of the meeting disengaged and when he did speak he had trouble explaining that he wanted to limit land-based missiles while preserving bombers and submarines from cuts (Fitzgerald 2000; Talbott 1984: 249–251). Given that the intent of the meeting was not to reach a decision, none was made at the end, but neither had there been any attempt to reconcile the opposing points of view. The different camps clashed again on April 29 in a Senior Interagency Group meeting. This time the antagonists were the Joint Chiefs of Staff's representative General James Dalton and Office of Secretary of Defense representative Fred Ikle (Talbott 1984: 254–257). The Chiefs had decided to support the reduction of launchers that was at odds with the military's civilian leadership. The Chiefs believed that a reduction in launchers would better serve the interests of the military, as it better met the requirements of the nuclear war plan, known as the Single-Integrated Operational Plan (SIOP).

NSC meetings took place on May 1 and 2 without the president in attendance. The purpose of these meetings was to create a common position in the administration that would be discussed on May 3 with the president, but what in fact took place was a hardening of differences that had implications for the ultimate proposal made to the Soviets. The two days of meetings produced a compromise between the Joint Chiefs and the State Department's positions. Burt and James Goodby (State's representative at the negotiations in Geneva) accepted the Chiefs reduction of 850 launchers and in exchange the Chiefs representative, General Paul Gorman, accepted a 2,500 sub-ceiling on land-based warheads. The Defense Department's representatives, Fred Ikle and Ronald Lehman and ACDA representative Rowny were isolated because they refused to compromise on the defense department's position and ultimately no common interagency paper was produced (Talbott 1984: 261–263).

Burt, in an attempt to advance his choice of cuts made on launchers, attempted to circumvent the interagency process by gaining the support of Robert McFarlane for a plan that was raised in the May 1–2 meetings, but was adamantly resisted. Burt presented McFarlane with a proposal that was only superficially a compromise between the Defense and State Department positions. The proposal required that reductions take place in two phases and in the first phase cuts would be made on launchers and in the second phase cuts would be made based on throw-weight. It was understood that this was not a true compromise because the probability of ever reaching a second phase was unlikely (Talbott 1984: 263–264). On May 3, McFarlane briefed Reagan on the variety of positions in the administration, but directed Reagan's attention to Burt's two-phase proposal which the president found favorable.

McFarlane opened the meeting presenting the consensus proposal produced from the previous two days of meetings, which, in fact, was the two-phase proposal formulated by Burt. Weinberger and ACDA director Eugene Rostow protested that the Burt plan did not go far enough in reducing the destructive capability of the Soviet arsenal. With no movement in any of the positions the meeting ended without Reagan making a final decision. Undeterred, Burt took this opportunity to further the two-phase option by holding a secret meeting with Reagan's Chief of Staff James Baker. Baker was convinced that the State Department plan was in the president's best political interest because of his concern that launcher reductions presented the best image for the president. Reductions in launchers were more tangible than throw-weight and was something that could be better understood by the public. Burt's ability to gain the support of McFarlane and Baker outside of the committee process resulted in the State Department plan forming the basis of the National Security Decision Directive on START. However, the two-phase proposal was not adopted unadulterated because McFarlane was conscious of the need to make a link between phases one and two and the president's vague agreement with Weinberger on throw-weight. McFarlane moved the discussion of cruise missiles into phase two, which meant cruise missiles were not going to be useful as a bargaining chip and he set an explicit target for throw-weight reductions in phase one.

The disagreements between Reagan's advisors during this initial stage of the START process resulted in a subset solution because of Burt's lobbying outside of the IG. However, the discussion was not a clear victory for either side, nor was it a compromise. Rather the resolution of the differences between the two camps resulted in a simple aggregation of the plans without any real reconciliation of differences. This resolution came at the end of a long deliberation in the Interagency Group meetings and culminated in Reagan's choice in an NSC meeting. Reagan announced the administration's START proposal at Eureka College, on May 9.

This first episode in the administration's efforts to formulate an arms reduction proposal perfectly reflects the decision-making process attributed to an advisory system that is formally structured with the president exercising low centralization over the process (Table 5.1). Reagan allowed proposals to be created and deliberated on within the Interagency Group without participating until it was time for him to choose the options that arose from the process. This was the case in the April 21 and May 3 NSC meetings. The discussions that took place within the Interagency Group and among Reagan's advisors demonstrate that there was a high degree of conflict and bargaining taking place outside of the president's view. William Clark at this stage was playing the role of gatekeeper, but his impact was negligible because of the ability of other advisors to circumvent the process. Richard Burt's appeal to James Baker outside of the interagency committee process and McFarlane's influence on the president's thinking prior to the May 3 NSC meeting demonstrate the ways in which advisors were competing to advance their preferences and willingness to circumvent the established procedures.

Table 5.1 The War of the Richards

Process	Characteristics
• Leader chooses between presented options	Yes
• Advisors compete to get preferences presented to leader	Yes
• Gatekeeper acts as honest-broker and presents options (opportunity for other advisors to appeal to leader)	Yes
• Bargaining and conflict take place at level below president	Yes
• Procedures may be circumvented	Yes
• Dominant-subset solution or deadlock	Yes

Stalemate (May 1982 – January 1983)

Before and after the start of formal talks in Geneva, the IG and NSC considered a range of technical issues that were important negotiating points that could make or break an agreement with the Soviet Union. The issues dealt with verification, refiring, and reconstitution, cruise missiles, and the ubiquitous throw-weight issue; neither the IG nor the NSC were satisfactorily able to resolve any of these issues. Consistent with his behavior in the formulation of the Eureka proposal, Reagan participated but did not a have strong set of preferences on these issues. In NSC meetings he would listen to the competing views and then make a decision. The work and the wrangling among advisors that took place prior to the NSC meetings occurred without the participation of Reagan. Preferences on how to deal with these issues came from the bottom up from advisors and specialists in the departments rather than down from Reagan himself (Talbott 1984: 286–295).

On May 21 the NSC held a meeting on the issue of a refire ban, meaning the discussion revolved around whether the treaty should require that both sides limit their inventories of ballistic missiles. For this provision to be successful, both countries needed to be able to verify that missile limits were being maintained. Aside from the principals in attendance, Fred Ikle, Admiral Bobby Inman (Deputy Director of the CIA), and Henry Rowen, a senior aid to DCI Casey, attended the NSC meeting. Again the meeting deadlocked and no decision was reached as division among advisors arose over the feasibility and utility of on-site inspections for verifying limits (Talbott 1984: 289–290). The disagreements persisted up until an NSC meeting held on June 25 — the day that Edward Rowny and the US delegation were to return to continue the formal negotiations in Geneva. It was decided that the president and NSC would resolve the issue of reconstitution and refiring at this meeting. But, once again, the stalemate at the interagency level permeated its way into the discussion among the principals and the delegation left for Geneva without the administration having a position on this issue.

The NSC took up the issue of refire, reconstitution, and verification again on August 9. The civilian Defense Department leadership had always maintained that the inventory limits were necessary and that they must be accompanied by on-site verification of designated sites. From the beginning the State Department had maintained that trying to negotiate for limits *and* verification was pointless because it would be impossible to ever know for certain that the Soviets were not cheating. It was not worth the diplomatic effort to negotiate an issue that the Soviets objected to in the first instance and one that would not ultimately be effective. Shultz began the meeting by presenting the established State Department side, which was in support of refire, but he unintentionally deviated from his notes and expressed concern that because verification was impossible this might give the Soviets the ability to cheat and establish an advantage that would be useful for political coercion. Reagan agreed with Shultz's main points, but he wondered whether it made a difference or not if the Soviet's did cheat. At this point, Chairman of the Joint Chiefs, General John Vessey, emphasized that if the Soviets could break out from the balance of terror between the two states that they would be able to use this to their advantage politically in the event of a crisis. This unique consensus among the principals on the nature of the threat posed by the lack of on-site verification, which Shultz unwittingly contributed to, swayed Reagan, who then decided in the meeting that although verification would be less than complete, it was still necessary (Talbott 1984: 291–292).

The decision-making on the disposition of cruise missiles during this period of time followed a similar pattern to the decision-making on strategic missile limits and verification. The START Interagency Group was supposed to be the forum where an administration position was formulated or a set of options was generated; however, the divisions within the IG prevented Reagan's advisors from coming to any conclusions. Richard Perle, who was the Pentagon's representative on the IG, wanted to exclude air-launched (ALCM) and sea-launched cruise missiles (SLCM) from START altogether. His position was that verification was impossible with cruise missiles launched from submarines and he would only accept reductions on cruise missiles if the Soviets reduced their air defenses. Instead of attending meetings and voicing his opposition and bargaining for an administration position that reflected the Defense Department's preferences, Perle at first chose to undermine the process by not attending IG meetings. The implications were that the IG could not seriously discuss the issue without the input of the Defense Department; consequently, the negotiators in Geneva could not broach certain issues with the Soviets (Talbott 1984: 293–294). On this issue Richard Burt wanted to link inclusion of cruise missiles in the talks with Soviet concessions on the Backfire bomber.

To move the negotiations forward and resolve the issue of cruise missiles, James Goodby, representing the State Department and John McNeil, a lawyer assisted on the development of SALT, constructed a proposal that presented the Soviets with the 'basic elements' of an agreement. Goodby and McNeil devised a proposal that was designed to maintain the phased approach proposed by the administration in May of the previous year, while at the same time permitting the administration to indicate to the Soviets the kind of limits that would be acceptable in the latter phase. Presenting a 'basic elements' package meant that the Pentagon would have to be willing to accept limits on cruise missiles, which Perle and his deputy Ronald Lehman refused to do. Moreover, Perle was suggesting that the two-phase approach should be done away with altogether, so the US and Soviets could negotiate on one agreement culminating in one treaty. Perle's position of doing away with the phases had a momentum. The new found momentum was a product of the changes in the membership of the JCS and Perle's ability to sway Rowny who had been sitting on the fence about the phases (Talbott 1984: 293–296).

Prior to a January 17 IG meeting, Perle cut a deal with Rowny, whereby Rowny would support Perle in collapsing the phases and in return Perle would allow Rowny to construct a basic elements paper similar to the paper created by Goodby. The result of this dealing meant that at the January 25 NSC meeting, Weinberger, Rowny, and the Arms Control and Disarmament Agency (ACDA) opposed Shultz and the Goodby basic elements approach; the Joint Chiefs refrained from participating in the debate. Consequently, McFarlane who was tasked with writing the National Security Decision Directive attempted to formulate the directive to include aspects of both sides' positions. The directive favored the Defense Department position because it allowed Rowny to present his basic elements paper to the Soviets, in addition to requiring him to inform the Soviets that the US would discuss cruise missile limits, but only on ALCMs; this discussion would be linked to discussion on throw-weight (Talbott 1984: 296–296). In theory, the phases were preserved, but in practice the delegation in Geneva was asking the Soviets to negotiate major issues in the first phase that fit with the Department of Defense's position.

Producing policy on refire and cruise missiles proved as difficult for the administration as it was for producing the administration's first proposal to the Soviets. Reagan and his advisors were confronted by a policy-making process that was rife with internal conflict. As Table 5.2 indicates, the hypothesized process characterizes the decision making within the administration on START between May 1982 and January 1983. Regan again remained primarily outside of the process with the exception of NSC meetings on May 21, August 9, and January 25 during which he listened to differing options and then made up his mind. Again, Reagan did not present any specific set of preferences to guide the formulation of options; thus, deliberations among the principals and advisors were driven by their own preferences.

Table 5.2 Stalemate

Process	**Characteristics**
• Leader chooses between presented options	Yes
• Advisors compete to get preferences presented to leader	Yes
• Gatekeeper acts as honest-broker and presents options (opportunity for other advisors to appeal to leader)	No Indication
• Bargaining and conflict take place at level below president	Yes
• Procedures may be circumvented	Yes
• Dominant-subset solution or deadlock	Yes/No

The State Department and Defense Department continued to clash over basic aspects of the administration's proposed policy, in addition to clashing over cruise missiles and verification. Like the previous episode, advisors chose to advance their preferences by circumventing procedures. Richard Perle engaged in this activity when he refused to participate in IG meetings knowing that it would prevent the committee from arriving at any conclusions because they lacked the Defense Department's input. Perle also cut a deal with Rowny in order to gain support for his position before the January 25 NSC meeting.

During this episode it is not clear if there is an advisor playing the role of honest-broker in the process. Caspar Weinberger has argued that William Clark in general played the role of honest-broker, but within the case there is no evidence of him having played this role. Robert McFarlane did not fully assume this role because his preferences tended to favor the State Department's. However, McFarlane, in structuring the January 25 National Security Directive, produced a policy that in the end favored the Defense Department. This solution to resolving disagreement differs from the other major decisions taken during this episode. In the case of verification, a consensus developed around including on-site verification within the US proposal. Reagan made this decision in an NSC meeting after all his advisors apparently agreed on this position. In two other instances on May 21 and June

25, NSC meetings resulted in deadlock with the administration being unable to address issues with the Soviets.

Enter the Scowcroft Commission (January 1983 – October 1983)

Robert McFarlane recognized that the divisions within the administration ensured that they would be unable to construct a proposal that was negotiable with the Soviet Union. In order to breathe new life into the administration's deliberations on START, McFarlane and other advisors encouraged the president to put together a commission composed of defense and arms control experts (Talbott 1984: 303). The president, as in previous episodes, remained outside the deliberation process until the end when it was necessary to make a final decision. A key element in the commission's efforts was to resuscitate START for the administration, in addition to creating proposals for the acquisition and basing of the new MX missile. Brent Scowcroft, former Ford National Security Advisor, and James Woolsey, lawyer and defense expert were selected to head the commission.[4] The commission held a series of meetings, small conferences and interviews with other arms control experts between January and April; the only contact with the administration came through McFarlane who maintained contact with Scowcroft and Woolsey (Talbott 1984: 304).

On April 6, the commission announced its findings for START and MX. The commission decided that the US should go forward and deploy MX missiles in fixed silos until the Midgetman missile (a mobile single warhead missile) could be deployed, which would result in a reduction of nuclear warheads. Again, the purpose of the commission was to have an outside group of experts set the administration's START policy despite the fact that competing factions in the administration continued to advance their preferred positions. In particular, Richard Perle saw the commission's findings as an opportunity to return to the discussion of throw-weight. Perle, with the assistance of Weinberger, proceeded to force the issue back on the agenda by sending a letter to the Senate indicating that the administration would adhere to the commission's recommendations, notably the commission's positive endorsement of throw-weight.[5] Members of the National Security Council Staff

---

[4] The commission also included Henry Kissinger, James Schlesinger, Harold Brown, William Perry, Lloyd Cutler, Thomas Reed, Nicholas Brady, Alexander Haig, Melvin Laird, Donald Rumsfeld, Richard Helms, John McCone, William Clements, John Deutch, John Lyons, Levering Smith, and Les Aspin.

[5] The Scowcroft Commission made references to throw-weight in an attempt to mollify ardent advocates of throw-weight. However, statements such as, 'attention to throw-weight limitations is consistent with the Commission's recommended program' or the claim that the Commission supported reducing 'the overall and destructive power of

blocked the letter, but Weinberger and Perle persisted in talking about throw-weight in public as if this was the administration's position. Weinberger and Perle, by going to the Senate and public with throw-weight, were, in effect, making throw-weight a central feature of the administration's negotiating position.

Throughout April and May, Weinberger lobbied Shultz on the issue of throw-weight, an issue that was new to the Shultz, since he had not been involved in the first round of discussions on throw-weight. Burt tried to persuade Shultz to ignore throw-weight because technological advances had rendered this form of measurement useless, but Burt failed to fully persuade Shultz that launchers and not throw-weight was the only way to go about making cuts in both arsenals. Burt could also not find support from the new Joint Chiefs of Staff, who were concerned about protecting Midgetman missiles that would not be deployed in hardened silos and as a consequence be vulnerable to large MIRVed ICBMs (Talbott 1984: 307–309). Because the JCS changed their position and Shultz did not fully object to throw-weight, Weinberger and Perle had an advantage going into the June 7 NSC meeting during which the administration had to decide on which aspects of the Scowcroft Commission's recommendations to adopt.

In the NSC meeting, Perle and Weinberger again presented their ideas on making cuts based on throw-weight. Richard Burt and James Goody, with the support of the ACDA, advised Shultz to present a compromise plan that allowed the Soviets to choose the manner of heavy ICBM reductions. The choice for the Soviets was accepting direct limits on throw-weight without excluding land-based ICBMs or a total of 210 heavy and medium missiles with no more than 110 heavy ICBMs. Reagan's decision in the meeting was far from clear and thus McFarlane was left with a considerable amount of discretion in constructing the president's decision directive. Reagan's comments on the correct approach were both contradictory and noncommittal. Reagan stated:

> I don't want to enshrine one specific approach, or one set of numbers. If there's another solution to the problem, I don't want to be precluded from trying that, too. I would like to get a good agreement, but I'm not going to grovel for just any piece of paper. On the other hand, let's not go for all or nothing if it means we end up getting nothing. (Talbott 1984: 312)

It was with this decision in mind that McFarlane composed and announced the NSDD in June. In the announcement, McFarlane noted that the administration, like the Scowcroft Commission, was concerned with destructive capability and that the administration would continue to indirectly pursue throw-weight cuts.

---

nuclear weapons' were taken by some as indications that the Commission wanted throw-weight as a key element of negotiations (Talbott 1984: 307).

In July, when the administration presented the text of the draft treaty, it contained three key points, two of which were proposed by Shultz in his compromise plan. The third point invited the Soviets to make a counteroffer if the previous two were not acceptable, but this counteroffer would have to reduce destructive capability, meaning throw-weight. McFarlane, playing the honest-broker, tried to bridge the differences between State and Defense, but the outcome was a simple amalgamation that was non-negotiable. In real terms Perle and Weinberger were able to obtain a subset solution by keeping throw-weight alive in the administration's proposals.

At the same time that the administration was trying to reconcile the Scowcroft Commission's recommendations and the administration's internal preferences, attempts were being made on the part of James Goodby, Richard Burt, and Ed Rowny to redirect START. Goodby proposed that sublimits not only be applied to missile launchers, which the Soviets wanted, but to warheads and bomber armaments. The result of this plan constrained the Soviet's ability to devote most of their weapons to missile warheads, which would allow them to keep an advantage over the US in missile warheads. This scheme moved in the opposite direction from the one pursued by the administration so far because it shared similarities with SALT II and the idea of an agreement based on SALT II was anathema to most members of the administration. Goodby presented the plan to Burt who had been thinking along similar lines for a year. Goodby and Burt then included Rowny at the ACDA, who helped to develop the plan; it was presented to Shultz on August 11.

Richard Perle again tried to use the Scowcroft Commission as a vehicle to forward the Office of the Secretary of Defense's arms control preferences. The Congress was eager to reinvigorate the administration's arms control efforts and sought to communicate their views to Reagan by way of Scowcroft and the Commission. Perle saw this linkage as an opportunity to indirectly change the kind of proposals that were being recommended to the president from the commission and build support for the Defense Department's views (Talbott 1984: 332). Perle entered into discussions with Walter Slocombe, who was close to commission members James Woolsey and Harold Brown. Slocombe communicated to Woolsey that he had spoken to Perle and that Perle had indicated that he did not need an overall limit on throw-weight but wanted an agreement that recognized the special threat posed by ballistic missiles. Perle would, in turn, be willing to accept an aggregate limit on bomber payloads and missile throw-weight. The idea of an aggregate bomber and missile weight limit appealed to Woolsey who, in turn, contacted Scowcroft and told him that he felt that Perle was open to 'massaging' on START. After meeting with Woolsey and Perle, Scowcroft contacted interested members of Congress and indicated that there was a means to move the negotiations forward with the Soviet Union with a new measure of destructive capability (Talbott 1984: 333–334). The resulting proposal was known as 'double build-down'.[6]

William Clark and Ronald Lehman believed that the administration could not allow the Commission to present a new proposal alone, lest the administration look as if it was ineffective. As a consequence, the NSC met on September 29 to formulate its own version of 'double build-down.' The NSC was unable to arrive at a version of double build-down that was anything like the original. Instead, the NSC constructed a watered-down version by excluding the combined limits on bombers and missiles until a later date. This change led to negotiations between Clark, Shultz, and Lehman with members of Congress and Scowcroft. Scowcroft was able to convince Shultz to make the case to Reagan that it was necessary to include limits on bombers and missiles to which, in subsequent discussions, the president agreed. The negotiations took place without the involvement of the president until the last day on October 3 when he gave his approval to the final proposal. The final agreement on the administration's arms control proposal called for presenting the previous START position, but at the same time established a Soviet and American committee to explore double build-down. The initial US position on double build-down required a five percent cut in missile warheads or reduction based on modernization. The combination of proposals and the persistent emphasis on cutting were not welcomed by the Soviets. When Rowny returned to Geneva to present the Reagan administration's proposal, he found the Soviets unwilling to discuss the old START agreement or double build-down.

The purpose of creating the Scowcroft Commission was to break the stalemate in the administration and generate new thinking on START proposals. But the events from January 1983 to October 1983 demonstrate that the Commission had no such effect on the policy-making process. Instead, the Commission was drawn into the conflict between Reagan's advisors. This episode indicates that the Reagan administration continued to follow the hypothesized pattern of policy-making (Table 5.3). Reagan participated in the process by choosing between options or by agreeing or disagreeing to the options presented to him. Despite the role of the Scowcroft Commission, conflict and bargaining were the modus operandi among the administration's principals. State and Defense, particularly Burt and Perle, continued to struggle to advance their preferred policy positions.

Perle used the findings of the Scowcroft Commission to support his argument for an agreement that focused on making reductions based on throw-weight. He even went as far as asserting this publicly, giving the impression that the administration had decided to make throw-weight the means for

---

[6] Double build-down required that both sides reduce a certain percentage of warheads and the number of standard weapon stations (gravity bomb, cruise missile, or ballistic missiles of a certain size).

reductions. Perle also tried to circumvent the committee process by intimating to Walter Slocombe that he was willing to make a compromise as long as the destructive capability of Soviet missiles was addressed. By taking this approach, Perle indirectly enlisted the support of the Scowcroft Commission in opposition to the proposals being brought forth by the State Department. These actions by Perle demonstrate the extent that advisors in the administration were willing to compete to get their preferences heard by the president.

Table 5.3 Enter the Scowcroft Commission

Process	Characteristics
• Leader chooses between presented options	Yes
• Advisors compete to get preferences presented to leader	Yes
• Gatekeeper acts as honest-broker and presents options (opportunity for other advisors to appeal to leader)	No Indication
• Bargaining and conflict take place at level below president	Yes
• Procedures may be circumvented	Yes
• Dominant-subset solution or deadlock	No

The solutions to disagreements within the administration for this episode vary. In the June 7 NSC meeting, Reagan did not clearly express his choice between the proposals presented to him and, as a consequence, McFarlane who was responsible for writing the national security decision directive cobbled together the proposals made by Perle and Burt. The September 29 NSC meeting produced an administration 'double build-down' proposal that was heavily watered down because the principals insisted on having their preferences included. Negotiations between the administration, Scowcroft, and members of Congress, resulted in a combined limit on bombers and missiles being reintroduced into the administration's proposal. Reagan ultimately accepted the final proposal that was in effect an aggregation of administration, congressional and commission preferences. In this episode neither dominant-subset nor deadlock solutions are evident, but instead, the solution to the disagreements was to produce a proposal that papered over differences.

A New Beginning: Rethinking START (January 1984 – January 1985)

After failing to resolve the disputes within the administration revolving around START, some of the major players in the administration met at the Wye Plantation to discuss the alternative approaches to START. The group included Burt, Perle, Lehman, Rowny, arms control negotiator Kenneth Adelman, Perle's aide Michael Mobbs, and Sol Polansky, Goodby's replacement at State. The group did not settle any old disputes but they did agree to establish an interagency committee tasked with constructing alternatives based on the Goodby plan formulated the previous summer. The outcome of the interagency committee meetings was that State, JCS, and ACDA each had their own preferred alternative. The exception was the Office of the Secretary of Defense that chose not to participate at all in the process. Shultz, wanting to avoid the inaction of the previous two years, decided that it was necessary to operate outside of the interagency committee to advance the version of the Goodby plan that he favored.

Shultz met with the president and McFarlane on January 13, and presented all of the proposals that had been discussed in the interagency committee.[7] Shultz wanted to demonstrate to the president that the administration was still as divided as it had been the previous three years. Reagan, in turn, asked if Shultz could find some way to 'mix them together' (Talbott 1984: 349). Shultz explained to the president that he would present to Soviet Foreign Minister Andrei Gromyko in an upcoming meeting in Stockholm the major points shared by all of his advisors in the administration, but in the event that Gromyko was interested, he would need to present something more. The 'more' was the State Department's set of talking points on the Goodby plan put together by Burt and Howe, which, Shultz told the president, had not been approved by the interagency process (Shultz 1993: 466). By appealing to Reagan's desire to avoid conflict among advisors, Shultz was able to advance his position over that of the Defense Department. It was only after Shultz's failed meeting with Gromyko that the Defense Department learned of Shultz's operations outside of the committee process.[8]

The continued inability of the administration to put together coherent and viable proposals on START initiated attempts by the administration to alter the decision-making structure. Shultz, with the support of McFarlane,

---

[7] In October 1983, McFarlane moved from Deputy National Security Advisor to National Security Advisor after William Clark left the position. McFarlane's Deputy was Admiral John Poindexter.

[8] Shultz (1993), in his memoirs, admits that the talking points discussed with the president were not vetted in the interagency process. But he goes on to assert that he had McFarlane approve the talking points afterwards with the interagency committee. Thus the Defense Department should have known that he presented the Goodby plan to Gromyko.

attempted to improve the decision-making process by streamlining it, first asking and then getting from Reagan the approval to make Paul Nitze chief of staff for arms control.[9] Shultz wanted to establish a chain of command under which 'interagency committees would meet and NSC members would fight for their views, but ultimately the decisions would be made through the Nitze-Shultz-Reagan lineup' (Shultz 1994: 498). With the inclusion of Nitze, the new director of the ACDA, Kenneth Adelman, and Rowny would now have to answer to Nitze.

Shultz did not stop at attempting to simplify and unify the decision-making process; he worked to create relations between the president's principal advisors by creating the 'Family Group,' so called because it met in the Old Family Dining Room in the White House. The members of the 'family' were Weinberger, McFarlane, DCI William Casey, and Shultz; they began meeting in December. For the most part, the Family Group tried to obtain a consensus on issues brought before it.[10] At the time of the formation of the Family Group, the administration was preparing to revive the stalled talks with the Soviets by holding a meeting between Shultz and Gromyko in Geneva on January 7 and 8, 1985. The planning for the meeting took place in a variety of forums. Shultz describes the process as being one where the Senior Interagency committee that was chaired by McFarlane produced issues that were then brought before the NSC at which time the president made final decisions — the normal operating procedure for the administration up until this point (Shultz 1994: 502—505). Now added to the process, Shultz met with Nitze and discussed issues as well as met with the Family Group; from these interactions the Reagan administration formulated policy. In theory, this alteration should have helped break the impasse created by the standoff between State and Defense and Burt and Perle specifically, but in the end it did not (Gwertzman 1984). The standoff remained because Reagan still needed to decide issues and the Secretary of Defense was still influential within the administration.

The Family Group met on December 1 and was unable to come to a decision on issues discussed in the meeting. Weinberger was not interested in compromise and spent most of the meeting arguing that he was unwilling to reiterate the administration's START positions, while also reasserting his

---

[9] Technically, Nitze was supposed to be the Secretary of State's special advisor on arms control. It is not typical for the president to appoint special assistants to cabinet members. The reason that Nitze can be considered more than just an advisor to Shultz is due to the position Nitze would occupy in the chain of command on START (Gwertzman 12/9/84).

[10] The Group not only focused on arms control but also on the fall of Ferdinand Marcos in the Philippines. The group met weekly, but eventually it fell into disuse; this was particularly true when the Iran-Contra affair captured the administration's attention (Weinberger 2002).

overall views on arms control (Shultz 1994: 504). Thus no decisions were reached during the meeting because none of the principals were willing to make concessions. This characterized all of the Family Group meetings with the exception of a December 21 meeting during which William Casey conceded that the administration had gone too far in insisting on strict verification. Although not a major breakthrough, it demonstrated that there was a possibility of compromise. The deadlock on issues continued through December as evidenced by the National Security Planning Group meeting on the 17, which made no movement toward a proposal despite Shultz's assurances to allies that the US would present one to Gromyko.

The talking points Shultz took with him to Geneva to discuss with Gromyko were in part produced from meetings held involving Shultz, Weinberger, McFarlane, and the president. Shultz argued that he should present Gromyko with aspects of the START proposal worked out over the previous year by Goodby that was pushed aside by 'double build-down.' Nitze, with the assistance of McFarlane, then wrote a set of talking points for a proposal to eliminate offensive and defensive weapons (Nitze 1989: 213–214). The outcome of this subset solution was that in January 1985, Shultz and Gromyko were able to agree to open talks on intermediate, strategic, and space weapons.

The decision making during this episode perfectly conforms to the predicted process (Table 5.4). Reagan as usual chooses from the options presented to him. The early January meeting between Shultz, Reagan, and McFarlane resulted in Reagan asking Shultz to essentially 'mix' together the principals' proposals. Reagan, in January 1984, did however participate in the deliberations on the talking points Shultz took with him to Geneva, but it was Nitze and Shultz who decided on the specifics.

Table 5.4 A New Beginning: Rethinking START

Process	Characteristics
• Leader chooses between presented options	Yes
• Advisors compete to get preferences presented to leader	Yes
• Gatekeeper acts as honest-broker and presents options (opportunity for other advisors to appeal to leader)	No
• Bargaining and conflict take place at level below president	Yes
• Procedures may be circumvented	Yes
• Dominant-subset solution or deadlock	Yes

In this episode, Reagan's advisors competed to advance their preferences, clashed over opposing policy approaches, and circumvented procedures. The START advisors were able to agree at Wye to think of alternative proposals, but afterward they continued to argue over differing policy preferences; this behavior continued throughout 1985 in 'Family Group' and National Security Planning Group meetings. This meant that most of the decision making throughout produced only deadlock. Shultz advanced his preferences by circumventing the agency process when he met with the president on January 13, 1984, and proposed a plan that had not been heard by any of the other principals. In the meeting, Shultz gained an advantage because he was able to appeal to Reagan's revulsion to conflict among his advisors that meant that the solution in this occasion for decision was a dominant-subset solution. The only exception to the deadlock and dominant-subset solutions in this episode was the compromise solution that was found in the January 1985 meeting among Reagan and his principals where it was agreed that the Goodby plan would form the basis for Shultz's talking points with Gromyko in Geneva.

Reagan and Gorbachev Summit: Round I (January 1985 – November 1985)

With the outcome of the Shultz-Gromyko meeting, the administration needed to decide on the positions it would take on each of the three parts of the talks. The first meeting took place on January 22 and was attended by the president, Shultz, Weinberger, McFarlane, Max Kampelman, John Tower, and Maynard Glitman; the latter three were the negotiators assigned to the arms control talks in Geneva (Gwertzman 1985). On February 1, Shultz met with the main negotiators and other advisors to set up a strategy for the upcoming talks and to address major issues, such as dealing with Intermediate Nuclear Forces Talks (INF) before START and the use of SDI and MX as leverage to get Soviet concessions. The problem with these discussions was that disagreements still remained on many of the issues dealt with in the past. Now divisions arose between advisors on the reduction of offensive weapons and restrictions on the Strategic Defense Initiative (SDI). Weinberger, in particular, was unwilling to make trade-offs between cuts and SDI. Indeed, he was pushing the president to withdraw from the ABM Treaty so that SDI research could proceed unimpeded (Shultz 1994: 523; Talbott 1988: 254). The outcome of these differing views was an inability of the administration to present a coherent set of instructions for the Shultz delegation in the next meeting with Gromyko in Geneva on March 12.

The meeting between Shultz and Gromyko failed because of the administration's willingness to withdraw from the ABM Treaty and the desire to develop and deploy SDI. Nitze proposed to move the talks forward by proposing a 'grand compromise' whereby each side reduced their arsenals by 50 percent and in exchange for making these cuts the US agreed to conduct SDI research within the limits of a perfected ABM Treaty.[11] Shultz supported the new plan developed by Nitze because a cut of 50 percent was significant enough that Reagan would be willing to accept limitations to the development of SDI. Shultz, McFarlane, and Nitze knew, however, that the plan would not make it through the interagency process because of the differences of opinion, particularly those expressed by the Office of the Secretary of Defense (Talbott 1988: 263–265).

At first, Shultz and McFarlane discussed the Nitze plan with Reagan at regularly scheduled Wednesday meetings, in addition to any other time that they could get the president alone. Both Secretary of State and National Security Advisor stressed the simplicity of the plan and the fact that if the Soviets made significant reductions, SDI would not be necessary. In these sessions, Reagan always agreed with his interlocutors, but, Weinberger also had access to the president, which meant that the issue was never settled. In his interactions with the president, Weinberger emphasized that SDI should be developed to find out what was possible because, if successful, the public would then have the technology available to protect itself (Talbott 1988: 264). The idea that with SDI the United States could not be threatened by the Soviets appealed to Reagan, but it also meant that McFarlane was not be able to sway the president to the National Security Advisor's and the State Department's side. This being the case, McFarlane and Shultz began to operate outside of the interagency process without the knowledge of Perle and Weinberger. Shultz and McFarlane decided that the best means to advance the Nitze plan was to get Reagan to approve a backchannel negotiation with the Soviets. The duo's hope was that they could come to terms with the Soviets and these terms could be presented to the president because, if the president approved the agreement, Reagan's other advisors would be forced to accept it.

Shultz wanted to intimate to Soviet Ambassador Anatoly Dobrynin that the US was willing to open a back-channel with the Soviets through Nitze and a Soviet official. Shultz, McFarlane, and Nitze constructed a set of talking points that addressed restarting the talks with a clear linkage between deep cuts in strategic and intermediate weapons and limitations on defensive weapons, meaning SDI. But in order to present this proposal to Dobrynin, they needed the approval of the president which McFarlane obtained by taking advantage of Reagan's propensity to not closely read many of the option papers given to him. McFarlane gave the president the talking points and gave him a 'low-key' and 'cursory' summary of the talking points after which Reagan signed off (Talbott 1988: 265). Nitze then met with the Chairman of the Joint Chiefs,

---

[11] A 'perfected' ABM Treaty meant removing ambiguities in the language of the document to prevent against cheating and disagreements over verification.

John Vessey, and afterward with the chiefs as a group. In both meetings, Nitze presented the 'grand compromise' with the intent of gaining their support. The Chiefs were not going to commit themselves to the plan unless it had support at the highest level. Given their apprehension in the meeting, the Chiefs did not directly support the plan, nor did they raise objections. With the Joint Chiefs neutralized and Reagan's unwitting approval, Shultz in June presented the compromise to Dobrynin who responded by presenting the established Soviet position. Shultz discouraged by Dobrynin's negative reaction to his ideas gave up on the Dobrynin back channel.

Reagan and the new Soviet Premier Mikhail Gorbachev planned to meet in the latter part of November, which meant that the administration again had to decide what kind of proposal was going to be presented to the Soviets. In October, the Soviets proposed a 50 percent reduction in strategic weapons to 6,000 charges of which no more than 3,600 could be placed on any one delivery system; in addition, they proposed a halt in the development of all defensive systems.[12] Unlike previous occasions, the interagency process produced for the administration a counter-proposal (Shultz 1994: 576–585). The 50 percent cut was accepted as was the reduction to 6,000 charges; however, Weinberger was able to ensure that Reagan's talking points included an endorsement of developing defensive systems (i.e., SDI). Again the administration, instead of resolving differences to make a more feasible position, chose to cobble together different positions and present them as a cohesive proposal.

The issue of interpreting the ABM Treaty remained a deadlocked issue among the president's advisors. Throughout October, differences over the issue intensified. Weinberger and Perle favored outright abandonment of the ABM Treaty while McFarlane publicly asserted a broad interpretation of the Treaty that permitted the administration to move forward with SDI. Nitze accepted that the Treaty could be legitimately interpreted in a broad fashion, but opposed doing so at this stage of negotiations. Shultz, while not fully objecting to the broad interpretation, believed that the administration should state that the Treaty was being studied in light of Soviet construction of the radar system at Krasnoyarsk that possibly violated the ABM Treaty (Shultz 1994: 579–581).

The issue of the ABM Treaty was discussed in the Senior Arms Control Group as well as informally between Weinberger, McFarlane, and Shultz. The president did not participate in any of these interactions and the issue was not offered up to Reagan at this point for a final decision. As a result of the division among advisors no administration position was reached and the issue of the ABM Treaty continued to linger. Despite the failure to resolve this

---

[12] 'Charges' refers to ballistic missile warheads, cruise missiles and gravity bombs. Cuts made under this definition benefited the Soviet Union because it forced the United States to make cuts in its bomber force and exempted the Soviets from cutting many of their intermediate range missiles.

issue, Reagan met with Gorbachev on November 19 in Geneva and the two leaders agreed that the nuclear and space talks needed to be accelerated and that a guiding principle of the talks was a 50 percent cut in both arsenals. Nonetheless, SDI continued to present itself as a barrier to further success in the talks.

Table 5.5 demonstrates the decision-making in the Reagan administration during this episode and it greatly approximates the decision-making predicted to be produced by formally structured and low centralization advisory systems. Reagan adheres to the established behavior of not participating in deliberations and enters the process when it is necessary for him to make a final decision. With McFarlane replacing William Clark as national security advisor, there is no longer anyone in the administration playing the role of gatekeeper. The implications of this change is that the National Security Advisor is now a full fledged participant in the internal struggles taking place between Reagan's advisors.

Table 5.5 Reagan and Gorbachev Summit: Round I

Process	Characteristics
• Leader chooses between presented options	Yes
• Advisors compete to get preferences presented to leader	Yes
• Gatekeeper acts as honest-broker and presents options (opportunity for other advisors to appeal to leader)	No
• Bargaining and conflict take place at level below president	Yes
• Procedures may be circumvented	Yes
• Dominant-subset solution or deadlock	Yes/No

This decision-making process contains three of the major elements characteristic of formal/low centralization advisory systems, conflict below the level of the president, circumvention of procedures, and competition to get the president's attention. Reagan's advisors clashed over the interpretation of the ABM Treaty and linkage of SDI to cuts. Specifically, Shultz and Weinberger competed to get the president's support for their preferred use of SDI; Weinberger wanted SDI to be developed while Shultz wanted to use SDI as leverage in negotiations. Weinberger, in effect, won because his views better matched Reagan's understanding of how best to protect the United States. In this episode the administration's solution was a dominant-subset because Weinberger's views prevailed by appealing to Reagan's beliefs. Shultz attempted to further his policy preferences by attempting to circumvent the interagency process (and to an extent the president) by deciding to directly raise the 50 percent cut in exchange for a halt in SDI development with the Soviets. In addition to this, McFarlane deceived the president by not fully informing him of the nature of the Shultz talking points that he had approved.

Aside from the dominant-subset solution achieved by Weinberger, deadlock and papering over differences are also evident in this episode as the administration struggled to resolve differences between advisors. Deadlock resulted from discussions within the administration prior to Shultz's trip to Geneva in March. Consequently, Shultz did not have a coherent set of instructions. Deadlock was also evident in October and November regarding the variety of interpretations of the ABM Treaty within the department. On the issue of the Soviet proposal in October, the administration's solution to differences was to paper over the differing viewpoints in the administration by accepting the Soviet cut in charges, but excluding elimination of SDI.

Dealing with Gorbachev's Big Idea (January 1986 – April 1986)

Gorbachev did not wait too long before he made a proposal that was designed to radically shake up the nature of the arms control talks. On January 15, Gorbachev proposed that by the end of the century both the Soviet Union and United States eliminate all nuclear weapons, with the proviso that both parties abandon the development of defensive space-based weapons systems. Because of the sweeping nature of the proposal, the administration was put in a position where it had to create a public response. Deliberations over the administration's response were restricted to the president, Shultz, Weinberger, the new National Security Advisor Admiral John Poindexter, Casey, Perle, and Nitze. Information and access were restricted because of the implementation of a new system of classification levels (Nitze 1989: 423). The contraction of the advisory system did not have an effect immediately because the deliberations over the response to Gorbachev's letter were taken up by the interagency process. The day the Gorbachev missive was received, Shultz called together Nitze, Perle, Douglas George representing William Casey, Roz Ridgway, and James Timbie. The group formulated a summary of Gorbachev's proposal and provided an initial analysis. Shultz presented the group's findings to the president and advised that the president not reject the proposal and that the administration quickly formulate a response (Shultz 1994: 700).

On January 16, the Senior Arms Control Group met and deliberated but the group was less than united when it came to deciding what to do. Peter Rodman of the State Department, Richard Perle, and the Joint Chiefs objected to the very idea of giving up ballistic missiles because of the implication such a move would have on the stability in Europe. But, more importantly, all those who opposed argued that the idea of a nuclear-free world was implausible.

Weinberger did not believe that Gorbachev was sincere and that the proposal was nothing more than a political ploy (Weinberger 2002). Shultz supported the idea of trying to eliminate nuclear weapons because it would mean that the Soviet Union would lose its superpower status (Shultz 1994: 701). The next day Shultz met with Perle and Nitze and once again Perle reiterated his objections to considering Gorbachev's proposal; but, Shultz insisted that they had to deal with this proposal. Reagan had initially alluded to eliminating all nuclear weapons to Gorbachev in 1985, so he was committed to accomplishing this goal. Aware of Reagan's thoughts, Shultz suggested that the US accept the phased approach to elimination proposed by Gorbachev. He also suggested that they use Gorbachev's proposal to counter the Soviets with a proposal to eliminate all intermediate-range ballistic missiles.

Shultz wanted to move the process along and take advantage of the flexibility the Soviets had been demonstrating. Therefore, on January 24, he met with the president and suggested that he be allowed to form a special group that would "get all the key people together outside of the petrified, stultified interagency process" (Shultz 1994: 702–703). The drafting of the letter to Gorbachev was formulated between the president, Shultz, Weinberger, Chief of Staff Donald Regan, and National Security Advisor Admiral John Poindexter, but even within this select group divisions remained, notably between Shultz and Weinberger (Nitze 1989: 423). The president finally sent a response to Gorbachev on February 23 and in April, to Anatoly Dobrynin, who told Shultz that 'Gorbachev thinks INF is possible' (Shultz 1994: 709).

The administration's policy process changed after Gorbachev presented his proposal to eliminate all nuclear weapons because many of the characteristics that were present in previous episodes do not appear in this one (Table 5.6). Reagan was presented with options, but unlike previous episodes, he participated in the construction of the letter sent to Gorbachev. Advisors

Table 5.6 Dealing with Gorbachev's Big Idea

Process	Characteristics
• Leader chooses between presented options	No
• Advisors compete to get preferences presented to leader	No
• Gatekeeper acts as honest-broker and presents options (opportunity for other advisors to appeal to leader)	Yes
• Bargaining and conflict take place at level below president	Yes
• Procedures may be circumvented	No
• Dominant-subset solution or deadlock	Yes

disagree about whether they should respond to Gorbachev's letter or not, but they do not compete to get their preferences presented to the president, nor do they circumvent procedures. Weinberger did not think that the letter should have been responded to but Shultz was able to convince Reagan that it was necessary for the US to respond. Shultz's arguments were particularly convincing because Reagan previously expressed an interest in eliminating all nuclear weapons. Shultz's ability to tap into Reagan's sentiment produced a dominant-subset solution. But what truly sets this episode apart from the others is the fact that advisors work within committees and that the final letter was the product of a meeting where all of the president's principal advisors participated.

The Road to Reykjavik (May 1986 – October 1986)

On May 29, the Soviet Union tabled a proposal that was a compromise on their SDI position. Previously the Soviets linked the research, testing, and development of 'space strike weapons' to a 50 percent reduction in strategic systems (excluding forward-based aircraft); now the Soviets were proposing that research, testing, and development would be permitted in a laboratory setting. In addition, neither side would exercise their right to withdraw from the ABM Treaty while negotiations were conducted on the future ABM measures and strategic weapons. Immediately following the Soviet announcement, both Shultz and Weinberger began lobbying the president. Shultz wanted the president to consider the proposal because it allowed the US to obtain cuts while at the same time continuing to develop SDI. The president, in Shultz's words, 'remained apprehensive' (Shultz 1994: 718). Weinberger argued separately to the president that SDI as a part of any negotiation would kill the program, and thus, the president should not even consider the Soviet proposal.

The deliberations over this new proposal occurred in the same small group that drafted the response to Gorbachev's January letter. In this group's first meeting, Weinberger proposed the elimination of all ballistic missiles, which was an idea that appealed to the president, and the group decided that the idea should be studied further. Days later, on June 18, Shultz tried to press Reagan to accept the idea that SDI could be used as leverage to get reductions, but the president was adamant and not willing to use compromises on SDI to obtain cuts (Shultz 1994: 720–721). Up until June 25, when Reagan sent his letter to Gorbachev, deliberations were restricted to the president, Shultz, Weinberger, and Poindexter, with Poindexter responsible for drafting the final letter. The proposal that finally emerged was mostly a rehash of positions already presented to the Soviets, notably a 50 percent reduction in strategic arms; the new ideas in the proposal were Weinberger's suggestion of eliminating all ballistic missiles and a commitment to non-withdrawal from the ABM Treaty. The ideas in the proposal, however, proved problematic because they permitted further development of SDI, despite the prohibition on withdrawal from the ABM Treaty. Once again Gorbachev took the initiative to move the process forward by proposing a meeting in Reykjavik that served as the basis for a summit in Washington.

The restriction of Reagan's decision-making group had the effect of altering the decision-making process (Table 5.7). Reagan at the outset had to decide whether he was going to accept the Soviet proposal; Weinberger and Shultz made arguments for and against. Initially each tried to persuade the president of the rectitude of their specific policy approach, so they both competed to present their preferences, but neither sought to circumvent procedures. Shultz was unable to get the president to accept any concessions on SDI. Unlike the previous episodes, the difference was that conflicting views were aired and discussed in front of the president over a series of meetings. There was significant division within the small group because proposals written again papered over the differences within the administration, by simply adding in all of the principals' views without any compromises.

Table 5.7 The Road to Reykjavik

Process	**Characteristics**
• Leader chooses between presented options	Yes
• Advisors compete to get preferences presented to leader	Yes
• Gatekeeper acts as honest-broker and presents options (opportunity for other advisors to appeal to leader)	Yes
• Bargaining and conflict take place at level below president	No
• Procedures may be circumvented	No
• Dominant-subset solution or deadlock	Yes/No

Washington, then Moscow (December 1986 – May 1988)

The next 18 months saw no change in the decision-making process within the administration, despite changes in personnel. Frank Carlucci replaced Poindexter as National Security advisor in December 1986 and then in December 1987 he replaced Weinberger as Secretary of Defense. Significantly, Richard Perle resigned from his position in March 1987. Weinberger and Perle, before leaving office, began pushing the president for a quick deployment of SDI but they were opposed by Shultz, Carlucci, and by Chairman of the Joint Chiefs Admiral Crow. Both sides argued for their preferred positions within the National Security Planning Group (NSPG) meetings and individually (particularly Weinberger) with the president. The president attended the NSPG meetings and when advisors confronted one another it resulted in no decision (Crowe 1993: 308–309).

The Soviets made further concessions in 1987, and, most significantly, they were willing to negotiate the ABM Treaty two to three years prior to the end of an agreed on ten-year prohibition on withdrawal. If in the two to three years no new agreement was made on the ABM Treaty, then it would no longer be binding. In Geneva, the Soviets tabled a proposal that called for the creation of a list of technology that would be prohibited in space if their characteristics exceeded certain agreed on limits. Nitze was the biggest advocate of the 'list' option, but he was challenged in interagency meetings by Weinberger and Carlucci; Shultz was, in general, reluctant about pursuing the idea (Talbott 1988: 341–357).

As the administration moved toward the Moscow meeting and the Washington Summit, the inability to break the deadlock over SDI remained in place because the president and his advisors could not find a consensus. Consequently, the rest of 1987 and 1988 saw the administration continue to make policy the way it had since 1983. The administration presented cobbled together strategic arms reduction proposals that were contradictory and unacceptable to the Soviet Union, and, as a result, the administration was unable to conclude a strategic arms reduction treaty.

The last two years of the administration saw no great changes to the established decision-making process in the administration (Table 5.8). Reagan continued to choose between the options presented to him by his advisors who

Table 5.8 Washington, then Moscow

Process	Characteristics
• Leader chooses between presented options	Yes
• Advisors compete to get preferences presented to leader	Yes
• Gatekeeper acts as honest-broker and presents options (opportunity for other advisors to appeal to leader)	Yes
• Bargaining and conflict take place at level below president	Yes
• Procedures may be circumvented	Yes
• Dominant-subset solution or deadlock	Yes

competed to advance their preferences on a range of issues, notably on SDI and the ABM Treaty. Carlucci, like Poindexter, played the role of honest-broker but this played no ameliorative influence on the conflict that took place below the level of the president. As a consequence, the administration became deadlocked on decision after decision and was unable to conclude an agreement with the Soviet Union.

Conclusion

The decision making during the eight episodes involved in the US-Soviet arms reduction case demonstrates that Reagan's decision-making process closely reflects the hypothesized policy-making process in the framework (Table 5.9). Three features of the decision-making process proved to be present consistently throughout all eight episodes: the leader chooses from presented options, advisors compete to get views presented to the president, and bargaining and conflict take place below the level of the president. With one very brief exception, Reagan did not participate to any great degree in deliberations on administration policy. Typically, Reagan entered the policy-making process after issues had been discussed by his advisors and when they were in a position to give him a consensus option (which was rare) or presented him with a range of options. After hearing the variety of views on the options before the administration, Reagan provided some kind of response, although his decisions were not always clear, in which case the National Security Advisor was be required to construct a National Security Decision Directive on his own. When he was unable to choose from among them, the options continued to be discussed until they were again brought to Reagan for his selection. The only exception to this case was during deliberations over Gorbachev's proposal to eliminate all nuclear weapons. On this occasion Reagan, with his advisors, participated in the drafting of the letter. However, this was the only time in that particular period that Reagan was a participant in deliberations and not only present in the process to make a policy selection.

Deliberations then, in the Reagan administration, primarily took place among his principal advisors as they bargained and clashed over policy, mainly outside the view of the president (six out of eight episodes). From the very beginning, the administration was split along the primary cleavage between the State and Defense Departments, personified by Richard Burt and Richard Perle. The bargaining over and differences over throw-weight quickly began to expand into other issue areas such as the interpretation of the ABM Treaty, the linkage of deep cuts to development of SDI, and the treatment of cruise missiles and bombers. Reagan's advisors presented their preferred options in meetings with Reagan, but the bargaining and deliberation over these options took place in interagency meetings. The exception to this was again during

Table 5.9 Reagan Advisory System: Formal/ Low Centralization

	War of the Richards	Stalemate	Scowcroft Commission	New Beginning	Reagan and Gorbachev	Big Idea	Road to Reykjavik	Washington Moscow	%
Leader chooses between presented options	Yes	Yes	Yes	Yes	Yes	No	Yes	Yes	87
Advisors compete to get ideas presented to leader	Yes	Yes	Yes	Yes	Yes	No	Yes	Yes	87
Gatekeeper acts as honest-broker and presents Options (opportunity for other advisors to appeal to leader)	Yes	No Indication	No Indication	Yes	No	Yes	Yes	Yes	62
Bargaining and conflict take place at level below the leader	Yes	Yes	Yes	No	Yes	Yes	No	Yes	75
Procedures may be circumvented	Yes	Yes	Yes	Yes	Yes	No	No	Yes/No	75
Dominant subset-solution or deadlock	Deadlock	Consensus, Deadlock	Paper over differences	Dominant-subset, deadlock	Dominant-subset, deadlock	Dominant -subset, Paper	Paper over differences	Deadlock	62

deliberations on the response to Gorbachev's May 29, 1986 compromise on SDI development. In this episode Reagan participated and was present while his principal advisors clashed over the draft response to Gorbachev's proposal.

Along with the bargaining and conflict taking place below the level of the president, there was the competition by Reagan's advisors to advance their preferred policy options (seven out of eight episodes). Both sides in the policy battles sought to influence the president at the expense of their opponents. Because of Weinberger's long-standing relationship with the president, he was able to visit the president and lobby for his options. Similarly, Shultz met with the president and discussed proposals that he had not deliberately presented in the interagency process. Robert McFarlane, as Deputy National Security Advisor and National Security Advisor, did not assume the role of honest-broker; instead McFarlane presented options that favored one set of policy options over others. McFarlane did this in May 1982 when he presented all the options to the president, but directed his attention to the two-phase approach suggested by State and Richard Burt. McFarlane also helped Shultz advance his plan to directly present the Soviets with a 50 percent reduction without going through the interagency process, by getting Reagan to approve the talking points without fully explaining them.

Also consistently found throughout most of the eight episodes are attempts by the advisors to circumvent procedures – to the extent that they were established (six out of eight episodes). Reagan's advisors resorted to a variety of extra-procedural means to advance their preferred policies. Weinberger and Perle used the Scowcroft Commission to support their position in the administration, by reinterpreting the Commission's findings and then stating publicly that throw-weight was the foundation of reductions, which had not been established as administration policy. Perle, in order to stop deliberations on those issues that he and the Secretary of Defense disagreed on, chose not to participate in deliberations with the effect of slowing down deliberations. This kind of behavior was not exclusive to the Defense Department civilian leadership as already noted. Shultz took measures to capture the administration's policy by discussing proposals with the president without discussing them with other principals; he also sought to present a proposal to the Soviets without the full knowledge of almost anyone else in the administration. The Secretary's hope was that the Soviets would accept the proposal and Shultz's proposal would become the de facto administration policy. Richard Burt, after failing to prevail in an NSC meeting, went outside the interagency process and appealed to James Baker (Chief of Staff) to talk to the president about his plan to base reductions on launchers, without the knowledge of Perle or the Defense Department.

In the latter stages of the negotiations and after the administration institutes some reforms in the decision-making structure, primarily by restricting access, the circumvention of procedures begins to taper off.

Disagreements within the administration continue and the president, for the most part, is not heavily involved in deliberations. By this late point in the negotiations, all of Reagan's principals had staked out their policy preferences and had tried to advance them outside the process and did not succeed. But the restriction of access and knowledge to only the principals made it far more difficult for advisors to go outside of the system without being held accountable by their counterparts. These changes also take place during a period of time when the administration was being challenged to respond to major concessions that were presented by the Soviets inside and out of summits. It is reasonable to speculate that this kind of pressure meant that the advisors could not put the administration at risk by engaging in internal maneuvering that would damage the administration's image. However, this pressure was not so great that it could not force the advisors to overcome their fundamental differences in their approach to the negotiations.

The remaining two characteristics were not always present in the administration's decision-making process. There was not always a gatekeeper playing the role of honest-broker (five out of eight episodes), nor was it the case that the unstructured solutions, dominant-subset solution or deadlock, were always present (five out of eight). Reagan, over the course of his administration, had six National Security Advisors, three of whom participated in the START deliberations. As Caspar Weinberger has pointed out, William Clark played the role of honest-broker and it is also evident that, in the case of START, Poindexter and Carlucci played a similar role. In two episodes there is no clear indication that a gatekeeper is present but it is possible to infer from Weinberger's comments that this is the role Clark is playing. McFarlane, on the other hand, played the role of an advocate and often sided with Shultz and the State Department. Yet, when writing National Security Decision Directives, he did demonstrate a willingness to try and construct administration decisions that represented the views of many of the principals. Overall, in five out of the eight episodes, a gatekeeper plays the role of honest-broker and advisors work around the gatekeeper to further their preferred policies.

Dominant-subset and deadlock unstructured solutions are found in this case, but there are several instances where disagreements within the administration are dealt with by papering over differences between advisors. In five out of the eight episodes dominant-subset solutions or deadlock occurred, and in three episodes efforts were made by the administration, in the process of creating a proposal, to paper over the differences among advisors. This outcome was not originally a part of the hypothesized process. The administration, out of necessity, had to make some kind of proposal to the Soviets because otherwise negotiations would be pointless. But the administration was handicapped by the internal divisions over policy, and, thus, given the need to come up with something, policy was cobbled together drawing on preferences from different advisors without any real effort to compromise or reconcile inconsistencies in the policy. Other than the presence of solutions that paper over differences, the only other deviant unstructured solution in this case is the formation of what approximates an integrative solution.

Chapter 6

Bill Clinton and Bosnia

Clinton's Advisory System

If one surveys the literature on the Clinton administration it is evident that Clinton's advisory structure was collegial and he exercised low centralization over the policy-making process. In fact, there is some consensus that Clinton had a collegial advisory structure, for example Margaret Hermann has argued that Clinton prefers an informal setting when shaping policy, which is compatible with a collegial management style (Hermann 1995: 157; Renshon 1995: 159; George and Stern 1998; Preston 2001). There is equally strong evidence that Clinton exercised low control over the decision-making process. Clinton was known for setting broad guidelines and paying "spasmodic" attention to foreign policy issues, as opposed to domestic policy, where he had a much greater interest and depth of knowledge (Friedman 3/22/93; Klein 2002: 68; Berman and Goldman 1996: 296, 298). It was not uncommon as Burns and Sorensen (1999) highlight for Clinton to cancel meetings on foreign policy when he felt that domestic issues were more pressing (Sciolino 11/8/93; Burns and McGregor 1999: 169).

Clinton wanted to adopt Franklin Roosevelt's style of making decisions, which meant a style of management under which deliberations where Clinton listened as his advisors debated issues in front of him (Renshon 1996: 260). However, Clinton was not the type of individual who could passively sit by listening as his advisors argued for different positions, instead his style was to be an active participant in the formulation and deliberation of policy. Stanley Renshon (1996) argues that Clinton's 'freewheeling staff system without clear lines of authority' actually indicates the degree of control that Clinton maintained over his advisory system. Clinton ensured that he would always be in control by establishing a system of decision-making that was impromptu and had no clear 'lines of authority.' Indeed it may have been Clinton's intent to implement a system that allowed Clinton to be in full control, but this does not seem to be fully supported by the evidence. Meetings during the administration were not managed and controlled by the president and often resulted in no decision being made, which frustrated Clinton. Despite the low level of centralization, Clinton was well known for his penchant to immerse himself in the details of policy, while at the same time demonstrating a willingness to listen to the views of those surrounding him (Renshon 1996; Burns & Sorensen 1999; Kessel 2001).

Formally, the Clinton national security infrastructure was fairly simple in organization. Decision making was intended to take place primarily within two committees, the Principals and the Deputies Committees. As dictated by Presidential Decision Directive (PDD-2), the Principals Committee (PC) was to be the main forum for consideration of national security policy. All meetings in the PC were to be chaired by the Assistant to the president for National Security Affairs, a position filled by Anthony Lake in the first half of the administration. The other members of the PC included the Secretaries of State and Defense, the US Representative to the United Nations, the Director of Central Intelligence, the Chairman of the Joint Chiefs of Staff, and the Assistant to the President for Economic Policy.[1] It was decided within the administration that the PC deal with large issues that required the attention of senior advisors. The Deputies Committee (DC), chaired by the Deputy Assistant to the President for National Security Affairs Samuel Berger, was responsible for making reviews of administration policy and overseeing policy implementation. PDD-2 also had a provision for Interagency Working Groups that could be established by the Deputies Committee as it saw fit in order to review a specific policy or to review and coordinate implemented policies.

The administration's Bosnia policy was primarily discussed within the Principals Committee. Clinton's PC included Anthony Lake (National Security Advisor), Warren Christopher (Secretary of State), Les Aspin (Secretary of Defense), Leon Fuerth (Vice President Al Gore's National Security Advisor), Colin Powell (Chairman of the Joint Chiefs of Staff), James Woolsey (Director of Central Intelligence), Madeline Albright (US Representative to the United Nations), and Samuel Berger (Deputy National Security Advisor). This group was unique in that they all had either served together in previous administrations or encountered one another while outside government. For the administration, the implication of this prior relationship meant that the president's main advisors were well acquainted with one another and were willing to engage one another on issues. Elizabeth Drew cites a member of the Clinton team who asserted that 'it makes it all very pleasant, but people interrupt each other and there's not enough discipline. We're there not as people brought together as representatives of institutions but as people who've been around tables with each other for a long time' (Drew 1994: 145).

---

[1] The PDD-2 also allows for other agency or department heads to attend meetings as they are needed, such as the Secretary of the Treasury and Attorney General. Although not stated as a member in the PDD-2, the Vice president was frequently in attendance at PC meetings and was an active member given his experience with foreign affairs. The PDD-2 also allows for other agency or department heads to attend meetings as they are needed.

The president rarely attended Principals Committee meetings and when he did meet with his advisors it was, more often than not, in informal settings (Holbrooke 1998: 81). The president, unlike his predecessors, held no regularly scheduled meeting with his advisors, aside from his morning briefing by Lake. The president's closest advisors on Bosnia — Lake, Christopher, and Aspin — met every Wednesday for lunch to discuss issues and frequently contacted one another throughout the day (Drew 1994: 141, 144).

Given the way in which Clinton went about structuring his advisors and the way in which he choose to control information and the interaction between advisors, the decision-making process should exhibit the following features:

- Willingness to delegate authority to others that have expertise
- Advisors instrumental in guiding policy
- Less emphasis on consensus building among advisors
- Conflict and bargaining between advisors
- No regular mode of interacting with advisors
- Subset solution/deadlock

Clinton's foreign policy team was comprised of seasoned veterans with a significant portion being former members of the Carter administration. Policy on Bosnia was most heavily influenced by National Security Advisor Anthony Lake, Secretary of State Warren Christopher, and Secretary of Defense Les Aspin. Anthony Lake was a veteran of the Nixon administration where he served as assistant to Henry Kissinger on the National Security Council staff and then as director of the Bureau of Policy and Planning Staff at the State Department during the Carter administration. Having witnessed the problems created by a National Security Advisor that was involved in the operation of foreign policy in the Nixon administration, as opposed to limiting involvement simply to its formulation, Lake believed that his role was to be an honest-broker presenting the president with a range of views and not to act as a diplomat. But Lake also believed that it was impossible to be simply an honest-broker and thought that it was important that he present the president with his own recommendations, 'because if you don't have views, you shouldn't be doing the job' (Deparle 1995; Lake 2002). As far as the Bosnia policy was concerned, Lake believed that intervention was necessitated on national security grounds, but he also believed that the brutality of the conflict created a moral imperative to act (Wayne 1997: 197).

During the Carter administration, Lake served with Warren Christopher who was Deputy Secretary of State under Cyrus Vance. Both had been witnesses to the conflict between National Security Advisor Zbigniew Brzezinski and Secretary of State Cyrus Vance and the conflict's debilitating effects on the policy process. Upon entering office, both figures agreed that they would avoid the conflict that plagued the Carter administration by agreeing that Lake would not be a spokesman for the administration on foreign policy, thus leaving diplomacy to Christopher. Christopher, a lawyer by training, led the Democratic Party search for a vice-presidential candidate before agreeing to be secretary of state. Christopher's deliberating style was very reserved; he preferred to let others recommend policies and debate points, and, afterward, he liked to address the risks associated with a particular policy (Drew 1994: 80). Some have attributed this style to the fact that Christopher was not interested in many of the new issues in international relations (i.e., environment or development). Critics have also assailed Christopher for not being an innovator or for not having a grand vision of US foreign policy like his predecessors (Holbrooke 1994: 140).

Secretary of Defense Les Aspin, former member of the House Armed Services Committee, was outgoing and deliberated by thinking aloud; an operating style that rankled the military leadership at the Pentagon. Aspin came to his position with a deep understanding of defense issues; in particular, Aspin was committed to reforming the operating and budgeting practices of the Department of Defense. On the issue of Bosnia, Aspin was generally opposed to intervening in a region where the US had no real security interest (Wayne 1997: 197). Aspin got along well with Chairman of the Joint Chiefs of Staff Colin Powell, who was a hold-over from the Bush administration. Like Aspin, Powell was hesitant to use force in Bosnia because of the possibility of the US becoming bogged down in the conflict without the options of resolution and exit. In August 1993, Powell was replaced by General John Shalikashvili who advocated that a more forceful policy on Bosnia was possible (Wayne 1997: 174).

Unusual for many administrations was the prominence on foreign policy issues of the vice-president. Al Gore had an interest in foreign policy that developed out of his years as a member of the Senate Foreign Affairs Committee. Unlike other vice-presidents, Gore attended NSC and Principals Committee meetings and made significant contributions to the policy deliberations. An indicator of the vice-president's interest in foreign policy was the regular attendance of his assistant on the National Security Council staff, Leon Feurth, at PC meetings. While it is known that Gore played a significant role in the decision-making process and participated in manner unlike any other vice-president, the amount of information on Gore's activities is thin. As a consequence, the case study potentially under-represents Gore's influence on the process.

Policy Environment: New World Order and Balkan Disorder

As the Cold War was winding down and, with it, the ideological stand-off that came to dominate international politics was diminishing, many in the world were heralding a new era of global cooperation between states. What was not readily apparent to many of those individuals who were talking of a new era in human relations was the possibility of new conflicts arising, conflicts that for outside observers were more complicated and vicious than those during the Cold War. President George Herbert Walker Bush constructed a foreign policy that was designed to cope with the dramatic changes taking place around the world, particularly in places that were vital to US interests. Bush marshaled an international coalition to eject Iraqi forces from Kuwait, he deployed troops to Panama with the intent of protecting American citizens and US interests in the Canal Zone by removing Manuel Noriega from power, but when it came to the issue of Yugoslavia, Bush was not prepared to intervene.

In 1991, Yugoslavia quickly began to disintegrate as Slovenia and Croatia declared their independence. The response by the government in Belgrade was to first compel Slovenia to reverse its decision and, when that failed, to do the same with Croatia, which failed too. Caught between these battling republics was the multi-ethnic region of Bosnia-Herzegovina. The president of Bosnia, Alija Itzebegovic, was forced by the actions of the other republics to either declare Bosnian independence or accept the dismemberment of the state by Croatia and Serbia, which sought to absorb territory populated by ethnic Croatians and Serbians. Itzebegovic chose independence, making war inevitable with between the rump state of Yugoslavia and the Bosnian-Serb population.

The response of the Bush administration was to avoid military intervention in the war breaking out in the Balkans arguing first, that military intervention was not in the United States' national security interest and, second, the European powers should take the lead in finding a settlement to a conflict in their own backyard. Even if the conflict had implications for US national interests, the administration argued, intervention was not feasible given that there did not appear to be a clear way for the US to exit the region. The shadow of Vietnam and concerns about the US being bogged down or on a slippery slope colored discussions about US intervention.

As the 1992 elections approached, Bush continued to refuse to get involved in the Balkans: this stance provided the inexperienced Arkansas Governor Bill Clinton the opportunity to distinguish himself from Bush by taking a stand on a foreign policy issue. During the election, Clinton called for greater US engagement in the Balkans, in particular supporting the use of air strikes against Bosnian-Serbs in order to protect the efforts of relief agencies. Shortly after taking a public position on air strikes, Clinton advocated that the US take the more controversial step of lifting the arms embargo on the warring parties that would allow the Bosnian-Muslims to acquire arms to better protect themselves. Despite taking a strong position on the war in the former Yugoslavia, Clinton primarily ran on a platform that addressed the domestic and economic concerns of the nation; he had decided that he would focus like a laser beam on domestic issues.

By the 1992 elections, the transition from a Cold War international environment to a Post-Cold War one was beginning. Containment, the principle that had underpinned US foreign policy for the past fifty years, no longer had any relevance which, in turn, raised the question of what new doctrine or strategy would act as a suitable guide for US foreign policy. Two general approaches arose during this period. One was essentially a form of neo-isolationism that recommended the US withdraw from all those areas where it had no direct national interest. National interest was very narrowly defined as those issues or areas that posed a direct threat to the continental United States and/or posed a threat to vital strategic resources. The second approach, which was internationalist, envisioned the opportunity for the US to spread liberal democracy through the support for and creation of international institutions and norms. Unfortunately, these debates about the direction of US foreign policy occupied the foreign policy establishment but not the candidates running for president. In short, when Clinton came into office there was no existing consensus on the direction of US foreign policy that he could adopt. And since Clinton's focus was on domestic issues, predominantly the economy, he did not have a clear vision of where he wanted to take foreign policy or the ideas by which it would be under-girded.

These were the conditions that Clinton and his advisors had to contend with upon coming into office. The Clinton advisory system (collegial with low presidential centralization) had to cope with an international environment going through dramatic change, while at the same time several severe conflicts were raging around the globe that demanded the attention of the incoming administration. An uncertain environment combined with a president that lacked experience in foreign affairs meant that Clinton was even more dependent on his advisors for advice. With this in mind, the hypothesized policy process is examined looking at the decision-making process of the Clinton administration on Bosnia from January 1993, when the administration first begins to formulate a policy, until November 1995, when the administration finally develops a strategy compelling the warring parties to agree to engage in talks at Wright Paterson Air Force Base in Dayton, Ohio.

Dealing with Reality (January 1993 – February 1993)

Given the stance Clinton had taken on the issue of Bosnia during the election campaign and the intensification of the conflict in the beginning of the year, Bosnia was one of the administration's number one priorities. The task for Clinton and his foreign policy team was to develop policy toward Bosnia that went beyond mere pre-election rhetoric. At the beginning of the year, Clinton issued a Presidential Review Directive (PRD-1) that called for a comprehensive evaluation of US policy towards Bosnia and the formulation of options by an interagency group. The options were discussed in the first Principals Committee (PC) meeting held on January 28. The president and vice-president came into the meeting at the end and participated in a discussion that proved to be inconclusive as the group raised and debated issues but could not come to any clear decisions on policy. Warren Christopher publicly stated that 'a wide range of options' were discussed in the meeting and in fact Clinton's advisors clashed over a variety of issues (Powell 1995: 575; Daalder 2000: 9). The PC met again on February 5 and once again the president and vice-president arrived at the end of the meeting. Clinton argued that not acting in Bosnia would jeopardize American leadership and that at least the US should participate in the humanitarian efforts. Clinton then decided in the meeting that the US should engage in a series of measures that included (1) asking the United Nations for authority to enforce the no-fly zone, (2) tightening of economic sanctions, (3) appointment of an envoy to the talks with Vance and Owen, (4) and reaffirming the Bush Administration's warnings about Serbia's expansion of the conflict into Macedonia and Kosovo (Drew 1994: 146). This decision included many of the ideas presented during deliberations and some of the options resulting from PRD-1.

Table 6.1 Dealing with Reality

Process	Characteristics
• Willingness to delegate authority to others that have expertise	Yes
• Advisors instrumental in guiding policy	Yes
• Consensus building among advisors	Less Emphasis
• Conflict and bargaining between advisors	Yes
• No regular mode of interacting with advisors	Yes
• Subset solution/Deadlock	Paper over differences

In this opening episode in the Clinton administration's development of policy toward Bosnia, the policy process fits the one indicated in the typology (Table 6.1). For the most part Clinton delegated authority to the Principals Committee to formulate administration policy. Clinton did participate in meetings though his participation came at the end of the meetings, which meant his advisors' deliberations dominated, which in turn meant that they were instrumental in guiding policy. While the PC met regularly to deal with the issue, Clinton's participation was irregular and abbreviated. Importantly,

Clinton's attendance at the end of meetings ensured that he missed aspects of group discussion and issues. There is no clear indication that after Clinton arrived in meetings late that he was briefed on previous discussions or was spared policy details. However, it was these meetings that caused Colin Powell to comment that meetings in administration 'meandered like graduate student bull sessions' which is further indication that bargaining took place. There is no indication that there was a desire for or against building consensus on a Bosnia policy and advisors disagreed about the direction of policy. The conflict between advisors was evident from the first meeting on January 28 where the PC came to no conclusion on policy recommendations. The president's choice of constructing a policy based on various ideas demonstrated an interest in making a policy that essentially papered over differences between advisors.

Looking for New Ideas (March 1993 – May 1993)

In March, the Serbians initiated offensive operations against specific Bosnian towns; the attacks on Srebrenica that were particularly ferocious attracted heightened media attention. On March 18, the day of the attacks on Srebrenica, Anthony Lake, Madeleine Albright and Al Gore agreed that the administration needed to create a more assertive policy to compel the Bosnian-Serbs to negotiate (Daalder 2000: 12). Lake decided to call a Principals Committee meeting on March 25 so that the advisors could figure out some new ideas to end the offensive and get the Bosnian-Serbs to negotiate. The principals with the participation of the president arrived at two different options. Secretary of Defense Aspin and Chairman of the Joint Chiefs of Staff Colin Powell supported the idea of getting a cease-fire and of offering protection to Muslim enclaves. The alternative was to resort to a mixture of lifting the arms embargo combined with air strikes against the Bosnian Serbs.

In the meeting numerous objections were raised against both courses of action. Gore and Albright were ardent supporters of bombing, while Powell constantly questioned whether or not there was an end-point if 'lift and strike' was chosen. The cease-fire option, Clinton argued, was at odds with the overall stated objectives of the administration in that it was perceived to reward Bosnian Serb aggression. Intelligence presented in the meeting emphasized that the Europeans opposed 'lift and strike,' arguing it to be an ineffective measure because the policy jeopardized humanitarian efforts and because it might instigate an all out Serbian offensive. Moreover, air strikes would not be effective because of the dearth of valuable targets. Like the previous meeting, the Principals Committee failed to arrive at any firm conclusion because of a lack of confidence in any one of the policies. Thus, the ineffective policy that was announced in February remained in place.

Deliberations among Clinton's principal advisors continued into April with the president attending several meetings early in the month. At an April 9 NSC meeting, Lake conceded that the administration's policies had failed and that it was time 'to start planning for Phase 2' which involved considering options that included force (Warner 5/10/93). In these meetings, the group discussed a range of possible options; the president was an active participant constantly pushing and probing his advisors for more information about the options they were discussing. Drew (1994: 149–150) notes that 'Clinton would press each advocate: What are our objectives with that option? What is the limiting principle? How do we extricate ourselves if we do x? What is controllable and uncontrollable with that option?' Despite the fact that the president was focused and involved in the process, he was unable to come to a final decision. Part of the reason that Clinton was unable to decide on a course of action was the influence of Stan Greenberg, the administration's pollster, who informed the president that the American public was generally not supportive of the US taking action in Bosnia and any action taken must be conducted multilaterally (Drew 1994: 150).

Clinton's advisors, as a group, were unable to generate a consensus on a choice of policy. The PC met without the president on April 17 and 18 in order to further discuss possible options. The group finally settled on the two options that were discussed in February: (1) 'lift and strike' and (2) cease-fire combined with the protection of Muslim enclaves. Lake, Christopher, Albright and Gore supported the option of lifting the arms embargo and using limited air-strikes to prevent the Serbs from engaging in offensive operations until the Bosnian Muslims were strong enough to defend themselves (Daalder 2000: 13). The Defense Department officials, both civilian and military, though, continued to advocate for the cease-fire. Consensus finally developed around a set of principles that all agreed were necessary for an agreement to be successful — Serbia needed to be in support of an agreement and bombing might be the means to get that agreement (Drew 1994: 152). On April 20, Clinton met with his foreign policy team and was presented with the two options; although the advisors built a consensus regarding some important principles of the policy they still remained divided over the appropriate course of action. Aspin, Lake, and Berger continued to favor options that required the use of force while Christopher cautioned that if force were to be used, there needed to be clear objectives. Clinton asked that all his advisors state what they believed to be the worst outcome under their options; he then asked them all to prepare papers on their positions. No final decision was made, essentially, in order to search for more information (Warner 5/10/94).

President Clinton called a meeting again on April 29 with the intention of coming to a final decision. In attendance at the meeting were Lake, Aspin, Christopher, Stephanopoulos, Berger, Feurth, and the Joint Chiefs of Staff and again the group examined the two options. Clinton asked very direct questions about the use of force because of his concern of becoming ensnared in the conflict and the risk to civilian lives. Air Force Chief of Staff General Merrill McPeak presented the president with an optimistic estimate of the effects of limited strikes in terms of effectiveness and risk to US personnel. This estimate happened to be a reversal of previous estimates given by Vice Chairman of the Joint Chiefs of Staff Admiral David Jeremiah. Colin Powell, who previously had been staunchly opposed to the idea of air strikes, found the idea more acceptable when cast in terms of limited use of force with clear objectives but he nevertheless commented that he found the estimates presented by McPeak to be excessive (Wayne 1997: 200–201; Drew 1994: 154-155). The meeting produced no final decision other than the president committing to making a final decision the next day.

On May 1, the same group met again for five hours and discussed a list of twelve options and objectives compiled by Lake. The only option that was not considered was the deployment of US combat troops to Bosnia. The members of the foreign-policy team essentially stuck to their positions, with Powell notably arguing the ineffectiveness of striking Bosnian Serb artillery (Drew 1994: 155). The president concluded that a policy of 'lift and strike' was the best position for the administration to take and shortly thereafter Warren Christopher left for Europe to convince US allies that lifting the arms embargo and engaging in limited air strikes was the best strategy. Although Clinton's advisors had different opinions, those with differing views understood that all available options were less than perfect. Drew cites one policymaker who stated that the whole situation was a 'no-winner' or as the president – quoting Richard Holbrooke — termed it 'the greatest security failure of the West since the 1930s' (Drew 1994: 155; Clinton 2004, 512). With no assertive action, the administration was being pulled in by competing sets of pressures from Congress that supported aggressive action, European allies and an American public that was adverse to the deployment of ground troops (Clinton 2004).

The collegial structure/low centralization decision-making process is represented in Clinton's efforts to find an effective policy toward the conflict in Bosnia. All of the framework's characteristics are found in this episode as described, with one exception (Table 6.2): The president participated in varying degrees during these months. Clinton's attention and participation varied between being heavily involved in deliberations to non-participation. In general, the process was driven by advisors who were granted authority to create and formulate options but not to make a final decision. As can be expected when advisors have authority and are guiding policy, conflict arose between the Defense Department on one side and Lake, Christopher, and Albright on the other. The advisors clashed over policy in meetings in March and April despite efforts to build a consensus on policy. The best that the advisors could do was to agree that the deployment of ground troops was not possible and that there were two options, a cease-fire and 'lift and strike.'

Table 6.2 Looking for New Ideas

Process	Characteristics
• Willingness to delegate authority to others that have expertise	Yes
• Advisors instrumental in guiding policy	Yes
• Less emphasis on consensus building among advisors	Emphasis on consensus
• Conflict and bargaining between advisors	Yes
• No regular mode of interacting with advisors	Yes
• Subset solution/Deadlock	Subset

The president brought about a subset solution by picking the 'lift and strike' options. The administration was divided between the ceasefire and 'lift and strike' options and Clinton chose the option advocated by the Lake, Aspin, and Berger subset of the administration. The principal advisors met frequently to discuss policy but Clinton's attention and participation fluctuated between being heavily involved in early April to being nonexistent during other times.

Changing Policy (May 1993 – July 1993)

Warren Christopher traveled from European capital to European capital trying to convince the US allies that they should adopt the 'lift and strike' policy but he ultimately failed in his efforts. The Europeans refused to participate in any policy that jeopardized the peacekeepers they had on the ground; they were especially opposed to participation given US unwillingness to commit ground troops. After Christopher returned, Clinton met with his foreign policy team on May 8 to hear Christopher's report and formulate a new plan of action (Hyland 1999: 37). At the meeting, Christopher explained that the only way to get the Europeans to accept 'lift and strike' was to pressure them, but he did not think the consequences were worth pursuing the issue any further. Christopher argued that the Europeans would not be pressured; and, moreover it would strain trans-Atlantic relations. After recounting his trip, the meeting touched on a variety of issues (Drew 1994: 158). Gore argued for the use of air strikes to eliminate the Bosnian Serb artillery. Christopher argued that it might be best to adopt a policy of containment by way of assurances and/or deployment of troops to Macedonia to ensure the conflict did not spread. Lake agreed that the administration should examine containment as an option, but also insisted that it should not give up on indicating an interest in lifting and striking (Drew 1994: 159). There was no consensus among the advisors and Lake was unable to push the president to make a final decision and choose a policy (Warner and

Clift 5/24/93). As the focus of the meeting wandered in different directions the president decided to consider the options, which meant no conclusions were arrived at by the time the meeting concluded.

Christopher concluded that the Bosnia policy was not viable and he tried to get the issue off the table by advocating the idea of containment, working outside of the Principals Committee to convince individuals close to the president of the virtues of containment with the intention of persuading the president to adopt this approach to the war in Bosnia (Drew 1994: 160; Wayne 1997: 203). He met George Stephanopoulos for dinner to sell him the idea of containment and then, a few days later, Christopher met with Stan Greenberg and emphasized the dangers to the administration if the US became too entrenched in Bosnia. At the same time, Christopher appealed directly to the president by holding private meetings with Clinton without the knowledge of any of the president's other advisors (Drew 1994: 160–161).

The Secretary of State next seized on initiatives being formulated by the United Nations to get the policy of containment adopted by the administration. On May 6, the United Nations passed a resolution designating six Bosnian towns as safe areas and called for the Bosnian Serbs to withdraw their forces to a stipulated distance from each safe area. Christopher seized the momentum created by this resolution and held a dinner for the foreign ministers of France, Britain, Russia, and Spain. Over dinner, and later at a meeting held at the State Department, Christopher constructed an agreement that he believed would be satisfactory to the Europeans and the American public. The foreign ministers ultimately signed a document, the Joint Action Plan, where they agreed to protect the safe areas with force, if that was necessary. An exception was made for the United States. The US commitment was to provide air support for the United Nations Protection Force (UNPROFOR) but not to deploy ground troops. The president, after the Christopher meeting with the Europeans, became convinced that 'lift and strike' would not work and supported Christopher's efforts to find a containment solution. Clinton found himself in a situation where, aside from the lack of support from the Europeans, he would have had to expend a considerable amount of political capital, which would jeopardize his domestic agenda (Daalder 2000:18). Lake acquiesced and did not oppose the signing of the agreement because he believed that, at the time, there was no other alternative (Drew 1994: 162–163).

The administration's shift to a containment strategy is again consistent with the process found in the framework (Table 6.3). This episode is dominated by Warren Christopher's efforts to change the administration policy. Christopher believed that 'lift and strike' was not feasible and sought to find an alternative means of dealing with Bosnia without being deeply involved. In Clinton, Christopher found a willing recipient of his new ideas. Clinton was willing to delegate his authority and allow his advisors to shape policy when he felt politically vulnerable. Christopher held meetings with the president and other individuals who were close to the president without the knowledge of the other principals. Christopher was able to get the European foreign ministers to support a policy of containment, which made containment an even more viable option for the administration. Because of Christopher's furtive actions, no consensus was really built on the new policy and deliberations followed no regular mode of interaction. The fact that Christopher went outside the system to change policy and the opposition — although weak — to containment presented by Lake demonstrates the degree of conflict in the administration over the Bosnia policy. When it came to a final decision the president settled on supporting Christopher's proposed containment strategy that did not have widespread support among other advisors, thus providing a subset solution.

Table 6.3 Changing Policy

Process	Characteristics
• Willingness to delegate authority to others that have expertise	Yes
• Advisors instrumental in guiding policy	Yes
• Less emphasis on consensus building among advisors	Less emphasis
• Conflict and bargaining between advisors	Yes
• No regular mode of interacting with advisors	Yes
• Subset solution/Deadlock	Yes – Subset

Air Strikes (July 1993 – December 1993)

In July, the Bosnian Serbs escalated their artillery assault on Sarajevo, producing an intensification of the humanitarian crisis within the city. As the situation progressively deteriorated the media attention also increased with the impact of inciting greater international outrage. Clinton, while in Japan at the Group of Seven annual economic meeting, viewed on television the plight of Sarajevo and was moved to take action. Clinton told Christopher that he wanted his foreign policy team to think of options that would bring relief to Sarajevo including the deployment of ground troops (Daalder 2000: 19; Wayne 1997: 204). Lake, in turn, contacted Aspin, Powell, and Vice Chairman of the JCS David Jeremiah and requested that the latter begin to work on a set of military options for a meeting among the principals on July 13.

At the July 13 meeting, Admiral Jeremiah presented the possible military options. He presented the principals with a range of options that required different numbers of troops, the largest requirement called for 70,000 troops, a figure higher than most of the principals were willing to accept. Differences did exist between the advisors. Les Aspin opposed the idea of ground troops completely because of the possibility of the US becoming ensnared in the conflict. Madeleine Albright fully supported the use of ground troops while Lake and the National Security Council Staff advocated the use of air power in order to ease the movement of relief supplies and as a coercive measure against the Bosnian Serbs. Christopher changed his position from containment to support for the use of air strikes against the Bosnian Serbs around all of the enclaves.[2]

A consensus formed that the deployment of troops was not a viable option and Lake, with Christopher's support, moved to revive the two-phase plan that he developed before Clinton's trip to Sarajevo. In the first phase of the plan the threat or use of air strikes would be used to break the Bosnian Serb siege of Sarajevo and then, in the second phase, the threat or actual air strikes would be used to force a settlement. On July 21, Lake presented his plan to a meeting attended by the president, vice president, and George Stephanopoulos; in addition to detailing the two-phase plan, Lake explained that the US would have to use its leverage on the Bosnians to make a deal. The president felt that lifting the arms embargo was a better policy but he was willing to consider the plan and wanted to hold a meeting the next day to make a final decision. At the next day's meeting with Lake, Clinton, and Stephanopoulos, the president decided that the administration should try the Lake plan. Two days later, Lake and Reginald Bartholomew, with general agreement within the administration, traveled to Europe to convince NATO allies to support the administration (Lake 2000). The result was that on August 2 the North Atlantic Council issued a communiqué stating that the alliance would carry out air strikes against the Bosnian Serbs around Sarajevo with the approval of NATO and the UNPROFOR command.

The response to the siege of Sarajevo again followed the pattern predicted by the framework (Table 6.4). Clinton indicated he wanted something done about lifting the siege on Sarajevo but it was left to his advisors to develop the policy; consequently, the advisors were again put in a position to guide policy. Most of the advisors differed over policy with the major players advocating slightly different positions, but they were all able to arrive at a limited consensus that ground troops were not to be deployed. The president was not a part of the process until Lake and Christopher began to advocate for the two-phase options; in a series of meetings with the president,

---

[2] Elizabeth Drew (1994: 274) cites an administration official who argues that his change in policy reflected Christopher's belief that the president was moving in a direction that favored the use of force.

Lake was able to convince the president to support their policy option, thus producing a subset solution.

Table 6.4 Air Strikes

Process	Characteristics
• Willingness to delegate authority to others that have expertise	Yes
• Advisors instrumental in guiding policy	Yes
• Less emphasis on consensus building among advisors	Less Emphasis/ Consensus
• Conflict and bargaining between advisors	Yes
• No regular mode of interacting with advisors	Yes
• Subset solution/Deadlock	Yes – Subset

Groping for Change (January 1994 – November 1994)

In the fall of 1993, after the United States and NATO issued its ultimatum to the Bosnian Serbs, the Serbians began to ease the pressure on Sarajevo and some of the safe areas; at one point it seemed an agreement settling the conflict might be at hand (Drew 1994: 282; Daalder 2000: 23). However, in December, the Bosnian Serbs once again placed pressure on the safe areas by increasing their attacks. These developments took place at the same time that the administration became distracted by other foreign policy issues (Drew 1994: 284). By January 1994, though, the administration was facing increasing pressure from Congress and the Europeans to take greater action to change the situation in Bosnia. In response, the State Department and National Security Council staff, in January, began to think about new approaches to creating a settlement and producing relief to the safe areas. An NSC meeting at the end of January that included Clinton, Lake, Christopher, and Perry produced a consensus for a more aggressive policy that included the use of diplomacy and air strikes (Daalder 2000: 24).

Subsequently, Christopher was directed by the president to construct a coherent strategy based on the ideas put forth in the meeting. Christopher, with input from Albright, Lake, and the new Secretary of Defense William Perry created a policy that called for presenting the Bosnian Serbs with the alternatives of negotiations or air strikes. Christopher advocated the threat of force against the Serbs in order to deter further attacks and force them to seriously negotiate (Elliot and Barry 5/9/94). Additionally, the United States sought to conclude an alliance between the Croatians and the Bosnians, thereby strengthening the negotiating position of the Bosnians. The president received the Christopher report on February 4, but before Clinton could decide on his own, the process of rethinking administration policy was jolted after a mortar landed in Sarajevo's main market on February 5 killing 68 civilians. The president met with his foreign policy team that day and asked them for suggestions on how the administration should respond. At the meeting the president decided to move forward with the plan proposed by Christopher that sought a comprehensive settlement. Clinton also asked for a more immediate plan to deal with the Bosnian Serb assault on Sarajevo. There was general agreement that air strikes were an appropriate response, although several advisors had reservations about it because it was not clear from where the mortar had originated. The doubt about the origins of the shell was great enough that the president decided that Albright should work through the UN to find out who was responsible for the attack and that Christopher should consult with the Europeans on a course of action (Daalder 2000: 25).

Christopher returned with a plan proposed by the French that called for air strikes and the enforcement of a demilitarized zone spanning a radius of 30 kilometers around Sarajevo. Two meetings were held among Clinton's principal advisors without the president where all in attendance agreed on a modified version of the French Plan. The group agreed that the 30-kilometer perimeter should be reduced to 20 kilometers, both sides' heavy weapons had to be placed under UN control, and that all violations of the demilitarized zones would be met with air strikes. The North Atlantic Council accepted the US plan on February 9, which was followed by a UN brokered cease-fire on February 10.

The collegial and low centralization characteristics are found in this episode of administration decision-making (Table 6.5). Clinton, at the outset, delegated authority to Warren Christopher to construct a strategy that was based on the discussion in an NSC meeting. Christopher was then in a position

Table 6.5 Groping for Change

Process	Characteristics
• Willingness to delegate authority to others that have expertise	Yes
• Advisors instrumental in guiding policy	Yes
• Less emphasis on consensus building among advisors	No indication/ Consensus
• Conflict and bargaining between advisors	Yes
• No regular mode of interacting with advisors	Yes
• Subset solution/Deadlock	Integrative

to guide the direction of the administration, with some input from the other principals. Even though other advisors were included, there is no evidence that there was consensus sought in formulating the final report that went to the president. Clinton, in the wake of the shelling of Sarajevo, finally made a decision after having consulted further with all of his advisors. Clinton accepted the Christopher report, making the decision outcome integrative. Authority was delegated to the principals and they guided policy by building a consensus around a modified plan that was presented to the president, thus bringing about an integrative solution. In both of these issues, Clinton is engaged in the process enough that he searches for more information before he makes a final decision. The ways in which the president engages the process ranges from active participation to deciding on a presented option. Clinton, in deciding on the use of force as an overall strategy against the Serbians, is more engaged in the process by participating in the initial and final meetings. When it comes to the strategy for dealing with the events in Sarajevo, Clinton decides at the end of the process.

Reconsideration (November 1994 – February 1995)

The Administration's decision to pursue a Croatian-Bosnian alliance bore fruit in March when the two parties decided to enter into a federation. In May the major powers holding interests in the Balkans, Britain, France, United States, Russia, and Germany formed a Contact Group so that they could better coordinate their efforts to find a settlement to the conflict. In July the Contact Group adopted and presented the Owen-Stoltenberg plan to the warring parties; the Bosnians and the Croats were willing to accept the plan while the Bosnian Serbs refused to do so. The possibility of a negotiated settlement was hampered by the Muslim-Croatian offensive begun in the fall that brought about reversals on the battlefield for the Bosnian Serbs. Most importantly, during this period the relationship between the US and the other Contact Group members deteriorated over concerns expressed by many NATO members that air strikes were only going to make a bad situation worse. The Serbs, undeterred by air strikes, continued the assaults on the safe areas and took 200 peacekeepers hostage resulting in the relationship between the United States and its allies reaching a nadir. The strain on the US-alliance relationship became great enough that Lake spearheaded a change in administration policy.

The amount of information on this period of time is not complete and does not lend itself to a complete analysis. But it is known that Lake, on November 10, sent a memo to the president arguing that the US should suspend the push for air strikes and that it should seek first to rebuild the relationship with its alliance partners. To maintain progress toward an agreement, the PC decided that several concessions should be made. The administration decided that it was reasonable to accept the Contact group division of Bosnia in a 51-49 split between the Bosnian-Croat Federation and the Bosnian Serbs, if all sides agreed. Constitutional linkages between the Bosnian Serbs and Serbia were acceptable as long as the same arrangement was a possibility for the Croatians. Legitimacy would be given to the Bosnian Serbs if they established contacts with the Contact Group. The president approved this course of action, but he did not attend the meeting when it was decided that this was the best approach to the Balkans (Hyland 1999: 38-39; Daalder 2000: 33–34).

Rapid Reaction Force (February 1995 – June 1995)

During the winter, fighting continued between the Serbs and Muslims but the fighting was not as intense as previous winters. Attempts by the United States and the Contact Group to open up negotiations with the Bosnian Serbs produced no results because the Bosnian Serbs lacked an interest in negotiations. In February, Lake began a review of the administration's Bosnia policy in anticipation of renewed fighting as the weather improved (Daalder 2000: 87–88). Sandy Vershbow, chair of the Bosnia Interagency Work Group (IWG), was tasked with generating a set of options that were to be discussed by the principals. The work of the Bosnia Working Group was completed by March and was reviewed by the Principals Committee; the president was not in attendance.

The Principals Committee was given four options on which to deliberate. Option one, supported by Christopher, called for the administration to maintain the status quo which meant continued containment, diplomatic efforts, and a focus on humanitarian relief. Leon Feurth, the Vice-president's security advisor, supported the option of quarantining the Bosnian Serbs by preventing the flow of material between Serbia and Bosnia. Lake and Albright both continued to support lifting the arms embargo while conducting air strikes until the Bosnians were in a position to better provide for their own defense. The president's advisors decided that it was best to get the warring parties to extend the cease-fire agreed to the previous year and open a dialogue with Yugoslavian president Slobodan Milosevic in order to pressure the Bosnian Serbs to negotiate (Daalder 2000: 82–88). The advisors reasoned that at this point more aggressive action would further destabilize the region and weaken the already fragile relations within NATO.

Lake agreed with the decision of the Principals Committee, but he still believed that this measure was inadequate and that the administration needed to rethink policy in order to find a longer-term solution. Lake had Vershbow and Colonel Nelson Drew examine the options the US would have if the UNPROFOR was withdrawn and if the arms embargo was lifted. The paper produced by Vershbow and Nelson argued that the deployment of US troops was too dangerous and that the US should encourage UNPROFOR to withdraw troops from vulnerable areas around the enclaves, and redeploy them, so that the troops could more vigorously enforce their mandate. The paper also argued that the presence of UNPROFOR was an impediment to a long-term solution, which meant that at some point in the future the UN mission needed to be withdrawn. This latter point was particularly crucial if the administration chose to proceed with lifting the arms embargo, training the Bosnian Muslims and engaging in air strikes (Daalder 2000: 88–89).

The Vershbow-Nelson paper was presented to the Principals Committee, in May, at the same time that intense fighting broke out in Bosnia. The Bosnian Serbs violated the heavy weapons exclusion zone and shelled the Tuzla safe area, which brought about NATO air strikes. The response by the Bosnian Serbs was to take several hundred UN peacekeepers hostage. In the May Principals Committee meeting there was agreement that the administration ought to advise the Europeans to keep their peacekeepers in place. In the event that UNPROFOR did withdraw, the Principals all agreed that the US should push for a multilateral lifting of the arms embargo, but this decision was not meant to be a commitment of the administration to lift, arm, train, and strike (Daalder 2000). Essentially, the administration's policy remained the same as it was in November, which was preventing a schism among the alliance members and pressuring the Serbs to negotiate.

On May 27, French president Jacques Chirac, in a conversation with Clinton, suggested that a rapid reaction force be created, tasked with supporting areas with vulnerable UNPROFOR troops, opening a six-mile corridor from the Sarajevo airport to the Bosnian controlled part of Sarajevo and redeploying UNPROFOR troops. On May 28, the president's foreign policy team met to discuss the direction of US policy. The meeting was chaired by Deputy National Security Advisor Samuel Berger because Lake was not in attendance. There was a consensus that the US should support the Rapid Reaction Force proposal with the understanding that the United States would not have to supply troops. Consensus was achieved also on the issue of US troop non-participation in the redeployment of UN forces protecting the various safe areas. Secretary of Defense Perry and Shalikashvili argued that the US should deploy troops for the purpose of redeploying UN troops that were in vulnerable positions and thus strengthen allied resolve (Daalder 2000: 51–52). Lake then sent a memo on May 29 requesting the president to approve the suggested policy discussion among his foreign policy team the day before. Clinton, in a meeting on May 30, approved the plan presented in the memo, stating that he agreed with the policy 'as you have set forth' (Daalder 2000: 53).

At the same meeting Lake recommended that the president refer to Bosnia in a speech at the Air Force Academy the next day given the attention it was receiving from the press. Lake, on the way to the meeting, suggested that the president provide a 'complete' and 'nuanced' explanation of the administration's policy. However, the comments made by the president were vague and were more broadly interpreted than the policy discussed in the Principals Committee. Clinton's foreign policy team, notably the representatives of the Department of Defense, understood that there were very narrow restrictions on the use of US troops. In the president's comments, he asserted that the US would 'help in a withdrawal or a reconfiguration and a strengthening of its forces' which was more open ended than the decision made by his advisors (Daalder 2000: 52). Clinton's comments publicly established administration policy towards Bosnia and UNPROFOR, and, consequently, the exact nature of the administration's policy remained ambiguous as it was interpreted in a variety of ways.

In Table 6.6 we find that the advisory system in this episode has many of the identified characteristics found in the framework. Clinton delegated authority to his advisors and it is their efforts that shape and guide policy. Policy was deliberated in the Principals Committee where there were disagreements among the advisors but they were often able to build a consensus on basic aspects of policy while still holding on to differing prerogatives. The ability to build consensus during this episode is in part the result of the changing events on the ground in Bosnia and proposals put forth by the European partners, such as Chirac's proposal for a rapid reaction force. The administration found itself reacting to events with tactical adjustments that avoided addressing strategic decisions. Thus, on a certain level, the solution to disagreements was superficially integrative in that advisors were willing to compromise to obtain a consensus on basic points, but the solutions were fundamentally papering over differences because the policy choices did not address the points that separated the advisors. During this episode, Clinton decided on the options that his advisors had formulated.

Table 6.6 Rapid Reaction Force

Process	Characteristics
• Willingness to delegate authority to others that have expertise	Yes
• Advisors instrumental in guiding policy	Yes
• Less emphasis on consensus building among advisors	Consensus
• Conflict and bargaining between advisors	Yes
• No regular mode of interacting with advisors	Yes
• Subset solution/Deadlock	Paper over differences

Endgame (June 1995 – July 1995)

The administration's discussion of Bosnia policy continued, since the overall direction of policy had not been settled in the following months. Clinton discussed with his most senior advisors US policy toward Bosnia in a meeting that was supposed to be in preparation for a meeting with French president Jacques Chirac on June 14. Clinton demanded that he and his advisors had to get the administration's policy straight because it was evident that there was no clear mission. Al Gore shared Clinton's sentiments and argued that the imperative to maintain alliance ties was not contributing to a policy that would bring a settlement to the conflict (Woodward 1996: 255). Other than demonstrating the president's frustration with the administration's policy nothing of substance came out of this meeting.

Lake decided during the June 14 meeting that now was an opportunity to change the direction of US policy that he had been discussing with Berger and Vershbow for most of the year (Daalder 2000: 90). Whether or not Clinton was fully aware of what Lake was trying to do is not clear. However, it is clear that Lake decided to hold a series of meetings in late June with the intent of formulating a new direction in US policy towards the war in Bosnia. On June 21, Lake held the first meeting to discuss alternatives to keeping UNPROFOR in place until the warring parties agreed to a settlement. Numerous ideas were raised, ranging from reviving the Owen-Stoltenberg plan to discussions of lift and strike. The meeting became focused on a memo presented by Madeline Albright who argued that UNPROFOR was an impediment to more assertive action by NATO and that Milosevic should be given an offer of relief from sanctions if he recognized Bosnia. If he remained recalcitrant, NATO would engage in air strikes against Serbia and rearm the Bosnians. Lake supported the idea and he presented the memo to Clinton who also agreed that this was generally the direction in which he wanted to take US policy.

Lake then proceeded to work with Albright to develop the ideas into an overall strategy, while at the same time holding meetings with his staff to fully develop a coherent strategy (Daalder 2000: 93–94). In the first meeting with his NSC staff on June 24, Lake set out a range of questions that, he hoped, would guide his staff's deliberations. One of the main decisions that came out of this meeting was that an agreement needed to be based on the 51-49 division of Bosnia that would probably include the swapping of territory in eastern and central Bosnia. At the end of the meeting, Lake directed Vershbow to create an integrated strategy that brought together the ideas discussed in the meeting. Lake next instructed Vershbow to present a strategy that defined the mix of incentives that the US could bring to bear on the combatants in support of the US diplomatic effort (Daalder 2000: 95).

Lake told Clinton that he wanted to develop an 'endgame strategy' and presented the president with the broad strokes of the new policy that sought a long-term solution to the Balkan War. He also told the president that there were significant risks attached to this strategy because it required the deployment of troops and, in the event the plan failed, would prove to be embarrassing to the administration. Clinton earlier in the month complained that 'we've got no clear mission, no one's in control of events.' The plan Lake was proposing was exactly the kind of new thinking about Bosnia that Clinton thought would give the administration a clear mission and give the president greater control over events (Woodward 1996: 257–258; Daalder 2000: 91). Lake, sometime after their meeting, showed Clinton a draft of the 'endgame strategy' produced by Vershbow without the knowledge of Clinton's other principal advisors. Once Lake was assured of the president's support, he told Perry, Albright, Christopher, and Shalikashvili that the president wanted a revaluation of administration policy and to make an assessment of what US policy should be in six months.

Lake, Perry, Christopher, Albright, and Shalikashvili met on July 17 to discuss their proposals. Lake had arranged for the president to stop by at the meeting so he could impress upon the other advisors that long-term policy was necessary and that the short-term, day-to-day responses to each new crisis were no longer adequate. Before Clinton arrived, Lake laid out his full strategy that included a variety of military and diplomatic options designed to be used as leverage on the warring factions. These carrots and sticks included using military force to relieve Sarajevo, encouraging third party arms shipments to Bosnia, unilateral lifting of the arms embargo, redeployment of UNPROFOR, air strikes against Serbia, the exchange of territory, international assistance for all sides post-settlement, and limited autonomy for Bosnian Serbs in a new Bosnian state (Daalder 2000: 99–102). Albright fully supported the strategy presented by Lake, but Perry, Christopher, and Shaliskashvili preferred to deal with the more immediate problem of Srebrenica which the Serbs had overrun days before (Woodward 1996: 261). Christopher, in particular, objected because he believed that the allies would not support this dramatic change in policy and that there was no leverage over the Bosnians and Serbs. Overall, Christopher argued there were more costs than benefits to changing policy (Daalder 2000: 101).

Clinton arrived toward the end of the meeting and told the group that he did not like the current state of US policy because it harmed the overall reputation of the United States and that a more forceful policy was necessary. The president pointed out that any success that US policy had was achieved when NATO was used as a real threat against the Serbs (Woodward 1996: 263). Clinton left the meeting and Lake suggested that the group consider his policy and devise their own long-term strategies so the president could consider these options. No immediate decision was made on the endgame strategy because of the events taking place within Bosnia.

The formulation and consideration of Lake's 'endgame' strategy follows the process predicted in the framework (Table 6.7). Lake decided to redirect policy and he was able to do so because of Clinton's delegation that gave Lake the ability to take control and redirect policy. Lake consulted with the principals at first to find any new ideas; afterwards, he developed some ideas with Albright because their views overlapped. However, most of the administration's deliberations took place between the National Security Advisor and his staff where ideas and options were developed. Lake then discussed his policy with Clinton without the knowledge of the other principals including Albright. This meant that no consensus was developed and the solution to differences among the advisors, although not final, favored Lake because he was able to influence the president's thinking on the policy. A critical variable in Lake's ability to influence was the siege on Srebrenica and the intense pressure this placed on the president and administration to act, which at this stage of the administration's experience with Bosnia was becoming a norm and exactly something Lake's plan was designed to overcome. Even with the support from the president, Lake's strategy was still opposed by Christopher, Perry, and Shalikashvilli.

Table 6.7 Endgame

Process	Characteristics
• Willingness to delegate authority to others that have expertise	Yes
• Advisors instrumental in guiding policy	Yes/No
• Less emphasis on consensus building among advisors	Less Emphasis/ Consensus
• Conflict and bargaining between advisors	Yes
• No regular mode of interacting with advisors	Yes
• Subset solution/Deadlock	Subset

Srebrenica to London (July 1995)

In the beginning of July, the administration was forced to deal with immediate consequences of the siege and fall of Srebrenica to the Bosnian Serbs. At the same time, Jacques Chirac called for the alliance to halt the Bosnian Serb offensive by a 'limited military action,' failing that, he argued, greater intervention would be necessary. Specifically, Chirac had a plan to defend the safe area of Gorazde with a thousand Rapid Reaction Force troops. On July 14, the day after Chirac's announcements, the NSC, including the president,

deliberated on the proposal presented by Chirac. No one at the meeting wanted
to reject the Chirac plan, but there was great reluctance toward the idea of
reinforcing Gorazde with ground troops; Perry in particular argued for the use
of air strikes instead. Clinton agreed and gave Shalikashvili the task of going to
Europe to decide on a specific military response with the allies.

The options produced by Shalikashvili and the British and French
military chiefs in London were discussed by Clinton's advisors without the
president on July 17. The British and French plans called for a more robust
enforcement of the UN mandate and the reinforcement of Gorazde. Clinton's
advisors recognized that the British and French would need convincing if they
were going to accept the US plan of significant air strikes. They agreed to
present the president with two options for a meeting scheduled the next day in
the Oval Office. One option required air strikes with no need for authorization
from the UN or NATO in order to defend Gorazde and Sarajevo; the other
option, the French plan, called for US transport of the Rapid Reaction Force
with air strikes. In the July 18 meeting, Al Gore spoke assertively about the
need to act in a decisive manner noting that the enclaves of Zepa and Gorazde
would be next to be attacked by the Bosnian Serbs. Clinton agreed that the
current situation was untenable and he was convinced that if air strikes could
be used to support the movement of the Rapid Reaction Force, they could be
effective on their own. Clinton then decided on the US option of unrestricted
air strikes and he sent a representative, this time Christopher, to get the
Europeans on board (Daalder 2000: 71–72).

Table 6.8 Srebrenica to London

Process	Characteristics
• Willingness to delegate authority to others that have expertise	Yes
• Advisors instrumental in guiding policy	Yes
• Less emphasis on consensus building among advisors	Less Emphasis
• Conflict and bargaining between advisors	Yes
• No regular mode of interacting with advisors	Yes
• Subset solution/Deadlock	Subset

This episode reveals that authority is delegated to Clinton's advisors,
specifically Shalikashvilli, who is allowed to develop the options for the
response to the Serb attack on Srebrenica, but this is only after Clinton engaged
in a lengthy debate with his advisors over the Chirac proposal (Table 6.8). The
president's advisors discussed the options developed by Shalikashvilli and
narrowed the number of choices to two, thus Clinton's foreign policy team

were guiding the direction of administration policy without the participation of the president. Advisors disagreed, but were able to reach a consensus on presenting the president with two options, although there was no consensus beyond this. It was up to the president with his advisors to decide on policy that resulted in a subset solution.

London to Endgame (July 1995 – November 1995)

Secretaries Christopher and Perry with General Shalikashvili went to London and met with representatives from Britain and France. After a period of reluctance, the three were able to encourage the Europeans to make three agreements removing the constraints on NATO air strikes.[3] Shortly after the Christopher mission returned from Europe the Senate passed a resolution on July 26 that unilaterally lifted the arms embargo against the Bosnian Muslims. Both events placed pressure on the administration to act in a decisive manner, which it had still not done despite the success of the Christopher mission. On August 7 Clinton met with Gore, Lake, Perry, Albright, Peter Tarnoff (who was representing Christopher), Samuel Berger, Leon Panetta (Chief of Staff), George Stephanopoulos (senior presidential advisor), Leon Fuerth, Sandy Vershbow, and Nelson Drew and discussed the series of long-term strategies on which they had been working. Christopher, although not in attendance, contacted the president by phone before the meeting to express his disagreement with the Lake 'endgame strategy.' Christopher objected to the idea of pressuring the Bosnians to accept the changes in the Contact Group map. He also did not believe that the American public would accept the deployment of US troops in Bosnia and that the allies would support any variation of lift and strike (Daalder 2000: 106).

Lake was aware of Christopher's thoughts and just before the meeting on August 7 he briefed the president advising him that it was necessary that there was a consensus on administration policy because of the magnitude of the decision and the consequences of failure of the diplomatic or military aspects. Lake began the meeting by laying out the differences between their positions. Then the president engaged in a 'seminar-type style of decision-making' where he went around the room asking each of the principals to elaborate on their respective options. After hearing all of the alternative positions, Clinton stated that he agreed with the political arguments that essentially supported the diplomatic approach laid out by Lake. To emphasize his point Clinton stated

---

[3] The three agreements included permission to respond with air strikes against Bosnian Serbs anywhere in Bosnia and not just in the area immediately surrounding Gorazde, air strikes could pre-empt a Serb attack, local commanders could call in close air support and the authority for wider attacks resided with UNPROFOR commander Rupert Smith. These agreements were the essential elements that structured Operation Deliberate Force begun in August.

that 'we've got to exhaust every alternative, roll every die, take risks' (Daalder 2000: 108-109).

The groups then focused on how the Lake plan would be implemented, with Lake advocating that he go to Europe and inform the allies that a settlement had to be found this year. This would be followed by efforts to start negotiations with the warring parties. Tarnoff presented the State Department plan of suspending sanctions in exchange for Serb recognition of Bosnia which would then be followed by negotiations between Milosevic and Itzebegovic and Tudjman. On this issue Clinton decided to go with the Lake Plan. Attention then turned to planning in the event that the administration did not succeed in getting an agreement in 1995. All those present agreed that the only alternative would be to pull out UNPROFOR and shift the policy to 'lift, train and strike' with the exception of Tarnoff, who argued that this was not necessary because Milosevic could help bring about a settlement if sanctions were used as leverage. The president listened to all the arguments and then adjourned the meeting stating that he would make a final decision by the next day, but he was probably going to go with the Lake 'endgame strategy' (Daalder 2000: 107–110).

On August 8 the same group met again with the president. Clinton began by stating that he was going to go ahead with the Lake strategy and that Lake should go to Europe to tell the allies that this was his final decision. Lake then went through a set of talking points he would use in his meetings with the allies that laid out the incentives that would be used to get the parties to negotiate. After each point, Lake asked for input from everyone in the group, thus ensuring that everyone agreed with his points resulting in a consensus. Clinton told his advisors that they would meet again in the morning to look over the final version of the talking points and, if there were no objections, Lake would leave on his mission to Europe (Daalder 2000: 110-111; Woodward 1996: 266). The next day the Secretary of State rejoined the group after his trip to Asia. Clinton fully supported the latest version of the talking points stating that 'the whole thing sounds pretty good' (Woodward 1996: 266). All the other advisors supported the talking points and the Lake mission, including Christopher, despite his concern regarding the dangers of lifting the embargo, training the Bosnians and engaging in extensive air strikes (Woodward 1996: 266).

The process that led up to the decision to finally adopt the Lake strategy sees Clinton engaged in the decision-making process more than in any other episode of decision-making. Despite his attention to the issue of Bosnia, Clinton still essentially allowed Anthony Lake to guide and shape the administration's policy. Lake had effectively convinced the president that the 'endgame' strategy was the only long-term solution. However, Lake's ability to be effective in advancing his policy preferences was in part aided by the fact that the rapidly deteriorating situation in Bosnia placed pressure on the administration to act. It was Lake who was the only advisor that was proposing a policy that held out the possibility of bringing about a resolution to the conflict. As indicated in Table 6.9, this process is consistent with that produced by a collegial structure with low centralization. In addition to delegated

Table 6.9 London to Endgame

Process	Characteristics
• Willingness to delegate authority to others that have expertise	Yes
• Advisors instrumental in guiding policy	Yes
• Less emphasis on consensus building among advisors	No
• Conflict and bargaining between advisors	Yes
• No regular mode of interacting with advisors	Yes
• Subset solution/Deadlock	Subset

authority and the direction of policy shaped by Lake, the process was also characterized by persistent disagreement between Lake and Christopher. Each had competing ideas about the direction of policy, but Lake was more effective in capturing the policy. The decision-making is also consistent with the typology because it demonstrates how Clinton shifted between disengagement with policy to being highly engaged. This episode differs from the typology in that there is a concerted effort by Clinton over a two-day period to ensure that there was a consensus on the new administration policy. In the end, when Clinton chose the endgame strategy, he settled the disagreements within the administration by going with a subset solution.

A number of factors came together during August that helped create the conditions for an agreement between the warring parties in the Balkans. First, Lake was successful in getting the Europeans to accept the new US strategy. After Lake returned from Europe, Richard Holbrooke was designated US Envoy charged with getting the Bosnians and Serbians to the negotiating table. As Holbrooke was beginning his mission, the Croats and Bosnians initiated an offensive that led to heavy losses for the Bosnian Serbians in terms of territory. Serbian losses were compounded by NATO air strikes conducted after a mortar attack on the main market in Sarajevo. Operation Deliberate force began on August 27 and ended on September 14 at which time the Bosnian Serbs and Milosevic were prepared to begin serious negotiations on a settlement. Proximity talks opened at Wright Paterson Air Force base in Dayton, Ohio, on November 21 and a final agreement was reached seven days later.

Conclusion

The nine episodes that compose the case of Clinton administration decision making on Bosnia are generally consistent with the process that results when a president chooses an advisory structure composed of a collegial structure and low centralization (Table 6.10). Three out of the five process characteristics consistently appeared in every episode found within the case. Clinton delegated authority to his advisors to construct administration policy. The Principals Committee (PC), based on presidential Decision Directive – Two, was tasked with being the main body to consider administration policy, but the examination of the administration's behavior reveals that not only was policy being considered within the PC but to a certain extent policy was being determined by the PC.

Because of Clinton's inattentiveness to foreign policy in general and his repeated absence from discussions of Bosnia, the direction of US policy was being determined by the PC, and given the low control that Clinton was exercising, policy was also deliberated outside of the PC. On several occasions authority was delegated to specific advisors to devise administration policy. Warren Christopher in early 1994 was directed by the president to develop a plan to bring about relief to the 'safe areas' in Bosnia. While Christopher accepted input from other principals, he had the authority to produce the final product. Similarly, Lake had the authority to go forward and develop his endgame strategy in 1995. In neither of these instances was Clinton playing a significant role in the process by participating in deliberations and raising alternative options or by monitoring the deliberations. It was typically very late in the process, when Clinton's advisors had already narrowed the range of options or a single advisor like Lake or Christopher presented a single option that Clinton would join the process and engage in extensive discussions on the virtues of the existing plans. Clinton's intense participation late in the process can be attributed to two factors. One, as events rapidly changed or as plans and proposals were made by actors outside of the administration, Clinton was placed in a position where he was forced to engage in the policy discussion. Two, as the situation worsened in Bosnia, particularly the later part of 1994 into 1995, the decision-making process began to resemble crisis decision-making, which would have demanded that Clinton participate.

Clinton's delegation of authority and intermittent participation meant that his advisors were instrumental in guiding policy in all nine episodes. Clinton's advisors are found to be guiding policy, even in meetings where Clinton was present and actively participating; his lack of clear goals combined with delegation meant that advisors could drive the direction of policy. This, to a certain extent, explains the tendency in many meetings for Clinton to constantly raise issues, discuss them at length, but arrive at no final conclusion. The ability of Clinton's advisors to guide policy is also a function of the fact that Clinton had no regular mode of interacting with his advisors. Clinton was inclined to focus more on domestic rather than foreign policy issues, which meant that he would give priority in terms of time to domestic issues. But over the course of these episodes we see Clinton meeting one on one with advisors whom he believed were presenting solutions to the immediate problems at hand, but the increasing reliance was a means to cope with the enormous amount of information that he had to process in order to make a decision. Lake and Christopher are the two main advisors that Clinton meets with to formulate policy, but pollster Stan Greenberg and George Stephanopoulos were two other advisors with whom Clinton consulted. Clinton also met with his principal advisors as a group and he participated in the formulation of options, although more often he held group meetings where he was presented with an option or two which would form the basis for intensive deliberations. The advisory system that Clinton established has a collegial structure in that the administration's deliberations took place for the most part in a 'team like' atmosphere, but this process differs from the Carter system in that Clinton's engagement in the open give-and-take during deliberations is infrequent and his control over discussions was minimal.

Conflict and bargaining also characterize the decision-making process within the Clinton administration. In eight out of the nine episodes in the Bosnia case bargaining and conflict are found to be a part of the decision-making process, the exception being one case where there was not enough information to make a solid determination. The presence of conflict and bargaining should not be surprising given that the collegial structure is designed to facilitate the interaction between different advisors with opposing policy views. What is surprising about Clinton's decision-making process is that for the most part advisors use group meetings to exchange ideas and present their preferred policy options without resorting to efforts to undermine the authority or role of other advisors. There are two notable exceptions to this case and they are Lake's selling Clinton his 'endgame' strategy and Christopher's advocacy of a containment strategy.

In both instances Lake and Christopher work outside of the committee system and without the knowledge of other advisors to shift the direction of policy. Each advisor was trying to change the direction of the administration policy knowing that they would not be able to make these changes in concert with other advisors. It might be the case that in this kind of structure when there are disagreements over aspects of strategy or when tactical issues are being discussed, the collegial setting, with little control by the president, can be effective. However, when it comes to changing the strategy in any fundamental way the president's involvement is required to provide guidance, because otherwise advisors will work outside of the normal group setting where there

Table 6.10 Clinton Advisory System: Collegial Structure/ Low Centralization

	Dealing with Reality	Looking for new ideas	Changing Policy	Air Strikes	Groping for Change	Rapid Reaction Force	Endgame Strategy	Srebrenica to London	London to Endgame	%
Willingness to delegate authority to others that have expertise	Yes	Yes	Yes	Yes	Yes	Yes	Yes	Yes	Yes	100
Advisors instrumental in guiding policy	Yes	Yes	Yes	Yes	Yes	Yes	Yes	Yes	Yes	100
Less emphasis on consensus building among advisors	Less Emphasis	Consensus	Less Emphasis	Less Emphasis/ Consensus	No Indication/ Consensus	Consensus	Less Emphasis/ Consensus	Less Emphasis	Consensus	55
Conflict and bargaining between advisors	No indication	Yes	Yes	Yes	Yes	Yes	Yes	Yes	Yes	89
No regular mode of interacting with advisors	Yes	Yes	Yes	Yes	Yes	Yes	Yes	Yes	Yes	100
Subset solution/ Deadlock	Paper over	Subset	Subset	Subset	Integrative	Paper difference	Subset	Subset	Subset	67

will be fewer powerful voices to challenge their prerogatives.[4] Lake and Christopher were both trying to change the direction of policy and may have felt that the opposition, mainly coming from the other, necessitated appealing more directly to the president or influencing those around the president.

The last two features of the collegial structure/low centralization process found in the Clinton case yield mixed results. The decision-making during the Clinton administration should, according to the framework, result in less emphasis on building consensus among advisors. Five of nine episodes within the case clearly demonstrate that there was no evidence of the president or any other advisor-building consensus before making a decision. In these cases different advisors held different policy positions and when a choice was made it was made without first getting them on board. The other four episodes provide mixed results. In two of the five episodes there is not enough available information on the decision-making during this part of the case to make an argument for or against the building of consensus among advisors. Two of these four episodes provide evidence for the formation of consensus with two of three episodes being mixed where there were decisions made with and without consensus. These findings support the argument that there was no preference for consensus in the administration at the highest level, but that at lower levels advisors attempted to reach a general consensus before engaging the president (Brookings 2000).

In the mixed episodes, the advisors and/or the president were generally able to arrive at consensus on a narrow range of options on whether or not the use of force should be a part of strategy or on whether ground troops were a viable option. However, when it came to making final decisions that preceded any administration action, consensus was not required. The one episode where there was full consensus among advisors was after Chirac proposed the deployment of a rapid reaction force in defense of safe areas. In this instance there was agreement that this was a suitable response to the events in Bosnia and that US participation should be limited. Overall, from these nine cases it is evident that consensus among advisors is less important when it comes to final decisions that would precede any external action. The consensus built for Lake's endgame strategy is a notable exception, which can be explained by the dramatic change in policy that was being proposed in the strategy and the costs to the administration. For the most part, however, consensus was generated among advisors within group settings by narrowing options, eliminating sets of options or in general by refining options.

---

[4] The ability to change policy direction in these cases also coincides with either previous policy failure or with a severe change of circumstances on the ground, which created an opportunity for an advisor to exploit the urgency in finding a new policy.

The unstructured solutions found in this case also present mixed results. Collegial structures with a low presidential centralization should produce subset or deadlock solutions. Six of the nine episodes in the case are subset solutions, which is consistent with the process identified in the typology. In a number of these episodes subset solutions are found in resolving disagreements regarding the final decision, but leading up to that subset solution there are periods of deadlock during which differences are not resolved. These are instances where Clinton allows debate to take place in meetings and the almost endless discussion of issues brings no resolution. However, this deadlock is often short lived and a final decision is usually made by the president with his advisors.

Of the remaining three episodes, the unstructured solutions differ from what was hypothesized in the typology. In two episodes, Clinton resolves differences by adopting a range of different policy options that essentially papers over differences within the administration. Clinton resorts to this kind of solution in the first episode in the administration when he is trying to formulate an initial approach to Bosnia. In this meeting Clinton agrees to a set of policy options that were raised during an NSC meeting without regard to consistency or coherence of these options. The other episode reveals that the disagreements are resolved by an integrative solution. In the episode dealing with the proposed Rapid Reaction Force, advisors were willing to compromise to obtain a consensus on basic points, but the solutions were fundamentally papering over differences because the policy choices did not address the points that separated the advisors. The episode where the administration finds an unstructured solution that is integrative, the president is involved in one decision and, in the other, the president's advisors integrate options. In one integrative episode, decisions were shaped by proposals made by the European allies, specifically by Chirac's proposal for the relief of Sarajevo. In the other integrative episode, which is not counted as a complete episode, there is an indication that the administration is influenced by the Contact Group's adoption of the Owen-Stoltenberg plan. In both cases, the need to support a policy in coordination with other states facilitates compromise by those deliberating on policy.

Overall, the process predicted to result from a collegial/low control advisory generally reflects the process of decision-making during the Clinton administration's decision-making on the war in Bosnia. Four of the identified characteristics consistently appear in all ten episodes of the case. Unstructured solutions and less emphasis on consensus, the other two characteristics, are also present but there are notable deviations from the process that were not anticipated. The consensus found in the episodes appears to have taken place on the policy parameters, but when final decisions are made consensus is not salient. The variety of solutions found in disagreements reflects the low control of the president, which is characterized by an absence from participation in the process; thus, the president does effectively condition how disagreements are settled. In these situations the prerogatives of the advisors and outside influences such as the rapidly changing nature of the international scene can alter the operating behavior of the deliberations as the episodes dealing with allies and the Contact Group demonstrate. The ability of actors outside the administration and events on the ground to influence the process can be explained by the fact that the collegial structure is designed to be open to external information. When this is combined with a president who does ensure that the process is centralized, it is very easy for new developments to overtake and lead the administration.

Chapter 7

Bush Decision-Making:
Pre- and Post-9/11

A candidate needs to focus on the big picture, his message his agenda, and let others worry about most of the details. (Bush 1999: 80)

I may not be able to tell you exactly the nuance of the East Timorian situation, but I'll ask people who've had experience, like Condi Rice, Paul Wolfowitz, or Dick Cheney. (Bush, quoted in Dowd 1999)

Although there have been countless book and articles published about George W. Bush and his administration, there exist few detailed accounts of the administration's policy making compared to earlier administrations. This is not surprising given the length of time before documents are declassified and key figures are willing to discuss openly and in depth their experiences in the administration. This is particularly true for an administration that from the outset has been extremely concerned about secrecy of internal policy discussions. The administration's dogged determination to keep secret from Congress and the public membership and discussions of Vice President Dick Cheney's Energy Task Force is an extreme demonstration of the administration's interest to hide from public view the administration's inner workings. As a consequence there is not a wealth of information that permits the kind of detailed analysis of the Bush administration decision making that characterized the previous chapters. Despite this, it is still possible to engage in analysis that allows for an examination of the administration's foreign policy decision making.

George W. Bush, prior to entering office, held strong views about how decisions should be made and how the decision-making process should be managed. Bush explicitly wanted to approach the job of policy making like that of a chief executive officer. With an MBA from Harvard Business School, experience as CEO of two companies, and witness to the inner workings of his father's presidency, George Bush believed that the best way to formulate policy was for an executive to surround themselves with knowledgeable experts and to rely on them to be responsible for the grunt work of constructing policy, while he would be responsible for making the final decision. In short, Bush believed that effective management meant delegating to a group of capable and loyal advisors. Bush, upon entering office, also believed that this delegation had to take place within an environment modeled on a corporation, where there was a clear and ordered hierarchy and the roles among actors were clearly delineated.

In the same way that Nixon wanted to avoid the mistakes of the Eisenhower administration and Reagan wanted to avoid the problems that afflicted the Carter administration, Bush was committed to a management style that would ensure that his administration was not plagued by the problems of the Clinton administration (Gregg II and Rozell 2004). The collegial structure and low centralization was something that Bush wanted to avoid because of the perceived propensity for that type of advisory system to devolve in to open-ended debates that roamed across issues, but often ended in no definitive decision. But the management style was also a departure from the Reagan administration's, in which Reagan's participation on the START deliberations were minimal. Bush, it is argued, approaches the policy process by being more active compared to Reagan, the president he shares similarities with in terms of personality and management style. Yet this involvement had limits and like Clinton, Bush tends to be more engaged when the issue is a part of his agenda; when the issue is not, he delegates more and relies more on the opinion of others (Burke 2004).

Bush's inclination to choose this type of management style is not surprising because of his business background, but it also fits with his type of personality. The comparison to Clinton is, again, instructive. While Clinton was inclined at times to immerse himself in the minutiae of a policy issue, Bush demonstrates a clear disinterest in engaging in details or 'intellectually sophisticated analysis' (Burke 2004: 110). This disposition has led to accusations that the Bush is either not smart or is intellectually lazy. Opposed to the extensive memos Carter, Clinton, and George H.W. Bush are known to have received, Bush prefers correspondence 'whittled down to one page memos' (Calabresi et al 2001). The president's propensity to treat issues that do not immediately concern him in a superficial manner needs also to be taken into account with his weak knowledge of international politics and world events. The implications of these two dimensions of Bush's character are that he must delegate to those individuals around him that have the knowledge and ability to deliberate on an issue. Bush potentially compensates for this deficiency by only surrounding himself with those he believes he can trust, so he can be assured that they will pursue policy compatible with his interests. Similar to Ronald Reagan, Bush insisted upon loyalty from those appointed to his administration. Again, this need can be attributed to his particular style of management. Interestingly, however, and in contrast to Reagan's personality, Bush has less of an aversion to dissention among the people that advise him, in fact he needed this if he was going to get the 'best' advice (Daalder and Lindsay 2003). This is compatible with this type of management style because the hierarchy and designation of roles should function to reduce conflicts that arise from internal dissent, however this is mitigated by the president's delegation and often lack of knowledge of the issues.

Bush's management style is reflected in the committee system put in place for the development of policy. In the National Security Presidential Directive—one (NSPD-1) established, as is usual for administrations, that the National Security Council Principals Committee (NSC/PC) is the forum for the most senior members of the administration to consider and develop policy. The committee is comprised of all the statutory members of the National Security Council with non-statutory members such as White House Chief of Staff, the Assistant to the President for Economic Policy, White House Counsel, Attorney General and Director of the Office of Management and Budget are either invited to attend or will attend when the policy relates to their responsibilities. Alternatively, they may be invited by the President's National Security Advisor who chairs the committee. Below the NSC/PC in the committee hierarchy is the National Security Council Deputies Committee (NSC/DC) which is tasked with prescribing policy options to the Principals Committee and review the work of specialized interagency groups. The Deputy National Security Advisor is responsible for chairing the meeting, thus putting the direction of both committees in the hands of the National Security Advisor. In some administrations, such as Richard Nixon's, this would have been a recipe for the National Security Advisor's dominance of the policy-making process, because if they chose they would be able to unduly influence the development of policy options, as well as the NSC/PC agenda (NSPD-1).

Below the two main senior interagency meetings are a series of specialized interagency committees known as National Security Council/Policy Coordination Committees (NSC/PCC) that are responsible for development and implementation of policy. Six of the NSC/PCC committees are responsible policy relating to six global regions (Europe and Eurasia, Western Hemisphere, East Asia, South Asia, Near East and North Africa, and Sub-Saharan Africa). There are a further eleven committees that are tasked with following policy along functional lines, for example International Development and Humanitarian Assistance, Arms Control, Counter-Terrorism and National Preparedness (NSPD-1). Each committee's chair is specified in the NSPD-1 and varies according to responsibility and area of expertise. The chairs for the regional Policy Coordinating Committee's are Undersecretaries of Assistant Secretaries chosen by the Secretary of State. This contrasts the functional PCCs that are chaired by different senior members of the administration. When determined necessary by the chair of each committee, these NSC/PCC can be supplemented by ad hoc subcommittees.

Given the president's predilection for a management style that is characterized by a hierarchic structure in which the president delegates responsibility for formulating policy to advisors and the president chooses at the end of the deliberation, the president's management advisory system is formally structured with low centralization. This type of management style is reflected in the fact that Bush implemented a committee structure that is hierarchically organized with the Principals Committee at the top of the system and the Policy Coordinating Committees at the bottom, which are tasked with developing and implementing policy that has been approved by the president and principals. Although he possessed a different committee structure, Reagan had the same kind of advisory system as the Bush administration, thus the decision-making process should look similar to that of the Reagan administration. This means that the Bush decision-making process should be characterized by:

- Leader chooses between presented options
- Advisors compete to get preferences presented to leader
- Gatekeeper acts as honest-broker and presents options (opportunity for other advisors to appeal to leader)
- Bargaining and conflict take place at level below president
- Procedures may be circumvented
- Subset-Dominant/Deadlock

With an emphasis on delegation in this type of decision-making process, Bush required a foreign policy team that he could entrust to formulate the type of policy that he wanted. In choosing his foreign policy team Bush selected a number of seasoned Veterans with experience in his father's, Ronald Reagan's, Ford's, and Nixon's administrations. Among these individuals were Vice President Dick Cheney, Secretary of Defense Donald Rumsfeld, Secretary of State Colin Powell, and National Security Advisor Condoleezza Rice. For most administrations the policy is driven by the principals in the administration, which makes sense given their position and authority. But just like the Reagan administration, individuals further down in the bureaucracy play a role in the formulation of policy.

Systems with low centralization of the process open up the possibility for a greater number of actors to have an influence in the policy process. Just as Richard Perle and Richard Burt—both Deputy Secretaries—were in a position to develop and drive the decision making on arms control policy during the Reagan administration, deputies and assistants in the Bush administration played an important role in the development of policy. The importance of these individuals is also attributed to the high degree of similarity between their views and the principals for whom they work. Combined, these factors ensure that this group has the ability to involve themselves in the process in a way that would not be possible in a hierarchic/high centralization system, unless the president deliberately pulled them directly into the process. This additional group of advisors includes

Assistant to the Vice President on National Security Affairs I. Lewis 'Scooter' Libby, Deputy Secretary of Defense Paul Wolfowitz, Deputy Secretary of State Richard Armitage, and Deputy National Security Advisor Stephen Hadley.[1]

Bush had developed a particularly close relationship with his National Security Advisor Condoleezza Rice. Former Stanford Provost and National Security Council staff adviser on the Soviet Union and Soviet defense policy, Rice was introduced to George W. Bush by his father at their home in Kennebunkport, Maine just as George W. was beginning to put together his presidential campaign. It is believed that during this brief period Rice and Bush 'bonded' on a personal level and shortly thereafter she would be appointed Bush's main advisor on foreign policy during his run for the presidency (Mann 2004: 250–251). Once the decision was made to make Rice the National Security Advisor it was understood that she would play the role of honestbroker; however, it is understood that because of the special relationship that she has developed with the president she has the ability be heard in ways that are not necessarily open to the other advisors. Rice had one disadvantage, because even though she was the close to the president she was serving in an administration where the other principals had more experience and knowledge of the inner workings of the policy process.

The individual who truly exemplified the status and the expertise of Bush's advisors was his new Vice President Dick Cheney. Cheney served as George H.W. Bush's Secretary of Defense and came to his new post with an interest in playing an active role in the development of foreign policy. As a demonstration of his interest in foreign policy, Cheney organized a number of national security specialists to serve him as a National Security Council staff. Cheney's staff was exceptional in that it was larger than previous VPs—twice the size of Gore's—and staffed with high caliber experts (Daalder and Lindsay 2003: 59). The vice president's interest in national security issues, in addition to extensive knowledge in the area potentially positioned him in competition with the two most important foreign policy advisors, the Secretary of State and the Secretary of Defense.

---

[1] Aside from the principals and this group of deputies there are other individuals inside and outside of the administration that are influential in the development of policy. Included in this group are Richard Perle (member of the Defense Policy Board), United States Trade Representative and former Undersecretary of State for Economic Affairs Robert Zoellick, White House Advisor on European and Soviet Affairs in the George H.W. Bush administration Robert Blackwill, Undersecretary for Policy Douglas Feith, United States Ambassador to Afghanistan and Director of the Strategy, Doctrine and Force Structure program for RAND's Project Air Force Zalmay Khalilzad, Assistant Secretary of Defense of International Policy in the Reagan administration Dov Zakheim.

Colin Powell served as Chairman of the Joint Chiefs of Staff in the Clinton and George H.W. Bush administrations, as well as a short stint as National Security Advisor during the Reagan Administration. Selected to be a member of the administration because of public stature and experience, Powell stood out from the other advisors in that he was not a die-hard conservative, in fact he tended to be quite liberal on social issues. But, as will be discussed below, Powell differed from those around him in terms of how to pursue US foreign policy. Powell had developed a reputation during his tenure as Chairman of the Joint Chiefs for his unwillingness to use military force unless that force was decisive and that afterwards there was a clear exit strategy. This, coupled with a belief in multilateralism, put Powell ideologically at odds with the rest of the administration, with the exception of his deputy Richard Armitage. Armitage, during the Reagan administration served under Caspar Weinberger as Assistant Secretary of Defense, but he was also close friends with Powell and shared similar views regarding the means to achieve the countries goals (Mann 2004). The relationship between deputy and principal at the Department of State was in a sense a mirror image of relationship that exited between the Secretary of Defense Donald Rumsfeld and his deputy Paul Wolfowitz.

Former Secretary of Defense during the Ford administration, congressman, and aspirant to the White House, Donald Rumsfeld had all the credentials to be Secretary of Defense. He was particularly a desirable choice given that prior to his appointment he headed a commission that contradicted the intelligence community's estimates on the ballistic missile capability of a variety of rogue states. Although Wolfowitz did not know Rumsfeld personally before taking the position as his assistant during the 1996 Robert Dole presidential campaign, they were compatible because of their political and policy views (Mann 2004, 231). When both were chosen for positions in the Defense Department they were familiar with each other's preference and styles. Rumsfeld also had another advantage as the Secretary of Defense, he was close friends with the Vice President. While Director of the Organization for Economic Opportunity during the Nixon administration, Rumsfeld hired Cheney to be his special assistant and they worked together throughout the Nixon and Ford administrations (Mann 2004: 10–11). Since both had compatible views on defense and national security, Rumsfeld with Wolfowitz ostensibly posed a policy counterweight to Powell and Armitage at the State Department.

Policy Environment: A Unipolar Moment

It is important to understand that the Bush administration's approach to international politics and foreign policy was not so much what was taking place in the world, but the administration's collective interpretation of international politics and the United States' role. Bush was a novice when it came to events abroad and as a result did not have what could be considered a sophisticated knowledge or understanding of foreign policy issues, which was not helped by the fact that he did not like to read briefing books or spend time learning about the intricacies of foreign policy (Sciolino 6/16/2000). Richard Clarke, National Coordinator for Security, Infrastructure Protection, and Counterterrorism in the Clinton and Bush administrations, has rejected the conventional wisdom that Bush was lazy or dumb and instead asserts that 'When he focused, he asked the kind of questions that revealed a results oriented mind, but he looked for the simple solution, the bumper sticker description of the solution' (Clarke 2004: 277). This is certainly true of Bush's view of US foreign policy and international politics. Bush characterized his view of foreign policy as a 'distinctively American nationalism' and that the United States needs to seek 'a balance of power that favored freedom' (Bush 1999; Callinicos 2003). Daalder and Lindsay (2003) note that during the 2000 presidential campaign the president outlined a policy philosophy, which was in part informed by an 'instinct' about international relations. But they, like others, have observed that to understand the administration's foreign policy it is requisite to understand the views held by the president's advisors, particularly those that can be characterized as holding a neo-conservative philosophy.

The Bush advisors are not monolithic in all of their views of policy, but they do tend to share a basic common view of the international environment and what the United States needs to do to ensure its security. The views held by the advisors in the Bush administration are in fact not different from many of the administrations before it in that US foreign policy is designed to promote interests and values that are beneficial to the United States, but it is also understood that these are interests that are beneficial universally. However, what separated the Bush advisors from those in previous post-Cold War administrations, notably Clinton's, was the understanding of how the United States was to achieve its interests.

The belief is that since the decline of Soviet Union, the United States finds itself at a moment in history where it is the dominant power in the international community and as such should actively use its economic and military strength to shape the world so that it is compatible with US interests. Of course in exercising its power the United States will be serving the interests of other states. Despite the United States' hegemonic status there is a concern that if the US is not vigilant and unwilling to use its power it will find its position undermined. So, even though there is recognition that the United States is a dominant power, it is understood that the new environment is one of competition between states and that the United States can be challenged, which means that in order for the US to pursue its interest, it must enact polices that will either deter or suppress challengers.

Two critical features of US foreign policy that are based on this view is a willingness to use US military power and act unilaterally. The common understanding is that there are limitations to diplomacy and that in a world with innumerable threats the willingness to use military power is of paramount importance. Aside from a coercive tool the use of military force is believed crucial if the United States is going to play a leadership role within the international community. The belief is that during the Cold War the United States distinguished itself by using military force in the effort to demonstrate to allies that the United States is willing to protect their interests, which serves to bolster United States' role as hegemon (Callinicos 2003; Daalder 2003). The emphasis on military force finds its greatest expression in the 2002 National Security Doctrine, in which the administration asserts that when necessary the United States will 'pre-empt' emerging threats. In fact the administration in this document is not asserting US willingness to use force to pre-empt, but in a preventative fashion where the United States can 'counter sufficient threats' 'even if uncertainty remains as to the time and place of the enemy's attack' (2002 National Security Doctrine). But for the United States to ensure that it can pursue its interests, the United States must be willing to act alone, unencumbered by the constraints of agreements or international institutions. The rejection of multilateralism that has been a fundamental principle in US policy since the Woodrow Wilson administration is not absolute. Bush's advisors believe that acting in concert with other states has advantages and at times is desirable, but the commitment to multilateralism can not come at the expense of vital interests. During the campaign, the administration rejected as at odds with US interests the Kyoto Protocol on the environment, the International Criminal Court, the Comprehensive Test Ban Treaty, and United Nations operations that involved 'nation-building.' The latter was of particular concern because Bush and his new advisors believed that the Clinton administration throughout the 1990s had participated in a series of humanitarian interventions in which the United States had no direct interest. Most importantly, these overseas adventures squandered resources and contributed to the decline in the militaries readiness to fight and win a war. Although Bush personally did not have a well-developed foreign affairs philosophy, those that served in his administration did, and as a consequence of the president's management style their views informed the nature and direction of US policy.

With this orientation toward international affairs, during his campaign Bush and his advisors asserted sets of foreign and defense policy goals, enabling the United States to deal with a variety of potential challenges. Perhaps at the top of the administration's agenda during the campaign was a desire to protect the country from the threat of ballistic missiles, which meant the development of a ballistic missile defense shield that was already under development in the Clinton administration, but was not a top priority. It also meant that United States would withdraw from the 1972 Anti-Ballistic Missile Treaty which essentially prohibited both the United States and the Soviet Union from developing and deploying Ballistic missile systems. The belief was that the United States does not face the danger of a massive attack from a heavily armed state such as the Soviet Union, but instead the concern was that terrorists or rogue states that couldn't be deterred by US nuclear superiority would be willing to attack the United States with a limited number of nuclear weapons.

The focus on rogue states is indicative of the administration's concern with emerging threats. Bush and his advisors believed that the Clinton administration had weakened the US standing in the world because of the unwillingness to use US and economic strength to bring rogue states to heel; of particular concern were the threats posed by North Korea and Iraq. But it was not only with rogue states that the administration claimed that the United States needed to be concerned. Bush and his advisors, prior to his election, discussed openly rethinking the approach toward Russia and China. The policy of engagement adopted during the Clinton administration was seen as problematic because it failed to account for the fact that China was an emerging competitor and that at some point in the near future it was reasonable to believe that United States and Chinese interest would conflict and this might require the US to confront the Chinese (McCormick 2004: 194–195). The relationship with Russia also had to change because internal instability foreshadowed a return to aggressive policies with its neighbors and in the near term put the Russian nuclear arsenal in a precarious position. Bush and his advisors had a well-defined sense of the policy environment and the policy required to advance United States interests abroad.

The means for the administration to achieve their goals was a departure from the previous administration, however the international environment that the administration had to deal with was not radically different from that of the Clinton administration. Essentially, the environment was more stable than the one Clinton had adopted from George H.W. Bush. Clinton came into office having to deal with an ongoing crisis in the Balkans that seemed to be worsening, then with a series of internal conflicts in Somalia, Haiti, Rwanda, and later with the escalation in tensions on the Korean peninsula and in India and Pakistan, because of nuclear weapons.

Bush and his advisors' approach to foreign policy seemed an even greater departure from the past given the conditions extant in the international arena at the time that Bush took office. Unlike Clinton who came into office and immediately had to deal with a series of crises, George W. Bush assumed office at a period when there was relative stability, domestically and internationally, with the United States' position politically and economically secure. The close election against Al Gore and the recount of votes in Florida created acrimony among the American electorate to say the least, but the administration was assuming leadership in a domestic context that was prosperous. The United States experienced a period of adjustment as a result of the decline in the growth of the high technology sector, but United States gross domestic product was outpacing the other major advanced industrial nations, such as Germany and Japan. In fact 1994 to 2000 was a period characterized by low inflation and an unemployment rate below five percent. Moreover, the United States was benefiting from the liberalization of the global economy by way of free trade agreements, such as the North American Free Trade Agreement and international institutions, such as the International Monetary Fund and World Trade Organization (Wilson 2004). The expansion of free trade and the liberalization of global economy was the centerpiece of the Clinton administration's foreign policy and by 2000—the year of Bush's election —it had clearly produced results.

Not only did the United States possess economic dominance internationally, the administration took office at a time of political and military superiority. US military spending had begun to decline during the George H. W. Bush's administration, but to an extent stabilized during the Clinton years. Despite this change the United States expenditures on defense outstripped Britain, Russia, Japan, France, Russia, and China collectively (Wilson 2004: 298). The United States throughout the 1990s had been critical of its allies for neglecting to modernize their militaries and failing to contribute their fair share to the preservation of global security. With the exception of a growing terrorist threat which had not yet fully gained US attention there were no immediate threats to US security. The United States had been able to take advantage of the political environment to participate in the settlement of the Northern Ireland and Middle Eastern conflicts, in addition to working with Japan and South Korea to convince North Korea to give up its nuclear weapons ambitions. Equally, significant was the influence of American culture. The processes associated with globalization had allowed the United States to export its culture ranging from language, food, to television and movies and despite the objections of individuals in the United States abroad, US culture was having a significant impact (Wilson 2004).

The following is an analysis of the Bush administration's decision making before and after the September 11, 2001 terrorist attacks. The analysis is divided into these two periods because of the assumption that the administration's decision making undergoes a change after September 11. In times of crisis, leaders are going to be more involved in the development of policy and overall more attentive during the process. Preston and Hermann (2004) have made this very argument and in the immediate aftermath there will be a movement away from the hierarchic low centralization style of management toward one with greater presidential participation and to a degree greater control. However, the change will not be so profound that the president will abandon his preferred management style entirely and that over time—and perhaps on issues that are not immediately related to the crisis—the decision making will conform to the process produced by a hierarchic/ low centralization management style.

Pre-September 11: The First Eight Months

In December 2000, the president with the assistance of Dick Cheney and Andrew Card began the process of selecting the members of the cabinet and other major appointees. Some of the choices were quite clear and easy, such as Colin Powell as Secretary of State and Condoleezza Rice as National Security Advisor. But other positions turned out to be more contentious given the personal and ideological animosity that existed among Bush's choices. Particularly problematic were the choices for deputy Secretary of Defense and deputy Secretary of State. The reason for the difficulty was that there was concern in the new administration that if Richard Armitage was selected deputy Secretary of Defense that Colin Powell's influence in the administration would be enhanced, thus putting him in a position to dominate policy.[2] The ultimate solution was to appoint Armitage to the deputy position at the State Department and give the deputy position at the Department of Defense to Paul Wolfowitz where he would be reunited with Donald Rumsfeld with whom he worked on the Rumsfeld Commission. The driving force behind this selection of advisors was in part influenced by the desire to limit the ability of Colin Powell to dominate the policy process (Daalder and Lindsay 2003; Mann 2004).

Powell stood out from the rest of Bush's advisors because he did not adhere to the same set of ideological principles as the rest of the advisors. Whereas individuals like Cheney and Rumsfeld emphasize military strength and the willingness to use it, Powell is reluctant unless there is a clear interest, rules of engagement, and exit strategy. Also, Powell places a greater importance on maintaining multilateralism as a central part of US foreign policy. The implications of this were that Powell and Armitage—who shared the same set of views—stood in opposition to the views of the Vice President, and the two highest officials in the Defense Department. The President's choice of personnel and the positions in the administration ensured that there would be two extreme poles in the administration that would clash with one

---

[2] James Mann argues (Mann 2004: 275) that had the president created ideological diversity in the major departments by pairing Wolfowitz with Powell and Rumsfeld with Armitage that some of the internal conflict could have been avoided. Conflict of policy would have taken place within administrations and would have to be resolved between the secretary and their deputy. But the chosen arrangement guaranteed that conflict would characterize the relationship between the two most important foreign policy agencies.

another over the formulation of administration policy. Condoleezza Rice's role in the administration was an honestbroker.

In the first meeting of the National Security Council on January 20, 2000, according to Paul O'Neill, the president explained the way he would interact with his advisors and how they would interact with each other. Rice was to chair the NSC meetings and report the advisors views to the president when he was not in attendance (Suskind 2004: 70). The president also stated that he would meet regularly with his advisors one on one. There is some question as to which side Rice favors; ideologically her views are more compatible with the Cheney, Rumsfeld, and Wolfowitz than with Powell (Daalder and Lindsay 2003; Walcott and Hult 2004). Given that the individual advisors had access to the president and that Rice was playing the honestbroker, it was difficult to manage advisors in the administration as they clashed over policy. Richard Clarke has the secretary of defense asserting that he was going to do what he wanted to do irrespective of Rice's or Cheney's relationship to the president (Clarke 2004: 229). If nothing else, the influence of the vice president was enhanced because the two departments were brought into direct conflict with one another, opening the door for the vice president to be influential on the formulation of policy in a way that is uncharacteristic for vice presidents (Mann 2004: 275).

Kyoto Protocol and North Korea

As a result of the president's choice of management style combined with the ideological cleavage evident in the administration, the formulation of policy in the first eight months of the administration was characterized by conflict among the president's advisors with efforts by the advisors to isolate one another and exclude each other from the policy process, resulting in a series of dominant sub-set solutions. This is particularly true in relation to the administrations policy toward Korea, Iraq, Terrorism, and China. The issue of North Korean nuclear weapons was a policy that early in the administration demonstrated the policy process associated with Bush's management style. None of the new members of the administration supported the policy established during the Clinton administration. At the end of his administration, Clinton was planning to hold a summit with North Korean President Kim Jong Il in order to build on the agreement made with North Korean, Japan, and South Korea where North Korea would receive support for the development of civilian nuclear energy in exchange for halting the development of nuclear weapons technology. Bush's advisors all felt that the agreement did not go far enough in ensuring the North Koreans halted the program and eliminated the ability to develop a nuclear weapons program.

During February, the administration debated the specific stance the new administration needed to take toward North Korea (this was an urgent matter as the president would meet with South Korean president Kim Dae Jung in early March). Former Secretary of the Treasury Paul O'Neill states that throughout February there was 'give-and-take on the issue with Powell supporting the administration continuing negotiations with an interest in compelling the North Koreans to end its development and production of ballistic missiles. Powell's position was in stark contrast to Rumsfeld, Cheney and Wolfowitz that believed that continued negotiations with North Korea without their dismantlement of their programs and full inspections was tantamount to appeasement' (Suskind 2004: 113–115). The day before Kim Dae Jung's meeting with Bush, Powell publicly stated that the United States was looking forward to future discussions with North Korea, but that any agreement would have to involve full verification of the dismantlement of the North Korean program. It is assumed that Powell was making his statements as a representation of the administration's policy on North Korea. But the wording of Powell's comments proved problematic because they were interpreted as meaning that the Bush administration might be willing to continue the Clinton policy and quickly engage in negotiations or a summit.

The next day, before the president was to meet with Kim Dae Jung, he met with Cheney, Rice, Communications Director Karen Hughes, and Chief of Staff Andrew Card. It was decided that it needed to be made clear that the Bush administration's policy was a departure from Clinton's policy and that Powell had not accurately represented the president's position. The forces in the administration represented by the group that met with the president were able to effectively shut Powell out of the process and advanced a different set of preferences. Moreover, in O'Neill's account he had the impression that the decision to contradict Powell's statements was made quickly and that the president had to 'digest unfamiliar facts, balance complex competing claims with little context' (Suskind 2004: 115). If true, this further indicates that the president was not an active participant in the development of the policy and was clearly not the driving force behind the change. It is reasonable to assume that the collected advisors presented the president with a set of options of which they argued that continuing with the Clinton policy would be mistaken.

A number of different sources indicate that over the first several months of the administration that this pattern of decision making was the norm. Internal discussions would be engaged over the direction of policy, but ultimately a decision would be made to the surprise of many of the president's advisors that were a part of the process. The individuals most often excluded from these decisions were Colin Powell and Richard Armitage, because they found themselves at odds with a core group of the president's advisors on a range of issues. Powell, O'Neill, and Whitman found themselves cut out of the decision making on the administration's policy on the Kyoto Protocol. Once again the administration sought to beak with Clinton's policy which was supportive of ratification of the agreement even though there was staunch opposition in Congress preventing ratification. Again, Paul O'Neill presents an indication of how policy on Kyoto was formulated. Christine Todd Whitman, Energy Secretary met with Andrew Card and Condoleezza Rice to discuss the position the administration was to take at meetings between world governments on the Protocol and carbon dioxide. Whitman presented both advisors her plan on carbon dioxide emissions and it was her impression that both Card and Rice accepted the plan. But in March, before a public announcement, Whitman was informed that the administration was rejecting the Protocol and withdrawing from the negotiation process, citing the concern that the agreement was unfair because states such as India and China were exempted. O'Neill also indicates that it was his impression that the lack of specific direction on policy through the first three months and the discussions held by the energy task force headed by the Vice President exhibited a general anti-regulatory bent that did not bode well for Kyoto or Whitman's plans (Suskind 2004). But it was not only Whitman that was surprised by the turn in the administration, Powell was also caught off guard by the dramatic turn of the administration (Calabresi et al. 2001).

It seems that there were discussions taking place in the administration about the Kyoto Protocol, but that individuals such as Powell and Whitman were often not in attendance. Both were supportive of continuing the negotiations, but on different terms from that of the Clinton administration. Whitman had meetings with Card and Rice on different occasions and they never indicated that the policy would take a dramatically different direction, which might mean that either one or both were playing a gate-keeping role and ensuring that Whitman remained isolated. Alternatively, there were other advisors in the administration, such as the vice president, that were advancing a different agenda and potentially were able because of proximity to the president and ability to appeal to his concern for the business community and consequently capture the policy. It is clear that with regard to Kyoto and North Korea, the decision making process is characterized by conflict, with Rice playing the role of the honestbroker, advisors competing, and procedures for policy development being circumvented. The president was not an active participant and made his decision at the end of the process.

Confronting Terrorism?

In the months prior to Bush's election victory, the intelligence community was becoming increasingly concerned by the threat posed by international terrorism, particularly al Qaeda. In fact outgoing National Security Advisor Samuel Berger urged Condoleezza Rice to focus on terrorism in general and al Qaeda specifically (Campbell 2004). The Clinton administration had decided that in order to cripple al Qaeda the best strategy was to target Osama Bin Laden by tracking his movements and attacking him with armed unmanned aerial vehicles. However, this technology was still underdevelopment and it was not yet certain that it would work. There was no explicit rejection of this strategy by the Bush administration, but neither was there a well-developed policy or a clear interest in immediately dealing with Bin Laden. In January 2001, Richard Clarke, in his capacity as National Coordinator for Counterterrorism—the position he held in the Clinton administration—held individual meetings with members of the National Security Council, with the interest in drawing attention to the seriousness of the threat posed by al Qaeda. Richard Clarke continued his efforts to attract the attention of the president's closest advisors by urging Rice to call a NSC meeting to discuss the issue and develop a strategy. Rice informed Clarke that the issue would not be placed on the NSC's agenda until it had been first discussed and framed by the deputies committee responsible for terrorism, the Counterterrorism Strategy Group (CSG).

The first CSG meeting occurred in on April 30 and was chaired by Rice's deputy Stephen Hadley. Richard Clarke began the meeting by briefing the group on current policy and available options. Both Richard Armitage and Richard Clarke supported the continued development of the predator drone project, in addition to significant financial and material support to the Northern Alliance, the only remaining force left in Afghanistan that could pose a threat to al Qaeda's position in the country and the Taliban government. The only departure from the Clinton administration was that Armitage advocated not just focusing the elimination on Bin Laden and al Qaeda leadership, but destroying all of al Qaeda (Coll 2004). Paul Wolfowitz objected to Clarke's focus on Bin Laden and expressed that when it comes to terrorism that there were bigger threats than that posed by al Qaeda, namely Iraqi terrorism. Clarke rejected the notion that terrorism either sponsored by Iraq or initiated by Iraq was a serious threat. Neither side was willing to bend on their positions and the meeting ended with a compromise proposed by Hadley. The committee would continue to review some of the major issues such as funding for the Northern Alliance, the threat posed by al Qaeda and United States–Pakistani relations, which were considered important for fostering greater stability in the region (Clarke 2004).

As the deputies continued to review options the president was receiving threat reports in his Presidential Daily Brief and his morning discussions with Director of Central Intelligence George Tenet. In a moment of exasperation during the summer, Bush exclaimed that he wanted to 'bring this guy down' (referring to Bin Laden) and that he wanted to stop 'swatting flies' (Clarke 2004; Coll 2004). Beyond this one reported episode the president nor his principal advisors were heavily involved in the development of policy. Through the spring and into the early fall the CSG met and reviewed possible options. It was not until September 4, 2001 that the National Security Council principals met to begin the process of deciding on the administration's strategy for dealing with the growing terrorist threat. Bush advisors were presented with a draft of a National Security Presidential directive that laid out US policy toward al Qaeda and Afghanistan. The draft declared administration policy to be the elimination of both Bin Laden and al Qaeda and the means to do this was through support for the Northern Alliance and other anti-Taliban forces in Afghanistan, to which all in attendance agreed. The problem was that there was no meaningful discussion of where the funds would come from to support this policy. Disagreement arose over the use of the predator drone. There was clear interest in making use of this type of technology in the effort to decapitate the al Qaeda leadership, however neither the Central Intelligence Agency nor the Defense Department were willing to take full responsibility for operating the program. George Tenet was concerned about the risks resulting from a mistaken attack and the Defense Department was apprehensive because the drone had not yet proven itself as a combat weapon (Coll 2004).

Colin Powell called for placing diplomatic pressure on Pakistan to help in isolating and the Taliban and combating al Qaeda, but like the plan for assisting the Northern Alliance there were no resources to support these efforts. Secretary of Defense Rumsfeld was also more concerned with terrorist threats emanating from states like Iraq, a position also held by Paul Wolfowitz. Rice ended the meeting by instructing Richard Clarke to finalize the Directive as it related to the administration's position on al Qaeda, which was the elimination of Bin Laden and al Qaeda (Clarke 2004). As a result of the disagreement over the predator program, the lack of funding for the proposals in the Directive and the reluctance on the part of the Defense Department, however, the policy existed in name only. The Directive was essential based on the lowest common denominator among all of the principals at the meeting. All could agree that al Qaeda was a threat and that the United States needed to assertively deal with the threat, but this concealed the fact that the administration was not committed to a course of action and agreed on little else.

The policy process in this episode of decision making is interesting because it conforms to the way in which policy is supposed to be made according to the process stipulated in the NSPD-1. Policy was developed at the lowest levels of the administration and options formulated and passed up the hierarchy from the principals committee and then finally to the president who made the final decision. Disagreements existed in both the CSG and the principals committee, but individuals did not go outside of the process to advance their preferred policy. The policy resulted in papering over differences as the final directive on terrorism. So this particular episode of decision making does not match that predicted to be produced by a formal management style with low centralization. This might be explained by the priority given to the issue by the president and key members of the National Security Council. Despite the efforts of members of the previous administration, George Tenet, and Richard Clarke most of the major foreign policy advisors did not find the al Qaeda threat worthy of the top of the president's agenda, thus the issue was left to be dealt with by the deputies. Presumably, if the issue was perceived to carry the same weight as nuclear weapons—as in the case of North Korea—the administration collectively would have approached the issue differently. This indicates that the type and perceived value of an issue impact the choice of management style. In this case the management was formal, but centralization was not a factor because the president and his advisors were not significantly invested in the issue.

Invading Iraq

Pre-September 11. Since the end of the Gulf War in 1991, several of George W. Bush's advisors advocated for regime change in Iraq; in fact they believed an opportunity was lost when George H.W. Bush refused to continue the war in Kuwait by removing Saddam Hussein from power. Cheney, Rumsfeld, and Wolfowitz were adamant that Hussein posed a threat to the United States and was a source of instability within the region. As the new president came into office, Iraq was on the administration's agenda, but it was not clear exactly what US policy would be, other than a departure from the past. It was believed that the Clinton administration had allowed the sanctions regime to be eroded and that Hussein might be actively reconstituting his 'weapons of mass destruction' programs. As president-elect, Cheney had the traditional briefings by the Secretary of Defense and the Director of Central Intelligence specifically focus on the situation in Iraq the type of threat that Hussein posed.

The first National Security Council meeting of the new administration on January 30, 2001 was devoted to policy in the Middle East, but the majority of the meeting focused on Iraq. George Tenet gave the NSC, including the president, a briefing on the most recent intelligence on Iraq's weapons programs. Discussion quickly turned to a focus on what needed to be done in response to the threat that Hussein posed. Colin Powell asserted that the sanctions had been weakening and that the sanctions were having a greater impact on Iraqi citizenry which resulted in a loss of public support. Powell proposed targeted sanctions on material that could be used for weapons production, which would effectively contain the threat yet allow needed supplies to reach the citizens of Iraq. Bush remained silent through the meeting as other issues such as the quality of intelligence and the nature of the Iraq's weapons program were discussed. At the end of the meeting, Bush instructed Powell to devise a new set of sanctions and for Rumsfeld and Chairman of the Joint Chiefs of Staff Hugh Shelton to examine military options (Mann 2004).

The National Security Council met again on several occasions in February to further discuss the possible ways of dealing with Iraq, but the president did not attend any of these meetings. These meetings followed a pattern whereby Powell would advocate for the implementation of targeted sanctions and the most effective means for containing Saddam Hussein. But with each meeting Powell was confronted by Rumsfeld's skepticism regarding sanctions and the threat posed by Hussein's anti-aircraft weapons. Rumsfeld's contention was that targeted sanctions would not prevent Hussein from acquiring dual-use technology, which referred to equipment that could be purchased and used for civilian purposes, but if needed, be converted to military use. The Secretary of Defense also was concerned that despite the sanctions and the no-fly zones that had been in existence in northern and southern Iraq since the end of the Gulf War that United States and British aircraft were continually exposed to Iraqi anti-aircraft fire. At the same time that the principals clashed over the sanctions policy, the deputies committee addressed the extent of support for the Iraqi opposition, with the State Department and Defense Department at odds with one another. Wolfowitz proposed a strategy whereby the United States would seize control of Iraq's southern oil fields and from this enclave the United States would support opposition forces in Iraq. The State department opposed this plan as unfeasible. The deputies committee, by August, presented the principals with a strategy for Saddam's overthrow by a graduated application of pressure through diplomacy and support for opposition. The proposal then incited a discussion at the deputies and principals level over the circumstance that the military would be used to support the strategy.

Despite the meetings held by the deputies and the principals through the spring and summer months, no concrete policy was passed on to the president. The only outcome was that the president's advisors staked out opposing positions on the issue. Policy on Iraq during the first eight months of the Bush administration essentially deadlocked as neither side was willing to compromise on its position toward sanctions and regime change in Iraq. If anything the State Department and the Defense Department went about formulating independent of one another. The president played no role in the process other than expressing an interest in bringing about change in the Iraqi leadership and for the principals to develop a policy. At this stage in the development of the policy towards Iraq there is evidence of either of the sides in the debate going outside of the committee system. However, based on comments made by Colin Powell during this period there is an indication that individuals in the administration were individually appealing to the president to take an aggressive stance on Iraq, which was compatible with the policy developed in the Defense Department. Powell's actions demonstrate the extent to which individual advisors were seeking to influence the direction of policy.

Iraq Post-September 11

The weekend after the terrorist attacks on the World Trade Center and Pentagon on September 11, 2001, Bush convened his national security team at Camp David to contemplate a course of action against the terrorists. Attorney General John Ashcroft, DCI George Tenet, and FBI Director Robert Mueller all gave presentations on efforts to enhance security. The conversation largely revolved around Afghanistan and what the possible options were for rooting out the terrorists hosted by the Taliban government. Paul O'Neill recounts that at this meeting National Security Advisor Rice raised the issue of combating threats beyond Afghanistan, which provided an opportunity for Paul Wolfowitz to address the threat posed by Iraq (Suskind 2004). In fact over the course of the weekend Rumsfeld and Lewis Libby raised the threat posed by Iraq. All three argued that attacking al Qaeda would be ineffective without addressing the states that supported and harbored terrorists. Wolfowitz specifically argued for a link between al Qaeda and Iraq and that Iraq was a greater threat because of its weapons of mass destruction. Given this link, Wolfowitz proposed pursuing Saddam Hussein since he would be easier to topple than trying to root out al Qaeda from Afghanistan. Powell objected to Wolfowitz's arguments, because he was a skeptical of a link and believed that there would be no international support unless there was clear evidence that Iraq was involved (Woodward 2002).

The first meeting of the weekend ended with no clear decision on a strategy, but the president let it be known during sessions that he wanted to focus debate on Afghanistan and Iraq. In between sessions Rice met with Powell, Rumsfeld, Tenet, and Chief of Staff Andrew Card and reiterated that the discussions needed to be more focused. In the second meeting of the weekend, the president went around the room listening to recommendations from Powell, Cheney, Rumsfeld, Tenet, and Card on what approach to take in dealing with the terrorists. Both Powell and Rumsfeld raised the issue of Iraq. Powell reiterated his contention that an attack on Iraq would be a mistake as there would be no international support for a campaign against Iraq. Rumsfeld argued against Powell, suggesting that another coalition could be formed to remove Saddam Hussein. However, Rumsfeld did not recommend that the president address Iraq at this point, nor did he reject the option (Woodward 2002). Powell was joined in his opposition to mounting military action against Iraq at this time by Cheney, Tenet, and Card. When the meeting ended there was still not a clear strategy in place for Afghanistan and it was unclear exactly what the president thought about military action in Afghanistan.

On September 17 after the weekend at Camp David the president met with the National Security Council. As it related to Iraq, the president decided that no action was to be taken at that time, because he believed that the administration did not have evidence of Iraqi complicity. There the issue remained until November 17, 2001 when after a NSC meeting Bush pulled Rumsfeld aside and asked him what kind of war plan was available for Iraq. Rumsfeld indicated that the plan was essentially an expanded version of the plan used in the Gulf War in 1991. The president directed Rumsfeld and Tommy Franks, Commander in Chief for Central Command, to begin reviewing and developing the war plan. In his instructions, the president made it clear that at this early stage that the only advisors to be involved should be Franks and Rumsfeld; others would be included later in the process. No other parties were involved until December 28 when Franks presented to the NSC his plan for an invasion. The president complimented Franks on his work and told Powell and Rumsfeld that they would have to work on the political dimensions of the plan. As Rumsfeld and Franks continued to develop the war plan, debate in the administration erupted around the means and the timing of removing Saddam Hussein from power.

The lines of division in the administration were the same as before September 11 with Powell, Armitage, and Tenet versus Cheney, Rumsfeld, and Wolfowitz. All agreed that something needed to be done about Saddam Hussein and that the ultimate goal was to bring about regime change in Iraq, but the two sides disagreed about the use of military force in creating change. Rumsfeld and Cheney believed that the Hussein regime was weak and that a combination of airpower and opposition forces in coordination with special forces could be effective in toppling the regime. Powell still believed that targeted sanctions supported by a credible threat of military force backed by a broad-based coalition could effectively contain Hussein. Powell was concerned that the president and those in the administration advocating for the use of force did not appreciate the difficulties of overthrowing Hussein. They were, in his view, underestimating the danger of the country descending into civil and religious conflict (Mann 2004). Over the course of the Summer, the war plan continued to develop, particularly after the president's January 'Axis of Evil' speech during which he highlighted the threats posed by Iraq, Iran, and North Korea. In effect, Powell had become isolated in the administration, as he had little time to discuss his views with the president on the planning and the use of force in Iraq (Mann 2004). This is significant given that Rumsfeld was constantly meeting one-on-one with the president during this time.

Because of the momentum building and his deepening isolation, Powell asked Rice to set up a private meeting with the president. Powell wanted the opportunity to present a point of view that he believed was not being represented or discussed by other individuals in the administration. In a dinner meeting on August 5, Powell presented his position to the president, emphasizing the potential fallout for the region if the United States invaded and the need to have an international coalition. Powell urged the president to consider requesting from the United Nations a return of weapons inspectors before taking any unilateral military action. The president asked few questions, but did not demonstrate any resistance to Powell's ideas (Woodward 2004).

The NSC met on August 14, without the president, with the purpose of building a consensus on the presidential directive developed in the deputies committee, specifying the administration's policy toward Iraq. Powell suggested the need to include in the policy an effort to build a international support, which would be particularly important if they were to keep the support of the British. Powell and Rice both supported the idea of the president speaking at the UN where he could call for a unified international effort to deal with the situation in Iraq. Cheney disliked the idea because he was concerned that if the UN had proved ineffective in dealing with Iraq it would result in no action (Mann 2004). But if it was necessary to go to the UN, Cheney and Rice wanted the president to highlight the UN's failure to deal with this problem and that the UN was a part of the problem. The meeting ended with all agreeing to recommend that the president make a speech at the UN. Two days later, the NSC met with the president and he approved the presidential directive, including the decision to make a speech to the United Nations.

Cheney was not satisfied with the idea of including the UN in the process and the possibility that the policy was shifting away from the assertive use of force. Cheney asked the president if he could state the administration's position in light of the challenges coming from many quarters outside of the administration. Bush agreed, but did not know the details of what Cheney would say in his speech. In his comments, Cheney rejected the utility of the UN as solution to the problem and that it was certain that Saddam Hussein had weapons of mass destruction. Cheney's statements were not official policy and were a departure from statements made by other members of the administration, including the president (Woodward 2004). Although the speech intensified the disagreements in the administration, the president was still committed to going forward with his UN speech.

Although the president weighed in and was committed to addressing the United Nations, his advisors continued to oppose one another as they began to debate what the president should say to the UN. The debate specifically revolved around whether or not the president should request a new resolution ordering inspectors back into Iraq. It was decided that the president would make his speech on September 12 and two days before the speech Cheney and Powell continued to argue over the virtues of a resolution calling for inspections. However, the night before the speech the president assured Powell that he was going to make the case for a new resolution (Woodward 2004).

Bush announced in his speech before the United Nations that the United States would work with international community to seek a resolution. For the administration this meant they had to ensure that a resolution was adopted that was compatible with their objectives, but this was a challenge since there were differences among Bush's advisors regarding what should be included in the resolution. Rumsfeld and Cheney urged the president to propose a resolution that required the creation of no-fly and no-drive zones in areas where the inspectors were working. In addition, there would be no areas exempt from inspections, as in the past and the permanent members of the UN Security Council would be allowed to deploy their own inspectors. Most importantly, if it was determined that Iraq was in 'material breach' there would be automatic authorization for the US or any other states to take whatever steps to gain compliance (Woodward 2004). This provision essentially authorized the US to use force. Powell presented the proposed resolution to the other permanent members of the Security Council, but all rejected it, because of the automatic trigger.

Powell informed the NSC of the Security Council's objections and he was able, with the approval of the president, to present a modified version, requiring the Security Council to assess the violation before taking action. But Cheney insisted that the administration add a provision to the resolution, calling for Hussein to present a full report on his weapons programs. Cheney believed that if Hussein did not present the report or claimed he had no weapons then he could be found in violation of the resolution. Rice supported this additional change and Powell was willing to present it to the Security Council.

Negotiations began between Powell and France's Foreign Minister Dominique de Villepin, because France had presented itself as the lead of opposition to the use of force in Iraq. As Powell negotiated he was able to make modifications, but was limited because he knew what the president and other advisors expected. A final agreement turned on whether there could be agreement regarding the conditions that qualified as a material breach. Ultimately, it was agreed that Hussein had to present a false declaration and fail to cooperate.

On November 8, 2002, the Security Council passed resolution 1441 authorizing renewed inspections and requiring Iraq to present a declaration of his weapons program. Iraq's report was presented to the United Nations' chief weapons inspector Hans Blix. By this time the president had grown increasingly impatient with the process as he received updates on the activities of the inspectors and actions of the Iraqis. In Woodward's account (2004), by the end of December the president decided that the inspections regime was not going to be effective and that the United States had to go to war. According to Woodward, Bush knew the views of all of his advisors and did not feel the need to ask them for their views. During Christmas vacation at his ranch in Texas, Bush told Rice that they were probably going to have to go to war and it was Rice's impression that the president had already made up his mind (Woodward 2004). In the first two weeks of January, Bush informed Rumsfeld of his decision and later Powell. The president decided privately, but it would be two more months before the administration publicly asserted its dissatisfaction with the inspections and committed itself to going to war.

Conclusion

In the months prior to September 11, the Bush administration's decision-making process is characterized by conflict among advisors, the attempt by advisors to circumvent the established procedures, a gatekeeper that represents the interests of all advisors, but has minimal impact on the conflict in the administration, and the president plays a role at the end of the process when he must chose an option. The decision outcomes examined were instances of dominant-subset solutions in the North Korea and Kyoto cases, but in the case of terrorism policy the disagreement in the administration was resolved by papering over differences. Thus, in the first eight months of the Bush administration his management style produced the type of decision-making process found in the advisory system framework. The notable deviation was the absence of conflict on the construction of the administration's terrorism policy. This episode is different because the advisors did not circumvent the process and worked through the main committees, but this result was due to the lack of interest by both the president and some other key advisors.

The decision making on Iraq in the period prior to September 11 is also compatible with a formal structure with low centralization. The president was not heavily involved in the process, which became deadlocked when the Defense Department and the State Department were unable to advance their vision of US policy on Iraq. There was a clear consensus that there had to be regime change in Iraq, but none on the means, level of force, or targeted sanctions. September 11 changed the dynamic within the administration for two main reasons. First, the attack on the United States confirmed the ideological beliefs held by members of the administration, such Wolfowitz, Cheney, and Rumsfeld. As previously discussed, all held a view that even though the United States was a dominant world power, there were threats in the international community that could endanger US interests. Although they believed that the main threats would come from states, particularly rogue states and not terrorists, September 11 made their arguments about US policy and interests all the more credible.

The second change was Bush's attitude toward foreign policy and attention to decision making. The type of crisis created by the terrorist attacks compels a leader to be more attentive to decision making. Leaders under these conditions often reduce the number of advisors they work with and become heavily involved in formulations and deliberation of options. Following the attacks, Bush met more frequently with his principal advisors and held longer morning briefings with George Tenet (Burke 2004). Hermann and Preston

(2004) assert that Bush's past patterns of delegation and lack of interest gave way in response to terrorism; however, the case of Iraq suggests that either his change did not apply to all issues or his change was not as transformative as believed.

In examining the decision-making process post-September 11 there are patterns consistent with the decision making in the first eight months of the administration. The conflict and bargaining continues on Iraq policy with a deepening divide between the Defense Department/Cheney and Powell. Advisors are still circumventing the process and attempting to advance their preferred policy. This was evident during with Powell's attempt to shift the move to war in August 2002 in his private meeting with the president, which was in response to the efforts by others in the administration to keep the Secretary of State isolated. This type of behavior was also demonstrated by Vice President Cheney when he made public statements on the administration's position on Iraq as if he were discussing the agreed policy, which was not the case. Rice continues to play the role of gatekeeper acting as an honestbroker among all of Bush's advisors. These similarities with previous decision-making processes are important because they indicate that on a certain level the president is not actively managing the process, he is not preventing individuals access, and has not put in place the means to either exclude opposition or manage conflict.

The difference between the Iraq decision-making process and previous episodes is that Bush is more involved in managing the development of policy. Bush begins the process of planning on Iraq by directing Rumsfeld to review the existing war plans. This is indicative of the fact that Bush is taking the lead in developing policy, but there is some question as to who could have been potentially influencing the president's thinking. While Bush was still president-elect, Cheney and others emphasized the danger from Iraq and after September eleventh Cheney was one Bush's advisors to suggest that the administration needed to deal with the Iraqi threat. The president was asked if he was influenced by Cheney in his decision to move forward with Iraq and Bush's response was that he could not recall if he had spoke to Cheney (Woodward 2004: 4). Bush delegated the actual planning to Rumsfeld and Franks, but he was continually briefed on the evolutions of the war plans, so the president was actively involved in overseeing the development of plans. Overall, the president was more definitive in stating his preferences and ensuring that these ideas were reflected in the development of policy. This in part contributes to Powell's difficulty in changing the course of administration policy, because Cheney, Rumsfeld, and Wolfowitz were constructing policy that best fit the president's desired goals. In looking at the president's final decision to go to war, a different approach is followed.

If it is true that the president decided on his own without any other consultation, this is an instance of the president deliberating on his own and choosing a policy. The argument can be made that the president was already committed to go ahead with an invasion, which may be the case, but the fact that he made the final decision to break with the UN and pursue unilateral action demonstrates a different approach to the policy process. This change by the president is significant because it means that the president increased his level of centralization over the process from the low levels that existed before the terrorist attacks, while retaining a formal structure. Bush changed his management style in the course of his administration moving to one that is more formal and centralized. Bush's decision-making processes were originally like that of Reagan; however, after the terrorist attacks Bush instituted mechanisms to control involvement and the flow of information, which is similar to Nixon's decision-making style.

Chapter 8

Advisory System Framework

This research elucidates variations in presidential decision-making, hypothesizing that four different choices of management style yield four different types of decision-making processes. The goal of the research has not been to take issue with how a given president chooses a management style. It is known that presidents will choose either a formal or collegial structure based on factors such as cognitive needs and experience. Presidents also make choices regarding how centralized they are going to make the process, and, this degree of centralization has implications for the decision-making process. Thus, a president's choice of advisory structure and level of centralization are key factors in determining how their administration will deliberate and formulate policy. In this sense, the interest of this research is not to completely dispense with the categories created by previous typologies that have used similar variables, but to improve upon their utility. The task in these pages has been to better specify the ideal policy processes that different management styles produce, thereby enhancing our understanding of how presidents make policy. This study has not sought to discuss how specific policies are chosen. There are both methodological and conceptual problems associated with determining what kinds of policies will be produced by a specific process. However, the typology has sought to move toward linking management style and policy outcome by determining the kind of decision outcomes that each decision-making process produces. Identifying decision outcomes is achieved by explaining how each decision-making process resolves internal disagreements over policy.

If a president alone decides the direction of policy, then disagreements among advisors at the deliberative stage have little impact on the decision-making process. In the event that the president has not made a unilateral decision then policy must be formulated, deliberated, and, finally, chosen. It is inevitable that during this process disagreements will arise among decision makers over the agenda, goals, and means for attaining their objectives. Disagreement and conflict are endemic parts of the policy process and as such are a critical link in the process leading to a decision outcome. An advisory system may resolve a disagreement by compromise, leading to the production of a policy that was not planned by any of the participants, or, one advisor or group of advisors may be in a position to end a disagreement by successfully advancing their policy preferences over other advisor(s). Alternatively, no solution to a policy dispute may be found and no effective action may be taken by the administration.

If we are to understand how policy is made then it is incumbent on foreign policy analysts to provide an accurate representation of the process of deliberation and choice. To date this has been an understudied area in US foreign policy scholarship. The process itself in many cases has been treated the same way many international relations scholars treat the role of governments in the international system, as nothing more than 'black boxes.' Mainstream International Relations theories explain how international and domestic factors come to bear on the decision-making unit and, like Athena from the head of Zeus, policy springs forth. What is missing from our understanding of decision-making is a clear understanding of how the interactions and deliberations between president and advisors shape and direct the nature of policy.

The Advisory System Framework was examined using the method of structured-focused comparisons, which presented a systematic assessment of the decision-making in the Nixon, Carter, Reagan, Clinton and Bush administrations. The five case studies examined in the previous chapters offer strong support for the proposition that structure and centralization create variations in the decision-making process in very predictable ways. The Bush case study was not full assessment, but a partial one, because of the lack of specific details on the administrations decision making. The episodes of decision making found in the four other cases of presidential decision making present strong support for the new framework (Table 8.1). But it should be noted that some of the characteristics were not consistently present and, although these expected differences are not enough to put the framework into doubt, they are worth noting not only because of what they say about the management and decision-making process of an individual presidency, but also because of what they say about a particular type of management style in general.

The Nixon administration's negotiations with the North Vietnamese from February 1969 to January 1973 are consistent with the decision-making process predicted for an administration that has a formal structure and there is high centralization over the process. Almost all of the features of the hypothesized decision-making process were present in the case. In almost every episode found in the Nixon case, Nixon expressed a general preference that shaped consideration of options, a gatekeeper (Kissinger) acted as an advocate who screened information, dissenting voices were actively excluded, Nixon evaluated presented options and almost all disagreements were resolved by dominant solutions, meaning the solution to disagreement reflected the president's preferences. There were some noteworthy exceptions. Nixon's active deliberation with Kissinger on policy was not a stated expectation of the

Table 8.1 Advisory System Decision-Making Processes

Nixon Administration	Carter Administration	Reagan Administration	Clinton Administration
Leader evaluates presented options **Percentage: 75%**	Leader is an active member of the group, guiding and shaping deliberations **Percentage: 57%**	Leader chooses between presented options **Percentage: 87%**	Willingness to delegate authority to others that have expertise **Percentage: 100%**
Leader expresses general preference shaping consideration of options **Percentage: 100%**	Leader pushes group to assess range of options **Percentage: 71%**	Advisors compete to get preferences presented to leader **Percentage: 87%**	Advisors instrumental in guiding policy **Percentage: 100%**
Gatekeeper acts as advocate and screens information and access **Percentage: 87%**	Emphasis on building consensus among core set of advisors **Percentage: 71%**	Gatekeeper acts as honest-broker and presents options (opportunity for other advisors to appeal to leader) **Percentage: 62%**	Less emphasis on consensus building among advisors **Percentage: 55%**
Discouragement of bargaining and conflict in group; dissenting voices excluded **Percentage: 87%**	Shared responsibility for decisions **Percentage: No Evidence**	Bargaining and conflict take place at level below President **Percentage: 75%**	Conflict and bargaining between advisors **Percentage: 89%**
Orderly policy-making with well-defined procedures **Percentage: 37%**	Meetings are regularized and frequent with core advisors **Percentage: 71%**	Procedures may be circumvented **Percentage: 75%**	No regular mode of interacting with advisors **Percentage: 100%**
Dominant solution **Percentage: 87%**	Integrative solution **Percentage: 71%**	Dominant-Subset solution or deadlock **Percentage: 62%**	Subset solution/deadlock **Percentage: 67%**

decision-making process. It was anticipated that highly centralized systems with a formal structure would produce a decision-making process in which the president institutes a rigid structure that allows them to remain aloof from deliberations. The president's role is to choose between options determined by advisors. However, Nixon's behavior deviates from this anticipated behavior because of his active participation in deliberations with his National Security Advisor. Nixon's behavior can be attributed to his need to maintain control over the process and ensure that policy reflected his views and/or a reflection of his interest in foreign affairs. Superficially, it seems as if Nixon has deviated from his preferred way of making decisions, but in fact his behavior is quite consistent. Active participation with his gatekeeper—Kissinger—ensured that the secrecy of the Paris talks was maintained and the talks were immune from internal opposition and leaks from within the administration. Thus Nixon continued to maintain high centralization with a truncated formal structure.

The sole characteristic of the decision-making process that was not consistently found throughout all eight episodes was a well-ordered policymaking process with well-defined procedures. Despite having constructed an elaborate committee structure and set of procedures for making decisions, most of this infrastructure was neglected or abandoned. The policy process and the procedures were subject to change as and when it suited Nixon's needs. When it was necessary to hold frequent meetings to decide on the escalation of bombing, Nixon did so; but when Nixon needed to act quickly without the complications brought about by lengthy consultations, he acted accordingly. What is important is that Nixon was conscious of the decisions he was making and these changes in procedure reflect the high degree of control he was exercising over the flow of information and participation.

Jimmy Carter's management style, like Nixon's, emphasized high centralization of the decision-making process, but Carter structured his advisors' deliberations in a collegial manner. As a result Carter guided and shaped deliberations, advisors assessed a range of options, building consensus was important, there was a sense of shared responsibility, meetings were frequent and regularized, and solutions tended to be integrative. In the seven episodes of Carter's negotiations with the Soviet Union on strategic weapons limitations, all of the characteristics of the decision-making process are found with the exception of two—shared responsibility and the characteristic 'emphasis on building consensus,' which was not anticipated.

There was no indication from any of the episodes for shared responsibility for any of the decisions made. The lack of any verbal indication might be explained by the fact that a sense of shared responsibility is implicit in the relationship between president and advisors and may not be readily observable. Shared sense of responsibility is perhaps better understood as loyalty and it can be inferred from the comments of Deputy National Security Advisor David Aaron (2002) that there was a high degree of loyalty at both the cabinet and sub-cabinet levels. The loyalty at these levels can be compared to the lower levels of loyalty found further down in the bureaucracy among those individuals that may not owe their position to the president or might possess different ideological views. A third alternative is that the ability to work toward a consensus when unprompted and the willingness to integrate ideas among advisors was driven by a belief that the deliberators had a stake in the policy chosen and in the final outcome. Which one of these explanations is most accurate is difficult to assess; the third is the most plausible explanation and seems the most unique to this kind of advisory system. The third explanation is the most plausible because it accepts that the advisory system characteristics are interrelated and that sense of responsibility is the product of the interaction between characteristics.

Unlike shared responsibility, emphasis on building consensus was found, but the president did not push for this consensus. In two episodes there is no indication that any kind of consensus was reached before a final decision was made and in four other episodes consensus was built, but it was built within the context of the Special Coordinating Committee (SCC). The reason that Carter's advisors used the SCC as a forum for building consensus without his prompting was that it was understood that this committee was the forum for generating and deliberating options and for building consensus on issues. The president's advisors operated according to the president's will, which was established at the beginning of the administration. This was one of the rare instances where a president gave very specific directions regarding how his advisors should conduct their deliberations. Thus the president explicitly established a norm for decision making that influenced the SCC proceedings. In addition to the activities of the SCC, consensus was further built by Vance, Brown, and Brzezinski during their weekly meetings. These meetings allowed the principals to engage in an open discussion on issues and problems without being encumbered by additional participants.

The building of consensus among advisors in committees is found in both types of collegial systems, exemplified by the Carter and Clinton administrations, which indicate that collegial advisory structures create an atmosphere that is conducive or requires advisors to generate consensus. But what is interesting is the lack of interest on the part of Carter in pursuing a consensus before making a decision, while Clinton on occasion did seek one. The answer to this discrepancy may be found, oddly enough, in the examination of the Nixon administration whose management style is not designed to produce consensus. In a couple of instances when Nixon was contemplating the increased use of force there is evidence that he pursued consensus among close political advisors like Mitchell and Connally, but also from Secretary of State Rogers and Secretary of Defense Laird, who were typically excluded from the process. In these episodes, the policies being deliberated could bring high costs for the administration if they were not successful, thus it was reasonable for the president to pursue broad agreement on administration policy. The same explanation can hold for Clinton who had to consider policies that required the use of force, which was a significant departure from previous administration's policy. Like Nixon, Clinton may have sought broad support and input on the policy before finally deciding. One conclusion that we can draw is that presidents might be inclined to build a consensus among a limited group of advisors when considering the use of force, particularly in instances where the use of force is considered a serious escalation of hostility or dramatic shift in policy.

Reagan's decision-making process, during the period under examination, is in line with a formal/low centralized system because he chose between presented options and advisors competed to get ideas presented to the president. For the most part, bargaining and conflict took place among the president's advisors, but on only two occasions did the intense conflict between the State Department and the Defense Department spill over into meetings where Reagan was in attendance. Similarly, in only two of the eight episodes did the advisors follow stipulated procedures. After access and participation in the deliberation process were confined to the National Security Council, the process became more organized and orderly, but, by this stage, differences within the administration were so entrenched that the production of policy became impossible regardless of changes in the decision-making structure. The divisions in the administration were so deep that dialogue and deliberation were impossible because no one was willing to make concessions to the opposition.

But, again, two features of the formal structure/low centralization system stand out because of the unexpected findings in a number of episodes. Anyone involved with foreign policy making would describe one of the roles of the National Security Advisor to be an honest-broker who ensures that the president hears all of the views of his principal advisors; during the Reagan Administration, not all of the National Security Advisors functioned in this way. Robert McFarlane acted as an advocate and sided with the State Department in bureaucratic battles, and yet, when it came to writing National Security Directives, McFarlane often tried to ensure that the views of the opposition were considered. McFarlane, when dealing with the president, pushed for specific sets of policy preferences, even though he recognized that those in the administration who held different views could not be ignored. In the second and third episodes, the data does not indicate that anyone was playing the role of honest-broker. Caspar Weinberger (2002) has noted that early in the administration, NSA William Clark was playing the role of honest-broker. The fact that there is no evidence for this behavior might be a result of an individual who is facilitating the access of others and has not insinuated himself into the process.

The exceptions discussed above are not sufficient to throw the framework into doubt, but they are significant enough that they should be noted. The same holds true for the unstructured solutions that were found in the Reagan case. In the Reagan type of advisory system, it was expected that solutions to disagreements will either be dominant-subset solutions or they will result in deadlock. However, in three of the episodes, instead of resolving disagreements with a dominant subset or deadlocking, Reagan's advisors papered over differences. Papering over differences is similar to deadlock in that both are ways of avoiding making decisions when none of the participants in the deliberations is willing to compromise.

The main difference between the two is that in instances of deadlock no decision is made with the implication being that the status quo is preserved. The status quo may mean no policy is formulated to deal with an issue or that the administration must continue with existing policy. Papering over differences, on the other hand, means that policy is made but that policy is comprised of the preferences of all those involved in deliberations, which is similar to the idea of a 'resultant' associated with the bureaucratic politics model. Since no group or individual is willing to compromise and the president is not controlling the process or has not imposed an effective mechanism for resolving disputes, differences are not overcome. The only way to construct policy to avoid absolute deadlock is to create a policy to which everyone contributes; the unintended consequence of such a way of making policy is that the policy is possibly internally contradictory and will not address an issue to anyone's satisfaction.

An alternative way of thinking about the relationship between deadlock and papering over differences is to consider that papering over differences is a means of covering up a deadlock instead of an inability to arrive at an agreed policy. When papering over differences is used for this purpose it allows the president and advisors the ability to conceal the fact that they have deadlocked over policy. In the intervening time, papering over differences presents an opportunity to break the deadlock between advisors or search for more information.

The analysis of the Clinton administration's decision-making on Bosnia, also, fits the pattern of decision making predicted by the collegial/low centralization system. Clinton showed consistently, throughout all ten episodes, a willingness to delegate authority to others and no regular mode of interacting with advisors. Clinton met with Anthony Lake, his National Security Advisor, in the mornings for his briefings, but when it came to deliberations on Bosnia the president participated in some meetings, at others he attended only part of the time, and some meetings he did not attend at all. Consequently, across all episodes Clinton's advisors were instrumental in guiding policy, which was evident from the inconsistent nature of the administration's attitude toward using force. Given this atmosphere, decision making was typically associated with conflict and bargaining.

It was hypothesized that during the Clinton administration's formulation of policy toward Bosnia there would be less emphasis on building consensus among advisors. In about half of the episodes this was the case; there was little evident emphasis on ensuring that consensus was established before a decision was made, but in the other half there were efforts to build a consensus. In these episodes consensus was not necessary when making a final decision, rather, consensus was generated among advisors while they were narrowing, eliminating, or refining options. If consensus played a role in deliberations, it did so at the early stages, but later when Clinton was finally ready to decide on policy in most cases there was no need to find a consensus among his core advisors.

The Clinton administration's decision making also presented a surprise in the variety of ways that disagreements were resolved. Consistent with this type of decision-making structure, most of the episodes contained subset solutions. Indeed, the final four decisions in the case were subset solutions, but prior to these final decisions, there were often periods of deadlock. This outcome is not surprising given the fits and starts of the policy-making process, but two of the four remaining episodes were integrative solutions and the other two were situations involving the papering over differences. Two integrative solutions are not surprising, given that the claim here is not that the policy process will result in only subset and deadlock, but that collegial/low centralization will tend more toward subset and deadlock. Interestingly, two instances of integration of policy ideas took place at times when proposals made by the allies served as the basis for making policy. The proposals put forth by the European countries acted to build a point of commonality between the opposing forces in the administration, which presented an opportunity for compromise. One could posit that had the president had been more effective in expressing a clear set of preferences, his preferences could have served as an engine for compromise within the administration.

In addition to the two unexpected instances of integrative solutions, the Clinton decision-making process, in two episodes, provided evidence for papering over differences. Like the instances of papering over differences found in the Reagan case, the resolution of disagreements in this manner was not predicted anywhere in the framework. When the papering over differences occurred, the president was not in a position or willing to resolve the disagreements that existed among his advisors and, consequently, he resorted to adopting a range of policy options that essentially drew on a range of proposals without reconciling differences. The presence of papering over differences in low centralization advisory systems may indicate that this type of outcome arises in decision-making processes in which the president is unwilling or unable to control the situation by expressing a set of preferences.

This would include instances in which the process does not have a gatekeeper that can help the president work at or force compromise. Two of the instances of papering over differences came at the beginning of deliberations on an issue, which may indicate that at the beginning of administrations with low centralization there is a tendency to engage in this behavior. At the beginning, when policy is first being formulated, there is a greater degree of uncertainty about objectives and there is an urgency for interested advisors to advance their preferences.

Despite the dearth of information on the specifics of the decision making in the Bush administration, there is enough information that allows an explanation of the decision-making process. Bush explicitly choose a style of management that called for an delegation and for the president to make the final decision. This is a management style where there is an emphasis on a formal structure with low centralization. As a consequence, the decision-making process will be characterized by conflict between advisors that circumvent established procedures in order to advance their preferences. The gatekeeper acts as honestbroker and the president chooses between presented options. Disagreements in the administration with either be dominant-subset or deadlock. The Bush administration's decision making should look very similar to the Reagan administration's, which was exactly the case in the months before September 11. The exception during this period of time was the administration's terrorism policy where the disagreements were resolved by papering over differences. Again this was not originally an expected decision outcome, but it is an outcome that is consistently found in administration's with low centralization. What is truly unique about the Bush administration is the change in decision-making process, which is a result of a change in management style. Bush became more attentive and active in the process after the events of September 11. The president, while not active in managing conflict and the flow of information, gave greater direction to the process by increasing his monitoring of the process and the assertion of his preferences. Combined this gave a greater degree of focus in the administration, by giving a voice for those in the administration that preferred an aggressive unilateral strategy against Iraq. But the president did not increase his control over the who participated in the process, thus conflict continued among Bush's advisors.

The framework presents foreign policy analysis with a better tool for understanding how different management styles create different decision-making processes. In sum, the major finding of this work is that the administrations under examination went about formulating foreign policy according to the advisory systems theory of decision making with a few notable exceptions. There are a number of findings that are significant because of their contribution toward our understanding of the decision-making process (Table 8.2). The second major finding highlights that the decision-making process is neither dominated by the president nor are presidential preferences all that matter. The variety of advisory systems demonstrates that depending on the centralization of the process presidents, to a significant degree, are constrained by their own advisory system, and, as a consequence, advisors can and will have the ability to shape and influence the direction of policy. The framework serves as a useful starting point in a further discussion of how advisors influence policy, particularly how they use tactics.

Table 8.2 Summarized Findings

- The four case studies overall support the decision-making processes represented in the typology.
- Presidents rarely change their advisory systems once they are established. Indeed, presidents become bound by their advisory systems and it is only after prolonged inability to formulate policy or policy failure that they will adjust the advisory system.
- The range of unstructured solutions goes beyond dominant, deadlock, subset, and integrative. Advisory systems often resolve internal disputes by resorting to papering over differences, which is related to, but distinct from, deadlock.
- In collegial systems consensus is not actively sought by the president, instead it is often generated among advisors as a function of the chosen collegial structure.
- In instances when force is being contemplated, presidents across advisory systems will open up the group of advisors and seek a broader consensus.

It is also clear from these cases that decision-making groups resolved disagreements by 'papering over differences' which was not an expected feature of the decision-making process. However, in low centralized systems this form of dispute resolution arose in a number of episodes and this indicates that the range of 'unstructured solutions' is larger than the four originally hypothesized by Charles Hermann et al. (2001). This discovery highlights the importance of better understanding the connection between management style and decision-making process, because it allows a greater understanding of the range of decision outcomes that can be produced. A further surprising finding is the lack of desire to build consensus among advisors in the Carter administration. This study assumed, like much of the advisory system literature, that in collegial systems the president will seek to build a consensus among advisors before a decision is made. While this was not true in the Carter administration, it was certainly true of Clinton who was not anticipated to have sought consensus.

An explanation for this role of consensus in these two advisory systems can be found in the role of centralization. In a highly centralized system, where the president is controlling information and is confident in that they have heard a range of alternative options they may have less of a need to build consensus. The difference between the Clinton and Carter administrations can also in part be accounted for by experience and interest. Carter, although no expert on foreign policy, had spent time before becoming president educating himself on major international issues. While in office, Carter continued to expand his knowledge, thereby deepening understanding of international relations. Carter's level of expertise also needs to be understood in light of his interest in foreign affairs. Carter's interest in foreign policy meant that he was an engaged and active participant in the policy process, while Clinton on the other hand came to office as a foreign affairs novice with very little interest in foreign policy. Thus, it is not surprising that Clinton would have greater need to rely on the consensus of his advisors before making a decision, whereas Carter with greater experience and interest had less of a need to be assured by a consensus before making a final decision.

Additional Influences on Decision-Making Processes

The advisory system decision-making framework like all typologies presents a set of ideal types and it is expected that past, present, and future administrations' decision-making processes may not exactly conform to the procedures described in the framework. But the cases in the previous chapters have demonstrated that in each administration a central tendency exists in terms of the chosen management style and the associated decision-making process. There are a host of variables that have not been directly taken into account in constructing the typology that most certainly influence the conduct of the policy-making process. Since decision-making takes place in a domestic political and social context and the domestic context is nested within an international context, the number of additional factors that can influence decisions is quite large. Nonetheless, it is important to address some of those proximate variables that intervene and influence the dynamics of the advisory system, altering the decision-making process. The five cases of presidential decision-making examined here give a partial insight into how variables such as interest and experience and domestic politics and international politics influence the decision-making process.

Interest/Experience in Foreign Policy

Unfortunately not every president comes to the White House with an interest in international affairs. Many during their election campaigns run on platforms that almost exclusively highlight domestic issues. Bill Clinton is the perfect case in point, because as governor of Arkansas, Clinton had no experience in foreign affairs; indeed the centerpiece of his campaign was the state of the US economy. Clinton did have to address some international issues given that he was running against an incumbent president that had won a war and was steeped in foreign policy experience. But the American public at the end of the Cold War was more concerned with domestic issues, and, consequently, Clinton's lack of expertise did not prevent him from being elected. In the four cases examined here the presidents that had the most interest in foreign policy were those presidents that had highly centralized advisory systems. Both Nixon and Carter had an interest in foreign affairs and were able to express a vision that US foreign policy should take during their terms in office. Although he did not have the same kind of experience as Nixon in foreign policy, before coming to office, Carter went out of his way to educate himself on the major issues, which was an ethos that he continued when he came into office. The outcome was a president that became adept and comfortable with being at the center of deliberations on foreign affairs.

Interest should not only be considered a characteristic that individual presidents bring with them at the outset of an administration. Interest can arise voluntarily as well as involuntarily during an administration. As new issues arise during an administration and compete for the president's attention, a president may be forced to shift focus over a range of policy problems. If a president is forced by circumstances to move their attention from one issue to another, it may have the effect of changing the policy process. This was exactly the case for George W. Bush, as September 11 forced the president to become more involved in the decision-making process. In this particular case the president changed his management style from low centralization to high centralization. In a different type of change, both Nixon and Clinton devoted more of their time to reelection activities, which meant that they were less involved in deliberations on North Vietnam and Bosnia, respectively. In the Clinton case, the shift in focus meant that deliberations on Bosnia languished, while during the Nixon administration Kissinger took the lead in directing the Paris negotiations.

Interest is not the only factor that needs to be considered when thinking about how presidents conduct the decision-making process, experience also matters. Experience has implications for how involved a president will be in the process, the way they are involved, and their ability to process information. What can we then say about those presidents, like Reagan and Clinton, that had little experience in foreign policy before coming to office? Although neither president had any background in the foreign policy issues found within the cases—Clinton had no experience in peacemaking or military interventions and Reagan was not steeped in nuclear arms or arms control negotiations—what is clear from Clinton's decision-making on Bosnia and Reagan's on strategic arms is that, over time, Clinton became a student of foreign policy and over time when he was engaged in policy he had a stronger ability to assert preferences and raise questions. There are fewer instances of Reagan involving himself in deliberations and demonstrating the depth of knowledge that Clinton showed, even considering the technical nature of arms control.

Clinton's ability to overcome his experience and knowledge deficit reminds us of the importance of individuals in determining foreign policy behavior. Perhaps a Reagan with a greater knowledge of arms control issues could have broken the deadlock between the advocates of cuts based on throw-weight and those who supported launcher-based cuts. Lack of experience, by itself, can be problematic for meeting objectives, but if inexperience is combined with a structural environment in which authority is delegated, then failure is assured or the inexperienced president will lose control to assertive advisors. The conflict in the first eight months of Bush's administration demonstrates what can happen when an inexperienced and uninterested president delegates authority. Policy was dominated by a small group of advisors or it resulted in policies designed to paper over differences and not fully resolve the problem at hand. Although Reagan surrounded himself with like-minded individuals and built an advisory system that was designed so he did not need to be a part of deliberations, his advisory system broke down. Reagan was able to establish the broad overall strategic objectives for the administration, such as reducing the size of the Soviet strategic arsenal, but he was unable to organize and rectify the problems that revolved around the means for those reductions. The combined effect of a lack of interest and inexperience is particularly detrimental because it practically ensured that the differences between Reagan's advisors were going to remain unresolved. Both experience and interest are important and the two interact over time and determine how a president will participate in the process. Presidents can develop interests on their own or may be forced to develop interests in foreign policy by external events and factors. Alternatively, a president might later in their administration develop more experience and use their experience with policy issues to guide future decision-making. Again, both interest and experience matter and each can be a dynamic variable that changes across time and influences a president's management of the process.

Advisory Systems Across Time

An advantage of examining the same advisory system over a range of decision-making episodes is that it provides an opportunity to assess the ways that advisory systems change across time. It is clear from the four case studies that across time administrations do not significantly change the nature of the advisory system once put in place. Instances in which there were attempts to change the decision-making process came very late in the cases, as is found in the Clinton and Reagan cases and the changes were brought on after a prolonged period of ineffective policy making. However, in the Nixon and Carter cases as negotiations matured both presidents were more removed from the process as the details of the negotiating positions were refined. This intuitively makes sense given that in the later stages after the strategic objectives and major issues have been determined, they would not need to be involved in the minutiae found in the final stages of the negotiations. For the Nixon administration this is the way in which his type of advisory system operates, but for Carter this is a slight deviation in that Carter is less an active participant than he was in earlier stages. The fact that presidents from two different systems become less involved in the process, and more or less begin to do nothing else but choose between options in the later stages of the process, gives an initial indication that this is an inherent part of the decision-making process associated with negotiations. The president is needed most in the earliest stages of the process rather than later in the process when much of policy has already been established.

There still remain, however, some differences between advisory systems across time. In the Reagan case, the administration does not expand the range of options it is evaluating across time, and instead, the administration endlessly debates the virtues of cuts based on throw-weight and launchers. This is markedly different from the Clinton case where in the majority of the case the idea of deploying troops is an option that is so objectionable that it is not even proposed, but as the crisis in the Balkans worsens the idea of troop deployment is raised and seen as a legitimate option. In general the Clinton administration has the ability over time to re-evaluate its position, whereas the Reagan administration does not. The same kind of characterization can be made of the Carter administration which can lead to a preliminary conclusion that collegial structures will be more inclined to change policy across time in ways that had previously been unacceptable, whereas the formal structures remain rigid. To take this point a step further, we can tentatively say, based on these cases, that systems with collegial structures are better at learning from past decision-making opposed to systems with formal structures that are resistant to change.

A further difference between these advisory systems is found in the number of participants in the process across time. For different reasons, in four of the cases the number of participants in the decision-making process declines. At the outset of deliberations the number of advisors participating in the policy process is at its largest. All of the president's principal advisors and even individuals at the deputy and undersecretary level are included in deliberations. But this number declines and for a number of reasons. In the Nixon administration, the restriction in participation is a result of Nixon and Kissinger's interest in excluding dissent and imposing greater control over the process. As previously discussed, it is only during decisions involving the use of force where the number of participants increases, but this change is episodic. In the Carter case, the narrowing is not pronounced and any that is detectable is better attributed to the stage of negotiations than any action by the president or advisors.

The Clinton case also demonstrates very little narrowing with the exception of the very end of the process where Lake effectively takes control of the process by developing and advocating the 'endgame strategy'; Lake consulted with other advisors, but the discussions about this plan and its implementation took place between Lake and the president. The fact that this decision involved only the president and Lake has to do with the deterioration of Bosnia and the long period of ineffective policy. In this case Lake had a strong sense that the prior policies had not worked and that the only way to change the situation was to move to a more 'radical' approach. Over time there is a contraction of participants in the Reagan administration, but here it is in part a response to the import of Gorbachev's proposals for cutting all strategic weapons, although this is not a complete explanation of the phenomenon. The Nixon administration is the most effective in narrowing the process as a means of control and this is a product of the design of the advisory system that is tailored to control access and participation.

Domestic and International Context

The impact of domestic political considerations has been debated among international relations scholars and foreign policy analysts. From the case studies described here, it is clear that public opinion and interest groups influenced the process by establishing the parameters of the debate for advisors and presidents. Each president in the four cases operated with a sense of the kinds of policies that would not be acceptable to the American public and as a consequence avoided discussion of such policy. Nixon, although willing to escalate bombing was keenly aware that the US public wanted to withdraw from Vietnam and that this sentiment was growing daily. For Nixon, this meant that he had to try to strike a balance between getting out quickly and not jeopardizing US credibility. Bill Clinton understood that the public supported US involvement in the resolution of conflict in the Balkans, but he also knew that the public had little tolerance for the deployment of ground troops into hostilities.

A crucial difference between the Nixon and Clinton administrations is the fact that Nixon's advisory system is better designed to arrive at quick decisions, whereas Clinton's permits disagreements and protracted discussion. This difference is significant because in instances where internal disputes extend deliberations the likelihood of external factors, such as public opinion or congressional prerogatives, become more influential (Hermann, Hermann, and Hagan 1987). External factors can have a greater influence because there are more opportunities to either build coalitions or use persuasion to change a decision-maker's mind. Added to this is the fact that Clinton's was a collegial structure that was designed to be more open to information than formal structures.

Public opinion can also contribute to setting the agenda for presidents as in the case of the Reagan administration where it was a public grassroots movement that was responsible for forcing Reagan to address strategic arms control. The anti-nuclear grassroots movement was strong enough that it caught the attention of members of Congress who in turn lobbied for the president to take action on arms control (Knopf 1998). In this sense, public opinion set the agenda creating the set of conditions that the president had to work with when deliberating and choosing policy. When the public, interest groups, and Congress are united in support or opposition of a particular issue it is very difficult for any advisory system to discount these interests. However, based on these cases it is reasonable to assume that some of these advisory systems will have greater openness to outside information than others. How the advisory system treats that information may vary given the interest and priorities of the actors, but, nonetheless, the advisory system must address domestic pressure.

There is also an indication from the four cases that elections serve to influence the timing of policy-making. There is no evidence whatsoever that any of these presidents were looking for an 'October Surprise' when deliberating on policy, but there is evidence that presidents and advisors allow electoral considerations to influence the pace of their decision making. A good example is Nixon's decision to continue secret talks with the North Vietnamese in the weeks before the 1972 election. Kissinger advocated that the US continue the negotiations, believing that the North would be more willing to make concessions before the elections than after. He concluded correctly that North Vietnamese feared the actions Nixon might take after receiving a new mandate at the election. Nixon, however, was concerned about restarting the negotiations fearing that something would go wrong and that this would impact the elections. Nixon was ultimately persuaded by Kissinger and allowed the talks to be restarted.

The other domestic consideration that any advisory system must contend with is Congress. The four cases studied here demonstrate that Congress acts as a constraint on a president in the same way as the public in that presidents are aware of the median opinion in Congress and are cognizant that certain policies will be vigorously objected to, such as the deployment of ground troops in the case of the Balkans. Members of Congress that can have an influence on public opinion or ratification preoccupy administrations as they engage in deliberations. Jimmy Carter sought input from Henry Jackson, being aware that the Senator was knowledgeable on arms control issues, but also that in any post-agreement environment Jackson's support would be critical for ratification. The influence of Congress does not just derive from its ability to ratify but also on occasion its ability to present alternative policies that find widespread support. In the case of Clinton and Bosnia, congressional support for the policy of "lift and strike" placed pressure on the administration, particularly at times when the administration was ineffectual in constructing policy (Drew 1994; Daalder 2000). Consequently, the Clinton administration was further driven by Congress to arrive at a resolute decision.

An understanding of different advisory systems alone is not enough to understand how policy is made, because advisory systems operate in a number of contexts and each context influences the process. International and domestic factors serve as both a set of opportunities and constraints on the behavior of the president and advisors during the decision-making process. The case of the Clinton administration and Bosnia again proves instructive in demonstrating this point. As we have seen, Clinton at numerous times from 1992 to 1995 was forced to make a decision because the pressure from external factors became too great. Bosnian Serb attacks on the safe areas and shelling of Sarajevo in 1994 and 1995 drew world attention and placed pressure on the administration to take resolute action. Perhaps more telling, in early 1994 when the Clinton administration policy making had stalled, the French presented a plan that served as a means to overcome divisions in the administration and move US policy forward. All of these factors influenced the process by forcing the administration to make a decision that it was otherwise uninterested (or unwilling) in making.

Most international relations scholars believe that knowledge about domestic and international variables provide enough information to understand the policy behavior of any state. Approaching an analysis of foreign policy in this manner is limiting because it ignores that policy behavior ultimately is the product of action taken by individuals alone or in groups. It is decision makers that must wrestle with the constraints placed on a state by domestic and international factors and it is out of those efforts that a state's behavior is produced (Figure 8.1). The process of agenda setting, deliberation, and choice that leads to a foreign policy outcome takes place between the president and his advisors and, as already noted, is additionally influenced by experience and

Figure 8.1 Advisory Systems Context

International
Politics

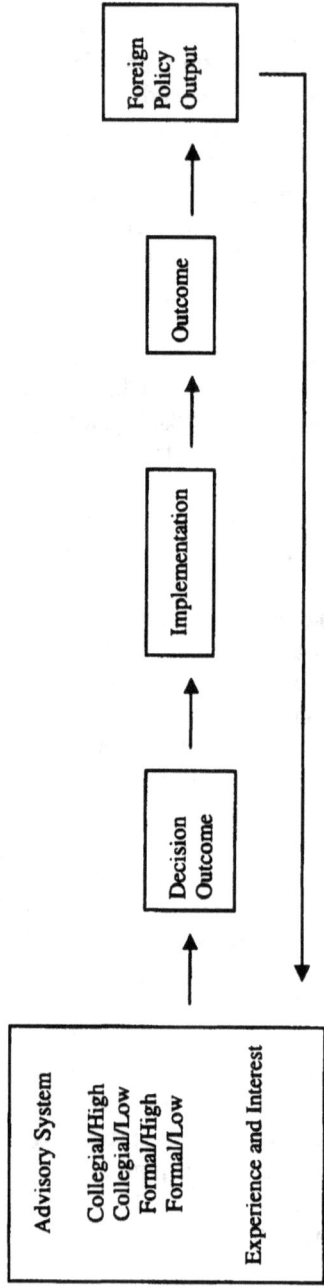

Advisory System				
Collegial/High				
Collegial/Low				
Formal/High				
Formal/Low				
Experience and Interest				

Decision
Outcome

Implementation

Outcome

Foreign
Policy
Output

Domestic Politics

time. The product of the advisory system is the decision outcome that leads to policy choice.

After policy is chosen it is implemented and the decision-unit—the advisory system—awaits an outcome which in turn feeds back to the advisory system for further deliberation and action. Throughout this process international and domestic factors act as sources of constraint and opportunity that influence the process. The extent that these external factors shape government behavior is contingent upon the kind of advisory system that is deciding policy. International and domestic factors can influence the process at any stage of the process, from setting the agenda to implementation. But again, at each stage of the decision-making process it is the advisors that must deal with these factors and the system they operate in will play a deciding role in what information from the external environment is taken into account and how it is processed leading to a decision.

Unless it is assumed that decision-makers have no affect on international and domestic politics then the actions and behaviors of decision makers must be taken into account. Essentially, the decision-making process has been treated as a black box in which inputs enter and miraculously policy comes out the other end. An understanding of the decision-making process allows us to open up the black box and explain the way in which information is processed and options for action are generated. The advisory system framework provides a better explanation of how the policy process functions, including its relationship with decision outcomes, which is a critical intervening step between international and domestic politics and foreign policy behavior.

Advisory Systems Framework: Future Directions

On its own, the advisory system framework is a valuable tool because it better specifies the links between management structure and decision-making process than the frameworks presented by Johnson and George. By the inclusion of the centralization variable, the advisory system framework expands the identified range of management structures and decision-making processes, while presenting an explanation of the variations in decision-making processes. In addition, the framework draws on the research by Hermann et al. (2001) and includes an explanation of the decision outcomes associated with each decision-making process. Identifying an advisory system with outcomes has been missing from the literature that has focused on the management of the foreign policy process. The implication of such a framework is that it explains the consequences of the choices made by leaders when they choose the means to formulate foreign policy, by constructing a set of ideal types that function as a baseline to understand both variations in management and processes.

Mediating variables such as the leadership's experience, time constraints, type of policy issue, and learning—to name a few—all potentially influence the decision-making process and subsequently decision outcomes.

Overall, the advisory system framework presents an explanation of the decision-making processes, their origins, and their outcomes. However, the advisory systems framework has a value beyond explaining how structure and centralization produce a particular kind of decision-making process; it has implications for how we think about other decision-making theories and models. If the framework's explanation of the decision-making process is accurate, then it is possible to addresses a range of questions regarding the decision-making process. For example, are some advisory systems more or less prone to engage in bureaucratic politics? Likewise, which advisory systems are more prone to lead to breakdowns or policy failures? In what ways do advisors go about influencing the decision-making process given a type of presidential management? An investigation of these types of questions presents the future possibility that once a set of management characteristics are identified, it is then possible to not only explain how decisions will be made by a leader and advisors, but whether the policy process will deadlock, result in groupthink, or be captured by a faction within the advisory system.

In some respects the advisory system framework functions along similar lines to that of Hermann et al.'s (2001) differentiation between decision-making groups according to the way in which those groups resolve disagreements. Once again, the three different models of small group decision-making are associated with four types of solutions deadlock, subset, dominant, and integrative. As already discussed, the advisory system framework incorporates elements of the Hermann model, but there are important differences that separate Hermann et al.'s model from the advisory system framework.

First, in the Hermann model a group's mode for resolving disputes is a function of the individual member's primary identity with the group. A small group in which the individual member's primary identity is based on being a member of the group leads to an environment where there is less disagreement regarding alternative options. The advisory system framework alternatively places greater emphasis on structure that is a product of leadership's choice of the best means to organize the decision-making process. From this perspective, the leadership's choice of management needs to be taken into account when considering foreign policy decision making, where there is often a hierarchic context and the leadership at the top of the hierarchy has the ability to shape the policy process. Group identity is not inconsequential, but needs to be accounted for, given the critical role leadership plays in influencing to nature of group relations. Given that the framework accounts for variations, in the prominence of the leadership in structuring and directing the policy process, it can also account for group decision-making where group identity will matter more, notably in instances of low centralization.

A second difference between Hermann et al.'s work and the advisory framework, is the fact that the framework provides a more detailed explanation of the decision-making process. Many of the features found in the framework are presented in the Hermann et al.'s model as mediating variables. Thus the framework is more definitive in linking choice of structures with a specific type of decision-making process and outcomes, which is different from Hermann et al. where the interest is in identifying outcomes. Nonetheless, both the Hermann et al. approach and the advisory system framework with their emphases, are two important ways of beginning the process of synthesizing foreign policy theories and it is critical that more of this research is conducted. The advisory system framework presents a context and/or fills in 'blind spots' of previous models and as a consequence presents an analysis with stronger explanatory power. The following sections present some ways in which the framework can be of assistance in synthesizing, as well as improving understanding of foreign policy processes, by functioning as a basis to reexamine bureaucratic politics, the use of tactics by advisors, and groupthink.

Bureaucratic Politics

As noted earlier there are a number of problems associated with the Bureaucratic Politics Model. First, the model assumes that the leader is an equal member of the decision-making body and consequently has no conditioning effect on the behavior of department heads that the leader—in many cases—has chosen. A second critique is that the participant's interests in the decision-making process are not determined by bureaucratic position and in fact a variety of interests ranging from self-interest, ideology, and loyalty to a leader can determine the preferences of an individual department head (Welch 1992 and 1998). It is a legitimate criticism of bureaucratic politics that advisors' interests do not derive from their bureaucratic position; however, the idea that policy is in part the product of the 'pulling and hauling' of advisors whose different interests can produce an outcome that does not reflect the intentions of any of the participants is not unfounded. David Welch (1992) has argued that 'since decision-making situations involve hierarchical distributions of authority, the process by which decisions are made should not normally be expected to result in a choice unintended by any player in particular.' This statement is true to the extent that the pinnacle of the hierarchy is engaged in the process and is exercising a centralizing force on the decision-making process; to be sure, this is not always the case.

When leaders are not a part of the process, or do not express preferences that function to influence the kind of options discussed, then it is reasonable that decision outcomes might not have been intended by any of the participants. However, in the case of advisory systems that are highly centralized, leaders have the ability to use their preferences to influence which policies will or will not be discussed, as well as determine the decision outcome. Richard Nixon, during deliberations on Vietnam for example, expressed his preferences during policy deliberations, which served to limit the number of options that were discussed, and, as consequence, the policy chosen reflected his preferences. Even in cases where the leader is exercising low levels of centralization, as in the case of Bill Clinton during the Bosnian conflict, leadership can still influence decisions. Bill Clinton made it clear to his advisors that he would not entertain policy proposals that included the deployment of ground troops to Bosnia, thus advisors did not raise this option during deliberations.

Bureaucratic politics model describes one of many different kinds of decision-making processes. As Stern and Verbeek (1998) note, 'The overwhelming majority of "bureaucratic politics" studies are event centric – this, they attempt to explain how bureaucratic factors lead to one specific decision rather than another.' The framework, unlike bureaucratic politics, presents an explanation of a variety of different policy decisions. The advisory system framework discussed here associates bureaucratic politics most closely with instances when there is low centralization in the decision-making process and is most prevalent in systems that are formally structured. Low centralization removes the leader from the process and allows bargaining and competition to take place among advisors. With a group of equal individuals and no gatekeeper, each can advance their preferences over the others. This is particularly problematic in a low centralization system where there is a formal structure because in this type of system a leader does not express a well-defined set of preferences that can act as a sufficient guide for the deliberation of policy; at best, advisors will have to work with the leadership's general beliefs.

Instead of conceiving of bureaucratic politics as being driven by the prerogatives of department heads or advisors, as Allison (1971) does, it is better to think of bureaucratic politics as a product of the nature of the leadership in a small group. Do some of the characteristics, like department heads advancing parochial interests, arise in other advisory systems where there is high centralization and/or collegial structures? Yes, but the difference in these advisory systems is that leadership is designed to deal with the competition that develops among advisors. Highly centralized, formal structures deal with this problem by putting in place a gatekeeper who manages the process on behalf of the president and highly centralized collegial structures manage bureaucratic politics by having the leader actively participate in decision-making—but not as an equal—openly encouraging differing views. Bureaucratic infighting is ameliorated by the fact that the leader harnesses conflict in an effort to construct better policy. Taken from the perspective of the social psychology literature, the leader functions to alter the 'resource and reward structures,' thus ensuring greater cooperation between group members (Kaarbo and Gruenfeld 1998). Consequently, when thinking of the outcome of bureaucratic interactions it is clear that a resultant outcome is not the only outcome or the most prevalent outcome, but one of many possibilities that are contingent on a chosen management structure and level of centralization.

For bureaucratic politics to be used as theory or model it needs to be better contextualized. Many of the assumptions such as the parochial interest of advisors and the absence of leadership do not hold when examining the decision-making process and the behaviors of decision makers (Rhodes 1994). It is reasonable to assume that given differences in structures, roles, and traditions, presidential advisory systems will differ from prime ministerial cabinet systems. Given these kinds of differences it would be a mistake to assume that the bureaucratic politics model that has been designed with US bureaucracies in mind can be seamlessly applied to other decision-making systems. Moreover, bureaucratic politics as a model has a limited ability to explain the outcome of a wide range of foreign policy behaviors within the US context, for it does not reflect the variety of ways in which foreign policy is made. Until a theory of bureaucratic politics can be conceived of in terms that account for this variation, it should not be thought of as a general explanation of foreign policy decision making but more as the product of a specific set of conditions.

Advisor Tactics

Often left unexamined in discussions of bureaucratic politics model are the means by which advisors engage in 'pulling and hauling' and attempt to determine the policy outcome. Bureaucratic actors have different bargaining advantages that they use in action channels to advance their set of preferences. Still this leaves unspecified the actual tactics that these advisors use to manipulate, control, or alter policy. The bureaucratic politics model does not fully address this issue, but other scholars have addressed this issue with an eye toward identifying the range of tactics available to an advisor (Garrison 1999; Hoyt and Garrison 1997; Maoz 1990).

Jean Garrison (1999) has argued that advisors influence the decision-making process through different kinds of manipulation. The tactics available to an advisor are influenced in part by individual ability, ingenuity, and drive, but individual capabilities are mediated by the available opportunities and constraints. Advisors will not use any tactic available to influence the policy process, but they will choose a tactic suitable given their immediate environment. Garrison (1999: 135) correctly notes that 'the structure of the advisory system sets the parameters of interaction but not all patterns of behavior.' The advisory system framework effectively provides a well-specified set of parameters to begin the process of hypothesizing the kinds of conditions that prevent or encourage an advisor to engage in one type of tactical manipulation or another. No policy making is free from manipulation; the key for the foreign policy analyst is to identify the advisory system and the conditions that the system provides for different tactics. The advisory framework permits a first cut at identifying which tactics are associated with a specific decision-making process.

The strategies used to manipulate the decision-making process fall into three categories (Garrison 1999). The first category focuses on advisors and their ability to manipulate who is allowed to participate in the process. The second deals with the ways in which advisors seek to influence the process by manipulating the processing of information; specific tactics of this kind include framing of the issue, leaking information, or resorting to 'salami' tactics (changing overall policy by making smaller incremental changes). Third, advisors can attempt to change the interpersonal relationships among the group by using threats, forming coalitions with other advisors, and by bolstering/legitimation (emphasizing the advantages of a policy while downplaying disadvantages often highlighting an advisors authority to set policy).

Table 8.3 Formal Advisory System Tactics

	Formal
High Centralization	Gatekeeper has advantage and uses range of tactics
Low Centralization	*Presentation of Information:* Framing, agenda-setting, leaking, and salami tactics *Interpersonal:* Coalition-building

Formal systems create the conditions that permit an advisor(s) to engage in manipulation (Table 8.3). This fact is clearly true for a formal/high centralized advisory system, like Nixon's, where an essential feature of the system is the gatekeeper that is in a position to determine access to the president, the information the president sees, and who will participate in deliberation. Kissinger's ability to persuade the president to accept secret negotiations and cut the Secretaries of State and Defense out of the policy-making on negotiations can be attributed to the range of tactics that he used. Throughout the case study, Kissinger controlled what others in the administration heard and knew about administration policy as it pertained to a negotiated settlement. Since exclusion is a constituent part of the formal/high centralized process, manipulation is expected, and to a certain extent limited, because the gatekeeper is effectively managing the system on behalf of the president. Other advisors may try these tactics but in a system with a gatekeeper the effectiveness of tactics may be limited.

In an advisory system such as Reagan's, where the president did not centralize control over deliberations, weak preferences existed, and Reagan waited to the end of the process to make a decision, it is reasonable to expect that his advisors resorted to a range of strategies to advance their preferences. The case of the START negotiations indicates that no advisor was in a position to exclude other advisors from participating in the decision-making process. Advisors sought to gain access to Reagan without the knowledge of other advisors, even though such behavior never resulted in anyone being excluded from the process for very long. The only time in the Reagan administration that advisors were excluded from the process was in 1987 when John Poindexter took over as National Security Advisor and limited access to the president. This change reduced the number of individuals involved in deliberations but it did not exclude any one of the competing perspectives in the administration.

There were significant efforts at trying to control the presentation of information and this case indicates that a full range of tactics—including agenda-setting, framing, leaking, and salami tactics—were employed. As mentioned previously, advisors attempted to gain access to the president without the knowledge of other advisors. These attempts were designed to set the agenda or frame issues, thereby gaining an advantage over competing advisors. Richard Burt appealed to Robert McFarlane whom he knew to be sympathetic to his views which resulted in at least one occasion of McFarlane structuring the NSC meeting that followed this appeal, so that the State Department option was the only option for discussion. Caspar Weinberger, who often met with the president alone, appealed to the president's deep anxieties about protecting the American public, thus, effectively allowing Weinberger to frame the way in which Reagan viewed the relationship between SDI and strategic cuts. Weinberger was successfully able to reinforce the president's view that SDI was a necessary part of arms control that could not be used as a bargaining chip to make the country less secure.

Of the three interpersonal tactics that Garrison identifies—coercive threats, bolstering/legitimation, and coalition-building—the last is perhaps the most constant tactic found in the Reagan case. From the very beginning, the two main combatants in the administration sought to vie for the support of other influential departments. At the outset, the Joint Chiefs of Staff's support for cuts based on throw-weight or launchers were up for grabs, but the Chiefs ultimately sided with the State Department while ACDA sided with the Defense Department. Throughout the negotiations, selection of the ACDA director and the Geneva negotiator and the role of Paul Nitze as arms control advisor were all associated with attempts by either side in the debate to gain more allies.

Leaking information was not uncommon during the administration. The Office of the Secretary of Defense was particularly active in leaking information on the 'administration's position' which, in fact, was often the Secretary of Defense's position and not the recognized policy of the administration. Very early in the process, salami tactics were used by Weinberger when formulating the National Security Directive where he was successful in getting language included that recognized the US interest in reducing the destructive capability of Soviet weapons, which was an indirect means of bringing throw-weight back into the discussions.

In the two collegial advisory systems, a variety of tactics are used, but here, the resort to interpersonal tactics does not seem to be as severe as it was in the formal/low centralization system (Table 8.4).

Table 8.4 Collegial Advisory System Tactics

	Collegial
High Centralization	*Presentation of Information:* Agenda-setting and framing
Low Centralization	*Presentation of Information:* Agenda-setting and framing *Interpersonal:* Coalition-building

The use of interpersonal tactics and coalition-building are far more prevalent in the Clinton system than in the Carter system. Given that in low centralization advisors are instrumental in guiding the direction of policy, advisors turn to others as a means for support in order to be more successful. At various points throughout the period of 1992 to 1995, Warren Christopher and Anthony Lake sought the support of other advisors in an attempt to advance preferred policies. Lake held discussions and meetings with Madeline Albright in order to generate support for more aggressive policies toward Serbia that included the use of air strikes. In early 1994, Christopher sought the support of various advisors for the report he designed that called for the US to bring about an alliance between the Bosnians and the Croatians. There is really no evidence for any high levels of coercive threats in either administration or even for legitimation for that matter.

Exclusion of advisors does not characterize either of the two collegial administrations. Because they are designed for open discussion and because both presidents desire to hear a range of opinions on policy, the decision-making process is inherently inclusive. In tactics designed to influence the presentation of information, there are some significant variations found in the collegial systems. First, there is very little from the cases to indicate leaking was taking place, although it is important to qualify this statement since this tactic was not covered by the case study questions. Likewise, salami tactics do not seem to play a major role in either the Carter or Clinton administrations, which can be explained by the open deliberations where access is easily obtained making it difficult to conceal the attempt at shifting policy.

Tactics found at high levels include framing and agenda-setting, which became a major issue for Carter as arms control was linked to Soviet behavior in Africa. Brzezinski framed the arms control talks as part and parcel of the larger strategic relationship with the Soviets, while Vance framed these issues as separate and as Soviet activities in the Horn of Africa having no bearing on arms control talks. During the Clinton administration, framing was an issue during the discussion of 'lift and strike' which was framed in terms of its impact on the conflict and its impact on the US relationship with its European partners. The push for a lift and strike policy was important in motivating Clinton momentarily to back away from the idea of US airpower as a remedy in Bosnia.

There are differences between the Carter and Clinton administrations in terms of the usage of agenda setting. As Garrison (1999: 123–126) points out, early in the Carter administration the president effectively set the agenda for SALT II, but later, as the international context changed, Brzezinski gained the ability to influence the agenda. But the fact that the agenda was set by the President in deliberations conforms to the hypothesized advisory system found in the typology. At various periods in Clinton's administration, Christopher and Lake were active in shaping the agenda. After his failed attempt to get the Europeans to support 'lift and strike,' Christopher attempted to change the agenda from US participation in resolving the conflict to US withdrawal from conflict resolution altogether. Lake, later in the process, was able to appeal to Clinton's frustration with the lack of progress in Bosnia and to convince him that the administration's objective was finding a policy that would lead to a long-term solution and not focusing on day-to-day events. Again, in the Clinton decision-making process where advisors are instrumental in guiding policy, the fact that advisors are competing to set the agenda is not surprising. This compares to the Carter administration where the president is more involved and can use his authority to set the agenda.

In sum, as these cases indicate, the kind of tactics that advisors can use to advance their preferences is shaped by the kind of advisory system that they operate within. Variation in advisory systems imposes constraints and creates opportunities for the president's advisors. Although these case studies have not been a complete examination of advisory tactics, they provide significant indication that there is a connection between advisory systems and tactics. Further research with different sets of cases needs to be conducted in order to derive stronger conclusions, but this can only be accomplished with a firm understanding of the context that this advisory system typology presents.

Groupthink

The reformulated typology also affords the opportunity to assess the conditions under which different types of management styles are more prone to create the conditions for groupthink. Fuller and Aldag (1997) have correctly argued that in constructing a model of group decision making, other elements aside from those identified by Janis need to be considered as a part of the decision-making process. They note organizational power, group cohesiveness, and directive leadership as examples of the types of antecedents that must also be included in explaining groupthink. (1997; 77). Fuller and Aldag present a general framework that serves as the basis for further research into groupthink phenomena and the relationship between these phenomena. Scholars have found that the presence of groupthink within a small decision-making group is contingent on specific antecedents, specifically the style of group leadership and group structure (McCauley 1989; 't Hart 1990; 't Hart and Bovens 1996; 't Hart, Stern and Sundelius 1997; Schafer & Crichlow 1996). 't Hart (1990) has hypothesized that there are three paths that lead to concurrence seeking that result in an abbreviated search of options, pre-existing cohesiveness, de-individuation, and anticipatory compliance. But of these three pathways to groupthink, the last, anticipatory compliance, is most likely to lead to concurrence seeking or groupthink. In the case of the former two pathways these conditions rarely occur in small groups, because it is rare that the members of high-level groups lose their identity in the case of de-individuation. In the case of pre-existing cohesiveness, it is also difficult to assume that high-level groups are going to be more united than fractured; in fact, 't Hart (1990: 197) argues that 'high-level administrative groups are characterized by fragmentation and divisiveness.' Thus, anticipatory compliance is more likely to result in a small group experiencing groupthink.

Anticipatory compliance is typically found in hierarchic systems such as the ones in which advisors operate. Shafer and Crichlow (1996) and 't Hart (1990) identify that the hierarchy within groups can induce groupthink because a leader that expresses predispositions or preferences creates a 'structure of incentives that induces many actors to comply with real or perceived stances and preferences of superiors or influential colleagues' ('t Hart 1990). Because of the traditional role played by many leaders and the prestige of their offices, anticipatory compliance should be found in many advisory systems. However, those with formal structures will have higher propensity for groupthink, because in the case of formal/high centralization systems, a leader expresses a set of preferences and in formal/low centralization systems a leader may not have preferences but he operates with broadly stated sets of views. 't Hart notes:

> Often, they [leaders] define and delimit the agenda and the kinds of alternatives to be discussed right at the outset of the deliberations by stating their premises. They may control the composition of the decision group, and may thus steer towards a likely outcome of the discussion. Leaders may narrow the range and depth of the group decision process by the manner in which they conduct the meetings, i.e. by 'opening' and 'closing' the discussion based on personal preferences for certain speakers or viewpoints. (1990: 200)

Given the prevalence of competing factions within any decision-making unit it is unlikely that groupthink will be found among all of the leader's advisors, instead we should expect that a subset of the group will display the symptoms of groupthink, self-censorship, mindguards, feelings of moral superiority, and so on ('t Hart 1990: 198). Internal divisions form a part of any of the decision-making systems, and, as a consequence, in-group/out-group distinctions are likely to arise. The formation of in-groups and out-groups in an administration may be necessary but not sufficient for the onset of groupthink. Formal structure and explicitly stated leader preferences may be required for groupthink to be induced. The formation of competing factions within the formal structure might be based on whether or not they are compatible with the leader's preferences. The group that most closely conforms to the leader's preferences may begin to perceive themselves as an in-group and feel that they are the 'true' defenders of the leader's interests.

In times of stress, which Janis explains is necessary for groupthink, the divisions within an administration can be intensified. A critical mediating variable in this process and in the functioning of advisory systems is the familiarity between advisors. Many advisors have worked together both inside and outside the government sharing the same ideological views or adopting similar stances on policy. Consequently, when called on to participate in a new administration, advisors may automatically form into in-groups and out-groups with new individuals (or those known to support differing policies) being seen as outsiders (Myers and Lamm 1976; Vertzberger 1984). Even in instances when there is not high stress, the formation of factions will create the conditions for the faction members to greatly resist dissenting voices and conform in their interpretation of incoming information (Vertzberger 1984).

An important distinction that might be made of advisory systems in relation to groupthink is that in systems where the process is highly centralized the leader's influence in the creation of groupthink might be more pivotal when compared to groups where there is low centralization. Under conditions of high centralization the president has established goals and/or parameters shaping advisor thinking on issues, thus, in these cases, anticipating the president's interest is much easier. This point fits 't Hart's argument that:

> In high-level decision groups, closed leadership styles combined with group or organizational norms of compliance may produce groupthink tendencies. This need not involve overt pressures for conformity; instead the group members are prone to excessive anticipatory compliance with the chief executive's assumptions, perspectives, and preferred alternatives. (1990: 177)

In groups with low centralization, groupthink may be found within a faction in the advisory system and whether this has implications for policy is contingent upon a faction successfully dominating the decision-making process. The perception that the Bush administration was resistant to considering alternative options in relation to Iraq, might be an instance of this type of groupthink. In looking at this case a number of factors make it possible instance of groupthink. The administration was divided into factions before the president was inaugurated. The members of each faction had a past history with one another and had personal relationships, increasing the bonds between them. The Cheney, Rumsfeld, and Wolfowitz faction shared a particularly rigid ideological view of United States foreign policy, especially on the issue of Iraq. So once the president asserted his interest in regime change and began the process of planning, it is reasonable to expect that groupthink would set in among the Cheney, Rumsfeld and Wolfowitz faction as they sought to defend their own and the president's policy preferences. Instances of low centralization are instructive because they highlight that the leader need not be an active member of the group in order for advisors to attempt to anticipate their wishes. Even in administrations such as Reagan's and Clinton's, where both presidents were less involved in the process, there is evidence that advisors tried to anticipate their wishes. The difference is that in the Reagan and Clinton cases, advisors attempt to 'preemptively comply with the real or perceived policy preferences of group leaders or high-status members' ('t Hart 1990: 187).

A difference between advisory systems is that those with collegial structures, as opposed to a formal structure, will have different paths to groupthink. While in systems with formal structures the path to groupthink begins with anticipatory compliance, in systems with collegial structures the antecedent to groupthink is consensus combined with an environment where the president is an equal participant in the process. Consensus is a feature of collegial systems with high and low centralization, the difference being that in collegial systems with low centralization there is less emphasis on consensus. Collegial structures, where consensus is a key component, will generate cohesiveness, which has been identified by 't Hart (1990) as one of the three paths to groupthink. The problem with taking this step and asserting that collegial systems follow a fundamentally different path to groupthink is that factions or the lack of cohesion permeates all the advisory systems. The one possible argument that could be made is that collegial structures with high centralization will be less prone to factions as compared to other systems. But this leaves unanswered the question of whether it is indeed cohesion, or, rather, the highly centralized role of the president that is producing anticipatory compliance. Tentatively, the advisory system framework is consistent with 't Hart's assertion of the centrality of leadership as a crucial antecedent necessary to account for when identifying and explaining the onset of groupthink.

As 't Hart, Stern and Sundelius (1997: 13) argue, groupthink is a contingent phenomenon that should account for the structural and environmental conditions specific to different decision-making settings. The advisory system framework found in this study acts as a starting point for better explaining the occurrence of groupthink in foreign policy decision making. The cases presented in this study have not been identified as cases of groupthink, and, therefore, it is difficult to make strong inferences based on their findings. Further research on groupthink needs to take place that accounts for the specific features of the decision-making systems that advisors inhabit.

Conclusion

Bureaucratic politics, organizational process, groupthink, and a number of other models and theories have dominated thinking on small-group decision making. However, some of this research remains underspecified, as in the case of groupthink, and more often than not is used to explain specific cases with little attention to explaining variations in behavior, as in the case of bureaucratic politics. With few exceptions, the literature on foreign policy decision making have been slow to move toward synthesizing many of these models, which would offer a more comprehensive understanding of decision making and the decision-making process. Greater emphasis needs to be placed on explaining when and why bureaucratic politics or groupthink will or will not characterize how a small group makes a decision. In order to do this, scholars in foreign policy analysis need to construct frameworks that identify both cognitive and institutional variations and commonalities in decision-making structures.

This essay presents one such framework where variations in leadership management style are used as a means to explain variations in decision-making processes and, as a consequence, variations in decision outcomes. The foreign policy analysis literature has relied on the Johnson/George typology of collegial, formalistic, and competitive management styles. However, as its critics have noted, the typology has not been fully adequate in explaining the range of ways in which leaders and advisors make decisions. By taking into account variations in levels of the leadership's centralization of the process the framework provides a more comprehensive explanation of decision making. With this reformulated framework as a foundation, it can serve as the basis to rethink, reevaluate, and develop existing theories and models on small group decision making. But this type of synthesis needs to expanded and existing frameworks need to be further refined. Without this type of effort, the study of foreign policy analysis will fail to progress and will find itself progressing not much further than the ideas presented over thirty years ago.

Chapter 9

Building a More Effective Advisory System?

Building a More Effective Advisory System?

The cases examined here demonstrate that once a president establishes a particular advisory system and sets that system in motion, it is rare that he will change the system or the decision-making process mid-stream. Only after prolonged periods of ineffectiveness in policy formulation, or after a massive policy failure, do presidents reevaluate the advisory system and its operation. Quite often it is not even the president that advocates for a change in the decision-making process, but, instead, it is advocated by an advisor or advisors that are painfully aware of the administration's difficulty in formulating policy. National Security Advisors who are tasked with the management and coordination of the deliberation process are key individuals that advocate for reforms to the process. Anthony Lake and John Poindexter both identified problems in the way that their respective administrations made policy and sought to make adjustments in order to streamline and enhance the effectiveness of the process. Poindexter's changes came far too late to reinvigorate the policy process while Lake was successful at improving the policy process on the issue of Bosnia by taking a lead. Despite the ability to make changes, it is clear that a president's management style influences the decision-making process, but, what is important to keep in mind is that once established presidents are bound by the systems that they create.

The structure and level of centralization once imposed determines how information will be processed, who is included in the process, and how disagreements will be resolved. A type of path dependency sets in and the chosen structure and level of centralization create the operating procedures for the advisory system. Changing the process means altering these operating procedures and potentially throwing the process into disarray as participants and information channels change. But all this assumes that the president and advisors are in a position to change the process. Unfortunately, the president and his advisors, when dealing with an issue, become preoccupied with the substance of policy and do not pay attention to the process of decision-making. Consequently, it is only at moments when policy is failing that someone in the administration may seek to improve the process itself. Therefore there are high costs for presidents that early on mismanage the decision-making process because of the difficulty in changing the process.

Given that the choice of advisory system can have a profound influence on foreign policy behavior, there has been an interest among scholars and practitioners (Hilsman 1967; George 1972; Destler 1972; Cosier 1978; Schweiger, Sandberg and Ragan 1986) to propose advisory systems that will ensure the quality of the decision-making process. These advisory systems are designed to ensure that decisions result from an evaluation of a range of options and that conformity that will undermine the search for policy alternatives is avoided. Having a devil's advocate and multiple advocacy have been proposed as two means for increasing the quality of the decision-making process (George 1980; Stern and George 2002). Both require that steps are taken to ensure that a variety of views within an administration are heard. Devil's advocate accomplishes this task by "institutionalizing" the role of opposition in the deliberation process. An individual or individuals are responsible with providing the group with opposing views; in this way the president is always assured of hearing contrary opinions.

The effectiveness of this approach in improving the quality of the decision-making process is questionable for a number of reasons. First, the formal creation of a position of devil's advocate while ensuring that dissenting views are presented can also lead to the marginalization of the presented options. The advocate does not stake a position based on a conviction, nor do they try to build the support to advance a particular position over others; others in the group may not find the advocate's arguments compelling and will fail to be persuaded (Stern and George 2002). Second, the advocate might serve the unintended consequence of being a means to stifle sincere dissention. The sincere dissenter that assumes the role of the devil's advocate can have their arguments in opposition to administration policy weakened as they fill the role of the 'official' group dissenter.

Proposed as an alternative to devil's advocate is multiple advocacy which calls for 'balanced debate among policy advocates drawn from different parts of the organization (or, as necessary, from outside the organization)' (George 1972: 751). The president must be an active participant monitoring and regulating the activities of the various advocates and they must select advisors in this capacity. The way in which Carter during the SALT II negotiations monitored the process, attended meetings, and gave direction to his advisors most closely reflects, from these cases, the kind of role that the president ought to play in this process. In addition, to an active president all the participants in the process must have equal access to bureaucratic resources (i.e., access to the president and adequate staff resources) and must be informed and well-versed in the policy issue. Supporting the president in this type of system is a 'custodian-manager' that monitors the activities of the advocates, ensures the equality of access and resources, maintains channels of communication to the president and ensures that a variety of views are represented (Stern and George 2002). Effective management by the president and his custodian manager ensures that a variety of options are evaluated and thoroughly assessed, debated, and presented to the president.

Multiple advocacy, like devil's advocate, is not free from criticism. Legitimate concerns arise regarding certain features of the system that are absolutely necessary for its proper functioning. First, multiple advocacy requires that the president not reveal personal preferences that could unduly influence the advocates' policy search. Even considering that presidents can still shape the policy process without explicitly stating preferences, the question still remains: is this process feasible, given that on a range of issues the president will let his preferences be known through public statements, campaign promises, and/or informal discussions. Stern and George (2002) argue that presidents should perhaps exclude themselves from early deliberations so as not to unduly influence the creation of policy options and, as an example, they cite Kennedy's deliberate absence from meetings in the early days of the Cuban Missile Crisis. This example highlights the problem of presidents concealing their preferences from advisors. The Cuban Missile Crisis was a unique crisis situation where it would be easy for the president to conceal preferences, given that he may have not had any. As Meena Bose (1998: 106) notes, 'Kennedy's actions during the Cuban missile crisis indicate that he could be receptive to some form of multiple advocacy in urgent situations, but his overall impulses were far more informal.' Bose is drawing our attention to the fact that the resort to multiple advocacy characterizes the decision-making during the Cuban Missile Crisis and not necessarily all of the Kennedy administration decision-making. When considering more routine kinds of policy-making or dealing with issues or problems that evolve over time, it may be impossible for advisors to stay away from encountering presidential preferences.

Regardless of the enunciation of his preferences, for multiple advocacy to work the president must be a constant participant in the policy-making process. There are many examples, principally Reagan and Clinton, where presidents find it difficult to be a constant participant in the policy-making process in the manner prescribed by multiple advocacy. The lack of attention may be a result of other policy commitments, but it also might be a result of an individual president's cognitive needs. Presidents choose advisory systems based on their cognitive needs, specifically based on their feelings of efficacy, the way they process information, how they deal with conflict and the level of control they require. By prescribing multiple advocacy as an advisory system, the expectation must be that presidents can and will adapt themselves to a system that may not fit their cognitive needs. A president like Ronald Reagan would find it difficult to make decisions as suggested by multiple advocacy, and, consequently, the quality of the process may in fact be worse off than the formal/low centralization system that he used during his administration.

It has been suggested that multiple advocacy not be used all the time by presidents, instead they should be selective and use this system when time permits and in instances when advisors fail to advocate a range of policy options. Is it possible for a president that chooses a particular system based on cognitive needs to change to a different system? For example, Nixon was able to switch from a purely formal style with high centralization to a more collegial process when needed to decide on escalating force. Those presidents that are removed from the deliberation process, like those that have formal low centralization, may be unaware that they need to change the process to produce a better range and evaluation of options. Reagan is the ideal example of a president removed from the process putatively unaware that his advisors were unable to construct policy. Instead of proposing that presidents adopt systems that are antithetical to their personalities, presidents should be encouraged to improve the systems that they adopt. In looking at advisory systems and learning, Paul Kowert (2002) argues that presidents should not choose systems that do not fit them, but rather they should be conscious of the advisory system becoming too extreme in design. A president needs to be aware that delegation, for example, can be an effective way to make policy but delegating absolute authority runs the risk of subjecting policy to the unrestrained competing desires of the president's advisors. Presidents with collegial and formal structures should be cognizant of the dangers of extreme centralization whether high or low, and the kinds of breakdowns in policy formulation that this can produce.

The above is not meant to suggest that there are no minimum requirements that need to be met by all advisory systems in order to create quality decisions. First, the president needs to be fully informed not only of the issues being deliberated, but also of the conditions surrounding the deliberations. The president should be aware of cleavages in the administration and the basis for the division among advisors. The president, irrespective of management style, must be prepared to intervene into a conflict between advisors that are not designed to help develop policy options. In the case of formal structures such intervention may mean making the National Security Advisor responsible for this task, but all advisors must know that the NSA is acting at the direction of the president. This behavior is in line with multiple advocacy to the extent that all administrations may need a 'custodian-manager' or 'honest-broker' to assist in managing the process. The responsibility for being the custodian traditionally falls on the National Security Advisor since this is one of the key features of the role of the special assistant to the president. However, it needs to be recognized that this role is at times a difficult proposition for the National Security Advisors given that they do often have policy preferences.

Anthony Lake has stated that a National Security Advisor must be a custodian for the president although, he acknowledges that the president's advisor should also be able to express preferences and make suggestions. Striking a balance between being a manager of the policy process and being an advocate is a difficult one as evidenced by the cases studied in this research. This problem highlights an important point addressed by multiple advocacy but advanced further by Burke (1984). Multiple advocacy suggests that each advisor is responsible for being the advocate of a different position, but it says nothing of their responsibility or obligation to the process. Thus, Burke asserts:

> [I]n official contexts other things are not equal, and we would certainly want the adviser not just to advance the interests of a particular incumbent but to take other facets of the office or the interests of others seriously, say those of the general public or those dictated by any constitutionally based-institutions or processes through which authoritative decisions are made. (1984: 824)

In some sense this idea is also reminiscent of the devil's advocate where an individual adopts a role in the advisory system and associated with that role are a set of explicitly defined responsibilities, such as, in the case of the devil's advocate, the responsibility of presenting opposing options. However, when an individual becomes an advisor to the president, it should be understood that their role in the administration is not just to give advice about 'means and ends,' but the advisor should understand they are obligated to deliberate fairly, meaning that policy views are represented accurately and there is no interest in distorting contrary or opposing policies. Advisors should seek to support other advisors and ensure that their views are represented and that no other advisor is attempting to misrepresent a point of view. In essence there is a role standard for advisors, and presidents, at the outset of the administration, ought to make clear to each advisor the standards to which they are expected to adhere.

The norms that guide the actions of advisors must go beyond ensuring that a range of options are presented, that advisors do not undermine one another, and that options are faithfully represented. It is also necessary that advisors adhere to a set of norms that guides the behavior regarding protection of public interest. Burke also advocates that advisor obligations not only apply to the decision-making process, but also to the larger institutional and political forces in which they are embedded. Specifically, he is referring to democratic institutions and the responsibility of the advisor to ensure that democratic values and goals, such as not deceiving Congress, are maintained. Responsibility to context can be taken a step further in that advisors also have a responsibility to consider the implications of state policy on other nations and the targets of foreign policy. With this obligation each advisor is forced to assess and reassess the options presented by asking if the process satisfies the requirements of a democratic society and whether or not the consequences of policy on another state are so high that they render an option unviable. Thus the adherence to an ethical standard has implications for the conduct of the policy process and ought to be recognized by any individual who assumes the role of advisor.

The construction of roles for each advisor is important if we begin from the assumption that although presidents determine the type of decision-making process with their choice of management style, they are bound by the systems they create. The quality of the process can be enhanced by requiring that a range of views are debated, but this will prove difficult if the advisors that are responsible for crafting policy do not have a commitment to the integrity of the process. A president must establish at the outset of the administration that each advisor has a role to fill that goes beyond acting as the head of their department or serving the president. Part of their role is comprised of an obligation to participate in the decision-making process in a fair, supportive environment. The president is then obligated to monitor the process to ensure that advisors fulfill their role.

By no means is this suggested as a cure-all, but it is important if we accept that the idea of a 'one size fits all' type of advisory system is unrealistic and that a president's choice of advisory system is best if it reflects their leadership style. Each advisory system has drawbacks, particularly when any aspect of the process is taken to an extreme, which is typically the source of problems within an administration. When bargaining and conflict go beyond the healthy give-and-take between competing policy visions and devolves to the point where it is impossible to formulate coherent policy, the process needs to be changed, but change does not mean imposing on a president a system that is incompatible with the way in which they 'best' make decisions. In short, the enunciation and establishment of norms regarding the nature of advisor participation in the process is one valuable means to begin to overcome some of the inherent weaknesses in all decision-making processes.

Bibliography

Adrianopolous, Gerry A. (1991) *Kissinger and Brzezinski: The NSC and the Struggle for Control of US National Security Policy.* New York: St.Martin Press.

Allison, Graham T. (1971) *Essence of Decision: Explaining the Cuban Missile Crisis.* Boston: Brown and Little.

Barnett, Michael and Jack S Levy. (1991) 'Domestic Sources of Alliances and Alignments: The Case of Egypt 1962-1973' *International Organization* 45 (Summer), pp. 369-395.

Bendor, Jonathan B. and Thomas H Hammond. (1992) 'Rethinking Allison's Models' *The American Political Science Review,* vol. 86, pp. 301-322.

Berman, Larry and Emily O. Goldman. (1995) 'Clinton's Foreign Policy at Midterm' in *The Clinton Presidency: First Appraisals.* Chatham, New Jersey: Chatham House Publishers.

Bose, Meena. (1998) *Shaping and Signaling Presidential Policy: The National Security Decision-making of Eisenhower and Kennedy.* College Station, Texas: Texas A&M University Press.

Brzezinski, Zbigniew. (1983) *Power and Principle: Memoirs of a National Security Advisor.* New York: Farrar, Straus & Giroux.

Brzezinski, Zbigniew, Madeline Albright, Louis Denend, and William Odom. (1982) Miller Center Interviews, Carter Presidency Project, Vol. XV, February 18, 1982 (Jimmy Carter Library).

Bundy, William. (1998) *A Tangled Web: The Making of Foreign Policy in the Nixon Presidency.* New York: Hill and Wang.

Burke, John P. (1984) 'Responsibilities of Presidents and Advisers: A Theory and Case Study of Vietnam Decision-making' *The Journal of Politics,* vol. 46 (August), pp. 818-845.

Burke, John P. (2000) *The Institutional Presidency: organizing and managing the White House from FDR to Clinton, 2nd ed.* Baltimore: Johns Hopkins University Press.

Burke, John P. (2004) *Becoming President: The Bush Transition 2000-2003.* Boulder, Colorado: Lynne Reiner Publishers.

Burke, John P. and Fred I. Greenstein. (1989) *How Presidents Test Reality: Decisions on Vietnam, 1954 and 1965.* New York: Russell Sage Foundation.

Burns, James M. and Georgia J. Sorenson. (1999) *Dead Center: Clinton-Gore Leadership and the Perils of Moderation.* New York: A Lisa Drew Book/Scribner.

Bush, George W., Mickey Herskowitz, and Karen Hughes. (1999) *A Charge to Keep.* William and Morrow Company.

Campbell Colin. (1986) *Managing the Presidency: Carter, Reagan and the Search for Executive Harmony.* Pittsburgh: University of Pittsburgh Press.

Campbell, Colin and Bert A. Rockman. (1996) *The Clinton Presidency. First Appraisals.* Chatham, New Jersey: Chatham House Publishers.

Campbell, Colin and Bert A. Rockman. (2004) *The George W. Bush Presidency: Appraisals and Prospects.* Washington D.C.: CQ Press.

Carter, James E. (1982) *Keeping the Faith: Memoirs of a President.* Toronto; New York: Bantam Books.

Carter, James E. (1982) *Miller Center Interviews, Carter Presidency Project,* Vol. XIX, November 29, 1982, (Jimmy Carter Library).

Chan, Steve. (1979) 'Rationality, Bureaucratic Politics and Belief System: Explaining the Chinese Policy Debate, 1962-1966' *Journal of Peace Research,* vol. 16, pp. 333-347.

Clarke, Richard A. (2004) *Against All Enemies: Inside America's War on Terror.* New York, New York: Free Press.

Clifford, Lawrence X. (1994) 'An Examination of the Carter Administration's Selection of Secretary of State and National Security Advisor' in Rosenbaum, Herbert, and Ugrinsky (eds.), *Jimmy Carter: Foreign Policy and Post-Presidential Years,* Alexej Westport, Conn.: Greenwood Press.

Clinton, Bill (2004) *My Life.* New York, New York: Knopf.

Coll, Steve. (2004) *Ghost Wars: The Secret History of the CIA, Afghanistan and Bin Laden, From the Soviet Invasion to September 10, 2001.* New York: Penguin Press.

Crabb, Cecil Van Meter and Kevin V. Mulcahy. (1986) *Presidents and Foreign Policymaking.* Baton Rouge: Louisiana State University Press.

Cronin, Thomas E. and Sanford D. Greenburg. (1969) *The Presidential Advisory System.* New York: Harper and Row.

Crowe, William. (1983) *The Line of Fire: From Washington to the Gulf War, the Politics and Battles of the New Military.* New York: Simon and Shuster.

Cyert, Richard M. and James G. March. (1963) *A Behavioral Theory of the Firm.* Englewood Cliffs, NJ: Prentice-Hall.

Daalder, Ivo H. (2000) *Getting to Dayton: The Making of America's Bosnia Policy.* Washington D.C.: Brookings Institution Press.

Daalder, Ivo H. and James Lindsay. (2003) *American Unbound: The Bush Revolution in Foreign Affairs*. Washington D.C.: Brookings Institution Press.

Destler, I.M. (1972) *Presidents, Bureaucrats, and Foreign Policy: The Politics of Organizational Reform*. Princeton, N.J., Princeton University Press.

Drew, Elizabeth. (1994) *On the Edge: The Clinton Presidency*. New York: Simon and Schuster.

Eckstein, Harry. (1975) 'Case Study and Theory in Political Science' in Fred I. Greenstein and Nelson Polsby (eds), *Strategies of Inquiry*, Reading, MA: Addison-Wesley.

Feagin, Joe R. and Anthony M. Orum. (1991) *A Case for the Case Study* Chapel Hill: North Caroline University Press.

Fischer, Beth A. (1997) *The Reagan Reversal: Foreign Policy and the End of the Cold War*. Columbia, MO: University of Missouri Press.

Fitzgerald, Frances. (2000) *Way Out There in The Blue: Reagan, Star Wars and the End of the Cold War*. New York: Simon and Schuster.

Foyle, Douglas C. (1997) 'Public Opinion and Foreign Policy: Elite Opinion as a Mediating Variable' in *International Studies Quarterly*, 41 (March), 141-169.

Fuller, Sally Riggs and Ramon J. Aldag. (1997) 'Challenging the Mindguards: Moving Small Group Analysis beyond Groupthink' *In Beyond Groupthink: Political Group Dynamics and Foreign Policy-making*. Ann Arbor: The University of Michigan Press.

Gaenslen, Fritz. (1992) 'Decision-Making Groups' in Eric Singer and Valerie Hudson (eds.), *Political Psychology and Foreign Policy*, Boulder, Colorado: Westview Press, pp. 165-193.

Galtung, Johan. (1967) 'On the Effects of International Economic Sanctions: With examples from the Case of Rhodesia' in *World Politics*, vol. 19 (April), pp. 378-416.

Garrison, Jean. (1999) *Games Advisors Play. Foreign Policy in the Nixon and Carter Administrations*. Texas A&M University Press.

Garthoff, Raymond L. (1989) *Reflections on the Cuban Missile Crisis*, Rev. edition.Washington, D.C.: Brookings Institution.

George, Alexander. (1972) 'The Case for Multiple Advocacy in Making Foreign Policy', *The American Political Science Review*, vol. 66 (September), pp. 751-785.

George, Alexander. (1980) *Presidential Decision-making in Foreign Policy: The Effective Use of Information and Advice*. Boulder, Colorado: Westview Press.

George, Alexander. (1982) *Case Studies and Theory Development* [draft]. Presented to the Second Annual Symposium on Information Processing in Organizations, Carnegie-Mellon University, October 15-16.

George, Alexander. and Richard Smoke. (1974) *Deterrence in American Foreign Policy: Theory and Practice.* New York: Columbia University Press.

George, Alexander and George Juliette. (1998) *Presidential Personality and Performance.* Boulder, Colorado: Westview Press.

Golembiewski, Robert T. (1962) *The Small Group: An Analysis of Research Concepts and Operations.* Chicago: University of Chicago Press.

Gregg II, Gary L. and Mark J. Rozeel (2004) *Considering the Bush Presidency.* Oxford University Press.

Greenstein, Fred I. (2002) 'The Contemporary Presidency: The Changing Leadership of George W. Bush: A Pre-and Post-9/11 Comparison' *Presidential Studies Quarterly,* vol. 32 (June).

Greenstein, Fred I. and Nelson W. Polsby. (1975) *Strategies of Inquiry.* Reading, MA: Addiston-Wesley Company.

Grieco, Joseph. (1982) 'Between Dependency and Autonomy: India's Experience with the International Computer Industry', *International Organization,* vol. 36 (Summer), pp. 609-632.

Haig, Alexander M. (1984) *Caveat: Realism, Reagan and Foreign Policy.* New York: Macmillan Publishing Company.

Halperin, Morton, Priscilla Clapp, and Arnold Kanter. (1974) *Bureaucratic Politics and Foreign Policy.* Washington D.C.: The Brookings Institution.

Haney, Patrick Jude. (1997) *Organizing for Foreign Policy Crises Presidents, Advisers, and the Management of Decision-making.* Ann Arbor: University of Michigan Press.

Hart, Paul 't; Eric Stern, and Bengt Sundelius. (1997) *Beyond Groupthink: Political Group Dynamics and Foreign Policy-making.* Ann Arbor: University of Michigan Press.

Hart, Paul 't. (1990) *Groupthink in Government: A Study of Small Groups and Policy Failure.* Amsterdam: Rockland, MA: Swets & Zeitlinger.

Hart, Paul 't and Mark Bovens. (1996) *Understanding Policy Fiascoes.* New Brunswick, N.J.: Transaction Publishers.

Heilbrunn, Jacob H. (1999) 'Condolezza Rice: George W.'s Realist' *World Policy Journal,* vol. 16 (Winter).

Henderson, Phillip G. (1988) *Managing the Presidency.* Boulder, Colorado: Westview Press.

Hermann, Charles, Janice Stein, Bengt Sundelius, and Stephen Walker. (2001) 'Resolve, Accept or Avoid: The Effects of Group Conflict on Foreign Policy Decisions' *International Studies Review*, vol. 3, pp. 133-168.

Hermann, Margaret G. (1995) 'Advice and Advisers in the Clinton Presidency: the Impact of Leadership Style' in Stanley Renshon, *The Clinton Presidency: Campaigning, Governing, and the Psychology of Leadership*. Boulder, Co: Westview Press.

Hermann, Margaret G. and Thomas Preston. (1994) 'Presidents, Advisors and Foreign Policy: The Effect of Leadership Style on Executive Arrangements' *Political Psychology*, vol. 15, pp. 75-96.

Hermann, Margaret G., and Juliet Kaarbo. (1998) 'Leadership Styles of Prime Ministers: How Individual Differences Affect the Foreign Policy Process' *Leadership Quarterly* vol. 9, pp. 243-63.

Hermann, Margaret G., Charles F. Hermann, and Joe D. Hagan. (1987) 'How Decision Units Shape Foreign Policy Behavior' in Charles Hermann, Charles W. Kegley, and James N. Rosenau (eds), *New Directions in the Study of Foreign Policy*. Boston: Unwin Hyman.

Hersh, Seymour. (1983) *Price of Power: Kissinger in the Nixon White House*. New York: Summit Books.

Hess, Stephen. (1988) *Organizing the Presidency*. Washington, D.C.: Brookings Institution.

Holbrooke, Richard. (1998) *To End a War*. New York: Random House.

Hollis, Martin and Steve Smith. (1986) 'Roles and Reasons in Foreign Policy Decision-making' *British Journal of Political Science*, vol. 16 (July), pp. 269-286.

Hoyt, Paul D. and Jean Garrison (1997) 'Political Manipulation within the Small Group: Foreign Policy Advisors in the Carter Administration' *Beyond Groupthink: Political Group Dynamics and Foreign Policy-making*. Ann Arbor: The University of Michigan Press.

Hyland, William G. (1999) *Clinton's World: Remaking American Foreign Policy*. Westport, CT: Praeger Publishers.

Janis, Irving. (1972) *Victims of Groupthink: A Psychological Study of Foreign Policy Decisions and Fiascoes*. Boston: Houghton Mifflin.

Johnson, Richard Tanner. (1974) *Managing the White House: An Intimate Study of the Presidency*. New York: Harper & Row.

Kaarbo, J. (1997) 'Prime Minister Leadership Styles in Foreign Policy Decision-making: A Framework for Research' *Political Psychology*, vol. 18, pp. 553-81.

Kaarbo, Juliette and Ryan K. Beasley. (1999) 'A Practical Guide to the Comparative Case Study Method in Political Psychology' *Political Psychology*, vol. 20, pp. 369-391.

Kaarbo, Juliet and Deborah Gruenfeld. (1998) 'The Social Psychology of Inter- and Intragroup Conflict in Governmental Politics' *Mershon International Studies Review,* vol. 42, pp. 226-233.

Kahin, George M. and John W. Lewis. (1969) *The United States in Vietnam: An Analysis in Depth of the History of America's Involvement in Vietnam.* New York: A Delta Book.

Kaplan, Morton A. (1957) *System and Process in International Politics.* New York: Wiley.

Kengor, Paul. (1998) 'Comparing Presidents: Reagan and Eisenhower' *Presidential Studies Quarterly,* vol. 28 (Spring), pp. 366-393.

Kennedy, Robert F. (1969) *Thirteen Days: A Memoir of the Cuban Missile Crisis.* New York: New American Library.

Keohane, Robert. (1982) 'The Demand for International Regimes (in Structural Perspectives)' *International Organization,* vol. 36 (Spring), pp. 325-355.

Kessel, John H. (2001) 'The Presidency and the Political Environment' *Presidential Studies Quarterly,* vol. 31 (March), pp. 25-43.

Kimball, Jeffrey. (1998) *Nixon's Vietnam War.* Lawrence, Kansas: University of Kansas Press.

King, Gary; Robert Keohane and Sidney Verba. (1994) *Designing Social Inquiry: Scientific Inference in Qualitative Research.* Princeton, NJ: Princeton University Press.

Kissinger, Henry. (1979) *Henry Kissinger: White House Years.* Toronto, Ontario: Little, Brown and Company.

Klein, Joe. (2002) *The Natural: The Misunderstood Presidency of Bill Clinton.* New York: Doubleday.

Knopf, Joseph. (1998) *Domestic and International Cooperation: The Impact of Protest on US Arms Control Policy.* Cambridge: Cambridge University Press.

Kowert, Paul. (2002) *Groupthink or Deadlock: When Do Leaders Learn From Their Advisors.* Albany, NY: State University of New York Press.

Kupchan, Charles. (1988) 'NATO and the Persian Gulf: Examining Intra-Alliance Behavior' *International Organization,* vol. 42 (Spring), pp.317-346.

Lake, Anthony. (2000) *6 Nightmares: Real Threats in a Dangerous World and How America Can Meet Them.* New York: Little, Brown and Company.

Light, Paul C. (1982) *The President's Agenda: Domestic Policy Choice from Kennedy to Carter.* Baltimore, MD: Johns Hopkins University.

Lijphart, Arend. (1971) 'Comparative Politics and the Comparative Method' *The American Political Science Review,* vol. 65 (September), pp. 682-693.

Lobel, Aaron. (2000) *Presidential Judgment: Foreign Policy Decisionmaking and the White House.* John F. Kennedy School of Government: Hollis Publishing Company.

Longely, J and Pruitt, P.E. (1980) 'Groupthink: A Critique of Janis's Theory' in by Ladd Wheeler and Phillip Shaver (eds), *Review of Personality and Social Psychology*, Beverly Hills: California, pp. 74-93.

Lord, Carnes. (1988) *The Presidency and the Management of National Security.* New York: Free Press; London: Collier Macmillan.

Mann, James. (2004) *Rise of the Vulcans: The History of Bush's War Cabinet.* Viking Press.

March, James G. and Herbert A. Simon. (1958) *Organizations.* New York: Wiley.

Marshall, Susan E. (1985) 'Development, Dependence and Gender Inequality in the Third World' *International Studies Quarterly*, vol. 29 (June), pp. 217-240.

McCauley, C. (1989) 'The Nature of Social Influence in Groupthink: Compliance and Internationalization' *Journal of Personality and Social Psychology*, vol. 57, pp 250-60.

McCormick, James M. (2004) 'The Foreign Policy of the George W. Bush Administration' in Steven E. Schier (eds), *High Risk and Big Ambition: The Presidency of George W. Bush.* Pittsburg, PA: University of Pittsburgh Press.

McLellan, David S. (1985) *Cyrus Vance.* Totowa, NJ: Rowan and Littlefield.

Minix, Dean. (1982) *Small Groups and Foreign Policy Decision-making.* Washington D.C.: University of American Press.

Moaz, Zeev. (1990) 'Framing the National Interest: The Manipulation of Foreign Policy Decisions in Group Settings' *World Politics*, vol. 43 (October), pp. 77-110.

Moens, Alexander. (1991) 'President Carter's Advisers and the Fall of the Shah' *Political Science Quarterly*, vol. 106 (Summer), pp. 211-237.

Munck, Gerardo. (1998) 'Canons of Research Design in Qualitative Research' *Studies in Comparative International Development*, vol. 33 (Fall).

Myers, David G., and Helmut Lamm. (1976) 'The Group Polarization Phenomenon' *Psychological Bulletin*, vol. 83, pp. 602-627.

National Security Council Project: Oral History Roundtables 'Arms Control and the National Security Council' March 23, 2000 http://www.brook.edu/dybdocroot/fp/projects/nsc/transcripts/20000325 .htm (April 2001).

National Security Council Project: Oral History Roundtables 'The Nixon Administration National Security Council' December 8, 1998 http://www.brook.edu/dybdocroot/fp/projects/nsc/transcripts/19981208.htm (April 2001).

National Security Council Project: Oral History Roundtables 'The Bush Administration National Security Council' April 29, 1999 http://www.brook.edu/dybdocroot/fp/projects/nsc/transcripts/19990429.htm (April 2001).

National Security Council Project: Oral History Roundtables 'The Clinton Administration National Security Council' September 27, 1999 http://www.brook.edu/fp/research/projects/nsc/transcripts/20000927.htm (August 2002).

Nitze, Paul H. (1989) *From Hiroshima to Glasnost: At the Center of Decision.* New York: Grove Weidenfeld.

Nixon, Richard M. (1978) *RN, The Memoirs of Richard Nixon.* New York: Gossett and Dunlap.

Perelmutter, Amos. (1974) 'The Presidential Political Center and Foreign Policy' *World Politics* 27: 87-106.

Ponder, Daniel E. (2000) *Good Advice: Information & Policy Making in the White House, 1st edition.* College Station, TX: Texas A&M University Press.

Porter, Roger B. (1983) 'Economic Advice to the President: From Eisenhower to Reagan' *Political Science Quarterly*, vol. 98 (Autumn), pp. 403-426.

Powell, Colin. (1995) *My American Journey.* New York, New York: Random House.

Prados, John. (1991) *Keepers of the Keys: A History of the National Security Council from Truman to Bush.* New York: Morrow.

Preston, Thomas. (2001) *The President and His Inner Circle.* New York: Columbia University Press.

Preston, Thomas and Margaret Hermann. (2004) 'Presidential Leadership Style and the Foreign Policy Process' in Eugene Wittkopf and James McCormick, *The Domestic Sources of American Foreign Policy: Insights and Evidence, 4th ed.*, Lanham, MD: Rowman and Littlefield.

Ragin, Charles and Howard, Becker. (1992) *What is a Case? Exploring the Foundations of Social Inquiry.* Cambridge, England: Cambridge University Press.

Ragin, Charles, Dirk Berg-Schlosser, and Giselle De Meur. (1996) 'What is a Case? Exploring the Foundations of Social Inquiry' in Robert E. Goodin and Hans-Dieter Klingemann, *A New Handbook of Political Science*, New York: Oxford University Press.

Renshon, Stanley. (1995) *The Clinton Presidency: Campaigning, Governing, and the Psychology of Leadership.* Boulder, Co: Westview Press.

Renshon, Stanley. (1996) *High Hopes: The Clinton Presidency and the Politics of Ambition.* New York: New York University Press.

Rhodes, Edward (1994) 'Do Bureaucratic Politics Matter? Some Disconfirming Evidence from the Case of the Navy' *World Politics*, vol. 47, (October), pp. 1-41.

Rosati, Jerel A. (1981) 'Developing a Systematic Decision-Making Framework: Bureaucratic Politics in Perspective (in Research Note)' *World Politics*, vol. 33, pp. 234-252.

Rosenbaum, Herbert and Alexej Ugrinsky. (1994) *Jimmy Carter: Foreign Policy and Post-Presidential Years*. Westport, Conn.: Greenwood Press.

Schafer, Mark and Scott Crichlow. (1996) 'Antecedents of Groupthink: A Quantitative Study' *The Journal of Conflict Resolution*, vol. 40 (September), pp. 415-435.

Schafer, Mark and Scott Crichlow. (2002) 'The Process-Outcome Connection in Foreign Policy Decision-making: A Quantitative Study Building on Groupthink' *International Studies Quarterly*, vol. 46, (March).

Scott, James M. (1996) 'Reagan's Doctrine? The Formulation of an American Foreign Policy Strategy' *Presidential Studies Quarterly*, vol. 26 (Fall), pp. 1047-1061.

Scowcroft, Brent. (2000) 'Recorded Interview' in Aaron Lobel (eds), *Presidential Judgment: Foreign Policy Decisionmaking and the White House*, John F. Kennedy School of Government: Hollis Publishing Company.

Singer, J. David. (1961) 'The Level-of-Analysis Problem in International Relations' *World Politics*, vol. 14 (October), pp. 77-92.

Shoemaker, Christopher C. (1991) *The NSC Staff: Counseling the Council*. Boulder, Colorado: Westview Press.

Shultz, George P. (1993) *Turmoil and Triumph: My Years as Secretary of State*. New York: Charles Scribner's Sons.

Sjoberg, Gideon., Williams, N., Vaughan, T. and Sjoberg, A., (1991) 'The Case Study Approach in Social Science Research: Basic Methodological Issues' in Joe Feagin, *A Case for the Case Study*, Chapel Hill: University of North Carolina Press.

Sloan, Joan W. (1997) 'President Reagan's Administrative Formula for Political Success' in by Eric J. Schmertz (eds), Ronald Reagan's America, Vol. 3, Wesport, CT: Greenwood Press.

Smith, Gaddis. (1996) *Morality, Reason and Power: American Diplomacy in the Carter Years*. New York: Hill and Wang.

Snyder, Richard, H. Bruck and Burton Sapin. (1962) *Foreign Policy Decision-making: An Approach to the Study of International Politics*. New York: Free Press of Glencoe.

Steinbrunner, John D. (1974) *The Cybernetic Theory of Decision: New Dimensions of Political Analysis*. Princeton, NJ: Princeton University Press.

Stern, Eric and Bertjan Verbeek. (1998) 'Wither the Study of Governmental Politics in Foreign Policymaking? Symposium' *International Studies Quarterly*, vol. 42 (November), p. 250.

Stern, Eric and George, Alexander. (2002) 'Harnessing Conflict in Foreign Policy Making: From Devil's to Multiple Advocacy' *Presidential Studies Quarterly*, vol. 32, (September).

Stogdill, Ralph M. (1981) *Stogdill's Handbook of Leadership: A Survey of Theory and Research.* New York: Free Press.

Strong, Robert. (1992) *Decisions and Dilemmas: Case Studies in Presidential Foreign Policy Making.* Englewood Cliffs, NJ: Prentice-Hall.

Suskind, Ron. (2004) *The Price of Loyalty: George W. Bush, the White House, and the Education of Paul O'Neill.* New York: Simon and Schuster.

Talbott, Strobe. (1984) *Deadly Gambit: The Reagan Administration and the Stalemate in Nuclear Arms Control.* New York: Alfred A. Knopf.

Talbott, Strobe. (1980) *Endgame: The Inside Story of SALT II.* New York: Harper & Row.

Talbott, Strobe. (1988) *The Master of the Game: Paul Nitze and the Nuclear Peace.* New York: Vintage Books.

Thompson, Kenneth W. (1994) 'Negotiations at Home and Abroad: Carter's Alternatives' in by Herbert Rosenbaum and Alexej Ugrinsky (eds), *Jimmy Carter: Foreign Policy and Post-Presidential Years*, Westport, Conn.: Greenwood Press.

Thompson, Kenneth W. (1997) *Presidents and Arms Control: Process, Procedures, and Problems.* Miller Center, University of Virginia: University Press of America.

Vance, Cyrus. (1983) *Hard Choices: Critical Years in America's Foreign Policy.* New York: Simon & Schuster.

Verba, Sidney. (1961) *Small Groups and Political Behavior: A Study of Leadership.* Princeton, NJ, Princeton University Press.

Vertzberger, Yaacov. (1984) 'Bureaucratic-Organizational Politics and Information Processing in a Developing State' *International Studies Quarterly*, vol. 28 (March), pp. 69-95.

Vertzberger, Yaacov. (1998) *Risk Taking and Decision-making: Foreign Military Intervention Decisions.* Standford, CA: Stanford University Press.

Walcott, Charles E. and Karen Hult. (1987) 'Organizing the White House: Structure, Environment and Organizational Governance' *The American Journal of Political Science*, vol. 31, pp. 109-125.

Walcott, Charles E. and Karen Hult. (1995) *Governing the White House From Hoover through LBJ.* Lawrence, Kansas: University Press of Kansas.

Walcott, Charles E. and Karen Hult (2004) 'The Bush Staff and Cabinet System' in Gary L.Gregg II and Mark J. Rozell, *Considering the Bush Presidency*, Oxford, UK: Oxford University Press.

Waltz, Kenneth. (1959) *Man, the State, and War: A Theoretical Analysis.* New York: Columbia University Press.

Wayne, Bert. (1997) The *Reluctant Superpower: United States' Policy in Bosnia, 1991-1995.* Ann Arbor, MI: University of Michigan Press.

Welch, David. (1992) 'The Organizational Process and Bureaucratic Politics Paradigm: Retrospect and Prospect' *International Security,* vol. 17 (Autumn), pp. 112-146.

Welch, David (1998) 'A Positive Science of Bureaucratic Politics?' *Mershon International Studies Review,* vol. 42, (November), pp. 210-216.

Welch, David and James Blight. (1989) *On the Brink: Americans and Soviets Re-examine the Cuban Missile Crisis.* New York: Norton.

Wilson, Graham. (2004) 'Bush II and the World' in Colin Campbell and Bert Rockman, *The George W. Bush Presidency: Appraisals and Prospects.* Washington D.C.: CQ Press.

Woodward, Bob (2002) *Bush at War.* New York: Simon and Schuster.

Woodward, Bob. (2004) *Plan of Attack.* New York: Simon and Schuster.

Yin, Robert. (1989) *Case Study Research: Design and Methods.* Newbury Park, Calif.: Sage Publications.

Zelikow, Philip and Ernst May. (1997) *The Kennedy Tapes: Inside the White House during the Cuban Missile Crisis.* Cambridge, MA: Belknap Press of Harvard University Press.

Newspapers and Magazine Articles

Calabresi, Massimo, Margaret Carlson, James Carney, Michael Duffy, Mark Thompson, and Douglas Waller. (2001) 'Odd Man Out'. *Time,* vol.158, no. 10, Pages 24-32. Online Lexis-Nexis Academic.

DeParle, Jason. 'The Man Inside Bill Clinton's Foreign Policy' *New York Times,* 20 August 1995: Section 6; Page 33; Col. 4. Online Lexis-Nexis Academic.

Elliot, Michael and Barry, John. 'Soft Hearts vs. Hard Heads' *Newsweek,* 9 May 1994: Page 42. Online. Lexis-Nexis Academic.

Friedman, Thomas and Sciolino, Elaine. 'Clinton and Foreign Issues: Spasms of Attention' *New York Times,* 22 March 1993: Section A; Page 3; Col. 1. Online Lexis-Nexis Academic.

Gwertzmann, Bernard. 'Nitze is Appointed Adviser to Shultz in Gromyko Talks' *New York Times,* 6 December 1984: Section A; Page 1, Column 4. Online Lexis-Nexis Academic.

Gwertzmann, Bernard. 'Shultz Scores a Backstage Victory.' *New York Times,* 9 December 1984: Section 4; Page 5, Column 1. Online Lexis-Nexis Academic.

Sciolino, Elaine. '3 Players Seek a Director for Foreign Policy Story' *New York Times,* 8 November 1993: Section A; Page 1; Col. 1. Online Lexis-Nexis Academic.

Sciolino, Elaine. 'The 2000 Campaign: The Advisor; Bush's Foreign Policy Tutor: An Academic in the Public Eye' *New York Times,* 15 June 2000: Section A; Page 1; Col 2. Online Lexis-Nexis Academic.

Warner, Margaret G. 'Clinton: Moving Toward "Phase 2"' *Newsweek,* 10 May 1993: Pg 28. Online. Lexis-Nexis Academic.

Warner, Margaret G. and Clift, Eleanor. 'The Road to Indecision' *Newsweek,* 24 May 1993: Page 20. Online. Lexis-Nexis Academic.

Jimmy Carter Presidential Papers

Memo, Brzezinski to Secretary of Defense and State, 2/4/77, 'Memorandum-Secretary of State and Secretary of Defense'folder, Vertical File, Brzezinski Collection, Jimmy Carter Library.

Chronology, SALT chronology, 3/7/77 – 7/10/78, 'SALT II and the Growth of Mistrust: A Chronology of Events,' USSR/US Conference 5/6-9-94, Vertical File, Jimmy Carter Library.

Meeting summary, Special Coordination Committee, 3/2/1977, folder, 5/6-9/94 (1), USSR/US Conference, Jimmy Carter Library.

Memo, Brzezinski to President, 3/8/77, 'Summaries of Recent SALT SCC Meetings' folder, Vertical File, USSR, Jimmy Carter Library.

Memo, SALT and Other Arms Control Issues Discussed in Moscow, 4/11/77, File Meetings SCC 1: 1/27/77 through Meetings SCC 15: 6/8/77, Box 26, Brzezinski Subject File, Jimmy Carter Library.

Memo, Brzezinski to Secretary of State and Secretary of Defense, 4/26/77, USSR/US Conference 5/6-9/94, Vertical File, Jimmy Carter Library.

Memo, Brzezinski to Secretary of State and Secretary of Defense, 4/29/77, USSR/US Conference 5/6-9/94, Vertical File, Jimmy Carter Library.

NSC Weekly Report, Brzezinski to President, 6/3/77, Weekly Report to President 1-15, 2/77-7/77, Brzezinski Collection, Subject file, Box 41, Jimmy Carter Library.

Memo, Brzezinski to President, 6/7/77, USSR/US Conference – USSR Related Documents, Box 1, Vertical File, Jimmy Carter Library.

Memo, SCC Meeting on SALT, 4/28/77, USSR Related Documents, Box 1, Vertical File, Jimmy Carter Library.

Memo, Brzezinski to Secretary of State, Secretary of Defense, Director of Central Intelligence, and Director of Arms Control and Disarmament Agency, 7/22/77, USSR/US Conference – USSR Related Documents, Box 1, Vertical File, Jimmy Carter Library.

Memo, Brzezinski to President, 7/25/77, USSR/US Conference – USSR Related Documents, Box 1, Vertical File, Jimmy Carter Library.

Memo, Molander and Utgoff to Brzezinski, 6/28/77, USSR/US Conference - USSR Related Documents, Box 1, Vertical File, Jimmy Carter Library.

Memo, Brzezinski to President Carter, 8/31/77, Meetings SCC 16: 6/4/77 through meetings SCC 47, Box 27, Brzezinski Collection, Jimmy Carter Library.

Meeting Transcript, SCC Meeting on Horn of Africa, 3/2/78, Meetings – SCC 50: 1/8/78 through Meetings SCC 100: 8/10/78, Box 28, Brzezinski Collection, Jimmy Carter Library.

Interviews conducted by author

Caspar Weinberger, June 26, 2002
David Aaron, June 24, 2002
James Goodby, July 24, 2002
Anthony Lake, December 16, 2002

Index

For Product Safety Concerns and Information please contact our EU
representative GPSR@taylorandfrancis.com
Taylor & Francis Verlag GmbH, Kaufingerstraße 24, 80331 München, Germany